Brothers of Coweta

Brothers of Coweta

Kinship, Empire, and Revolution
in the Eighteenth-Century
Muscogee World

BRYAN C. RINDFLEISCH

THE UNIVERSITY OF
SOUTH CAROLINA PRESS

© 2021 University of South Carolina

Published by the University of South Carolina Press
Columbia, South Carolina 29208

www.uscpress.com

Manufactured in the United States of America

30 29 28 27 26 25 24 23 22 21
10 9 8 7 6 5 4 3 2 1

Library of Congress Cataloging-in-Publication Data
can be found at http://catalog.loc.gov/.

ISBN: 978–1-64336–202–1 (hardcover)
ISBN: 978–1-64336–203–8 (paperback)
ISBN: 978–1-64336–204–5 (ebook)

CONTENTS

ILLUSTRATIONS

ACKNOWLEDGMENTS

Acknowledgments are hard. How can one thank all the people and institutions that have provided such invaluable support in the process of researching and writing a book? With that said, I do know where to start. As I promised, this second book is dedicated to Elliana. I love you so much, and you have been incredibly patient with me throughout this project. You are worth more than the world itself, I cannot imagine a day without your smile, your laugh, and your beautiful tantrums. And while I promise this book is yours, we have your mother to thank just as much for her support and patience throughout this process. I love you both so much.

The origins of this book are a somewhat funny story. I was in the middle of researching a different book when I ran across James Hill in Pittsburgh for a conference. James and I have known each other a long time, and our work intersects all over the place. So when he saw that I was presenting on the "same ol'" Escotchaby and Sempoyaffee, he laughed and told me something to the effect of "You're really getting a lot of mileage out of these guys." I laughed too, but then it dawned on me, James was onto something. There was a story here I wanted to tell, I just didn't know it until James pulled it out of me. Thanks, James!

I also need to thank my incredible group of friends who have listened more than enough about Escotchaby and Sempoyaffee and have provided invaluable support and love throughout my life. Jeff Fortney and Rowan Steineker (and now little Thaddeus!), you guys mean the world to me. Liz Ellis, Brooke Bauer, and Christian Crouch, I cannot imagine my world without you three. Cedric Burrows, Jenn Finn, Sergio Gonzalez, Alison Efford, Kristen Foster, Sam Majhor, Ben Linzy, Mike McCarthy, Sam Harshner, Karalee Surface, Lisa Lamson, Abby Bernhardt, Cory Haala, you are all a godsend to Marquette; may it be a better place because of you all. And Nadine Zimmerli, your enthusiasm and laughter make this world a better place.

As a scholar of the Native South, I extend my friendships and relationships to all the people in that circle. And while I list all your names, it does not do justice to how much you all mean to me and have been a critical part of my personal and academic life. Thank you so much to Josh Piker, Robbie Ethridge, Angela Pulley Hudson, Steve Hahn, Alejandra Dubcovsky, Hayley Negrin, Kathryn Braund, Dustin Mack, Fay Yarbrough, Andrew Frank, Tyler Boulware, Natalie Inman, Jamie Mize, John Juricek, Greg O'Brien, Steven Peach, Jeff Washburn, Jason Herbert, Kris Ray, Nate Holly, Jeff Washburn, Gregory Smithers, Theda Perdue, Michael Morris, and Claudio Saunt.

I would also not be the person that I am today without my Bright Institute cohort. Your generosity and example, your challenges and love, have meant so much to me these past three years—I cannot put it into words. Thank you so much to Cate Denial, Monica Rico, Serena Zabine, Courtney Joseph, Carl Keyes, Cathy Adams, Tamika Nunley, Jonathan Hancock, Will Mackintosh, Doug Sackman, Angela Keysor, Lori Daggar, Bridgett Williams-Searle, Michael Hughes, and, again, Christian Crouch.

And I would be remiss if I did not thank all the scholars whose work has had a profound impact on me and to whom I owe so much: Jeanie O'Brien, Erica Armstrong Dunbar, Ned Blackhawk, Jenni Monet, Sarah Deer, Jodi Byrd, Alyssa Mt. Pleasant, Daina Ramey Berry, Roxanne Dunbar-Ortiz, Julie Reed, Kathleen DuVal, Brett Rushforth, Michael Witgen, Lisa Brooks, Nick Estes, Michael Leroy Oberg, Helen Rountree, and so many others that the list honestly could go on forever.

A special thanks to Ehren Foley, my editor at University of South Carolina Press. He took a chance on me and this book, and I sincerely hope it pays off in some way or another, because this book would not have happened without him. *Seriously.* For any young scholar that is looking for someone to fight for you and to care for your project, talk to Ehren. *Please.*

To the institutions and archives that supported this project, thank you for also taking a chance on me. This list includes the incredible staff of the American Philosophical Society (special thanks to Linda Musumeci!), Huntington Library (Steve Hindle!), Filson Historical Society (LeeAnn Whites!), Hargrett Rare Book and Manuscript Library, South Carolina Historical Society, and the British National Archives. In addition, the Bright Trust at Knox College has been an invaluable source of financial support for my work.

In Milwaukee thank you to my incredible department chairs—James Marten and Lezlie Knox—and my "mates" Laura Matthew, Rob Smith, Jolene Kreisler, Tim McMahon, Dan Meissner, Phil Naylor, Fr. Steven Avella, Dave McDaniel, Chima Korieh, Mike Donoghue, Peter Staudenmaier, Alan Ball, Carla Hay, and Patrick Mullins. Special mention to Sameena Mulla, Jodi Melamed, Amelia Zurcher, Phil Rocco, Grant Silva, Amber Wichowsky, Paul Nolette, Gerry Canavan, Enaya Othman, Melissa Ganz, Steve Hartman

Keiser, Theresa Tobin, and Darren Wheelock, whose teaching and research at Marquette inspire me every day.

To my family who has provided the most generous understanding, space, and love. Deb and Mark Hilstrom, this book would not have been written without your care for me and our family—that, and the use of your basement to write. To Brian, Paige, Amira, Vivi, Drew, Cass, Eliseo, and Mayahuel, I miss you all every day. Mom and Dad, thank you for making me who I am today.

To my other "extended" family, this book is indebted to Jacqueline Fontaine-Schram and Ron, Mark Powless and Eva Martinez-Powless, "Doctor" Mark Powless and Terri, and Bryan "Maza" Brookbank and family. Y'all inspire me so much; I again cannot put it in words.

Finally, a quick "shout out" to my game group (you know who you are) and, even though it sounds weird, my neighbors/friends who have similarly heard way too much about this project, namely, Andy and Anna Kerr (and Johnny and Lincoln!) and Paul and Stephanie.

NOTE ON TERMINOLOGY

It is important to note that whenever possible, the author refers to eighteenth-century Creek peoples by their present-day spelling as *Muscogee,* in recognition of their nationhood and sovereignty today. While Europeans overwhelmingly referred to Muscogee peoples as "Creeks" in the past, it is far more important to recognize the sovereign status of Muscogee peoples—and the Muscogee nation—today. The author also considered using the spelling *Mvskoke* rather than *Muscogee* but made the conscious choice to employ modern-day spellings in accordance with the identity of the nation and its peoples today.

Meanwhile, the author employs the terms that Muscogee peoples would have used for themselves and their kinsmen, community, leaders, and ceremonies whenever possible. Such terms include *huti* for one's larger family or matrilineage, *talwa* for town/community, *mico* or *tustenogy* to identify specific leadership roles in eighteenth-century Muscogee society, and certain rituals or ceremonies such as the Busk or Boosketau, drinking *cassina,* among others.

Finally, when referring to the collective Indigenous Peoples of North America or the Native South, the author privileges capitalization and as often as possible utilizes "Indigenous" rather than "Native."

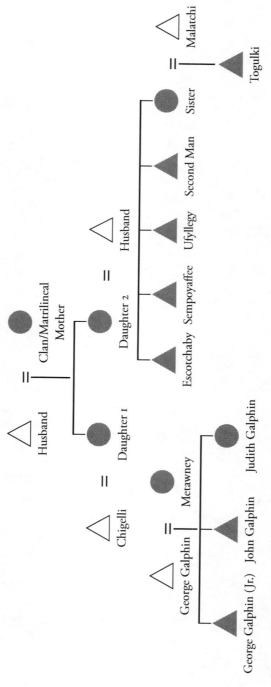

Sempoyaffee and Escotchaby's Matrilineal Kinship Tree—their *huti*.
(Bryan C. Rindfleisch)

Introduction

In January 1760 Britain's superintendent for Indian affairs in the South, Edmond Atkin, sent a letter to Henry Ellis, the governor of Georgia, in which he reported on the state of affairs between the Muscogee (Creek) Indians and the English colonies. Writing from Cusseta, a Lower Muscogee *talwa*, Atkin had recently learned that several "English scalps" were received in nearby Coweta, one of the most politically active *talwas*. The grisly trophies had been sent by the Savannah and Cherokee Indians, who were currently at war with the colonies. In response Atkin had imposed a boycott on the trade to Coweta and ordered all the English traders to leave that *talwa*, in hopes of pressuring Coweta's *micos* to reject the invitation to war. But at the time Atkin wrote to Ellis, Coweta's *micos* "have done nothing yet to deserve [trade] being restored." To make matters worse, Atkin tried to enter Coweta and talk with its *micos*, but he was refused entry because they were engaged in "private consultation" with French agents. It was bad enough that Coweta might join the Savannahs and Cherokees against the colonies, but it was even worse that Coweta's *micos* conversed with Britain's enemy in the middle of the Seven Years' War.[1]

The reasons for Coweta's estrangement in January 1760 were many. Despite decades of mutual trade and alliance, Muscogee *talwas* such as Coweta had always entertained relationships with multiple European powers—the British to the east, Spanish to the south, and French to the west—continually playing the empires against one another to Coweta's benefit. Therefore, Atkin contended with shrewd and calculating *micos* who sought to exploit the imperial conflict for the good of their people and, in this case, invited French envoys who desired Muscogee peoples to "remove to near the Alabama Fort." As Atkin and English authorities feared during the war, the Alabama Fort—or

Fort Toulouse—was the main contact point between Muscogee and French peoples, a permanent fortified garrison among the many *talwas,* whereas all efforts by British officials to convince *micos* to let them build a similar fort had failed in the past. As the French diplomats retreated from Coweta to Fort Toulouse, Atkin gloomily concluded that "the French have not better Friends any where among those who pretend to have any Connection with us" and that he could "scarce speak bad enough of those who bear sway" in Coweta.[2]

The deteriorating situation in Coweta was further complicated by the encroachments upon Muscogee lands prior to the war. As Atkin noted in his letter to Ellis, there existed in Coweta and the other *talwas* a "natural jealousy" when it came to their lands, which had been "raised within a few late Years . . . to a pitch beyond Imagination." Only a few months earlier, a delegation of *micos* had vented their frustrations with such encroachments and in Atkin's presence had asserted how the land "belongs to all the Red People"; if the English did not stop such proceedings, the delegation maintained, they "will then go to the Fork & tell them not to stay there." Atkin not only understood the threat for what it was but also knew from personal experience that violence could easily be the answer to such encroachments. In fact, part of his mission among the *talwas* was to resolve a recent incident that resulted in the death of an English family. But when Atkin tried to broach the subject of "satisfaction" with several *micos* of Coweta and Cusseta, talks quickly broke down, and he foolishly declared "that while the Indian who was the most guilty of that Murder was living, I should never look upon" Muscogee peoples as "friends." After the fact a troubled Atkin wrote to Ellis that "this was productive of a great deal of Trouble in Negotiation," although he wisely deferred any more demands for satisfaction. In short Atkin had nothing but bad news to report to his superiors about Britain's relationship with Coweta in January 1760.[3]

Curiously enough, Atkin blamed all of the discontent in Coweta on one source: the "4 vile Brothers" whom he regarded as the "Owners of the Town Ground . . . who over rules all when on the Spot" in Coweta. He thus singled out a particular family in Coweta as responsible for all of Britain's problems in January 1760. This is incredibly significant, since Europeans rarely paid attention to the familial dimensions of the Muscogee world during the eighteenth century, let alone identified a specific family line or lineage of individuals in the process. More specifically Atkin took issue with two brothers: Escotchaby, also known as the Young (or Coweta) Lieutenant, who was the "Chief Warriour & greatest Offender about the Affairs of the Scalps," and Sempoyaffee, at times also known as Fool Harry, a *mico* without whom "nothing could be done effectually" in Coweta. Sempoyaffee and Escotchaby were joined by their two other brothers, Ufylegey and the Second Man of Coweta, in receiving both the French envoys and the Savannah-Cherokee message. As Atkin concluded to Ellis, the "4 vile Brothers" were all prone to "Deceit" and in "firm Attachment to the French."[4]

But nothing could have been further from the truth. While Atkin derided Sempoyaffee as one of the most "Frenchified" *micos* and Escotchaby "the worst person we could have amongst us at this Juncture," Sempoyaffee and Escotchaby continually reached out to British authorities (those not named Atkin) throughout the war. At a council with Governor Ellis in October 1759, Sempoyaffee confessed "there have been many lying Talks given out concerning Us," meaning himself and his brothers. Or when secondhand accounts placed Sempoyaffee, Escotchaby, or their other brothers at Fort Toulouse, it was Escotchaby who put the rumors to rest, stating that he and his brothers had indeed visited the French fort but with the intention of learning more about France's plans for attacking Fort Loudoun—a British stronghold—and establishing a second fort on the Cherokee River. In fact Sempoyaffee and Escotchaby consistently met with British officials in 1759 and 1760, where they declared that "the Nation was not to become a Party in the present War; and had advised the . . . other Indians to remain neuter." Even Ufylegey, who Atkin accused of conspiring with the French, presented his "French Commission" to Atkin, although Atkin believed Ufylegey "pretended to be deceived by the Commission, for that he took it as being only to keep the Path white and clear." If one was to believe Atkin, then, the "4 vile Brothers" were firmly in the French interest. However, the situation was far more fluid and complicated than Atkin led others to believe.[5]

Apparently Atkin's bad blood toward this family stemmed from his confrontation with Sempoyaffee and Escotchaby at the *talwa* of Tuckabatchee in late 1759. During a council meeting between Atkin and the Lower and Upper *micos,* he alleged that Sempoyaffee and Escotchaby had "behaved excessively ill" toward him, although he failed to mention specific details. But as Governor Ellis later learned, it was instead the "conduct of Mr. Atkin" that angered Sempoyaffee and Escotchaby and also alienated many of the *micos,* who remained "in a very ill humour" and "kindle[d] such a spirit of dissatisfaction and resentment" toward the British. Atkin offended so many at Tuckabatchee that, in his words, the head warrior of Cusseta, "seized with a Fit of Madness, suddenly started upon on the Cabbin behind me, and with a Pipe Hatchet fell on me & by repeated Blows brought me to the Ground." Even though Atkin survived the ordeal, he had no one to blame but himself. Meanwhile Ellis was forced to clean up Atkin's mess and reassured their superiors in London that Muscogee peoples remained at peace with the colonies, although he confided that several *micos* "candidly opened to me all the causes of their discontent," all of which revolved around Atkin's behavior. As Ellis lamented, "Mr. Atkin's Journey and Negotiations have hurt our Interest with the Creeks," and he advised that Atkin be recalled to London.[6]

Despite Atkin's blundering of the entire situation, it is somewhat astounding that both Atkin's contemporaries and future historians maintained the fiction of the "4 vile Brothers" as the adversaries of the British Empire and its colonies. Imperial agents not only continued to characterize Sempoyaffee, Escotchaby, and their relatives as "Heads of the French party" during the war, but twentieth- and twenty-first-century historians have also perpetuated the fictions that these individuals led the "pro-French party in Coweta." This is partly a cautionary tale, then, about the dangers of historical evidence and interpretation, due to the severe limitations when it comes to documents related to Native American history and the colonial nature of the archival record.[7] In Atkin's case his bias suffused the documents he left behind, with consequences for the ways in which scholars have interpreted those documents. It is also worth noting that scholars in this case have not fully put the pieces together and unassumingly adopted Atkin's bias as their own. While the characterizations of Sempoyaffee, Escotchaby, and their relatives as "Francophile" do not necessarily have repercussions for our understandings of the Seven Years' War in Muscogee territories and the broader South, and North America more generally, it does relegate the members of this Muscogee family to an ahistorical role, one that fails to convey the complexity of choices and actions undertaken by a specific family amid the conflict of empires.[8]

Atkin did, though, dedicate an excessive amount of attention to the four "vile" brothers in his brief career as superintendent of Indian affairs, and in doing so he identified several individuals who belonged to a specific Muscogee family that was at the heart of imperial anxieties during the mid-eighteenth century. Often, scholars of early America and Native America are unable to reconstruct fully the kinship and familial dynamics of Indigenous groups in North America, largely because Europeans rarely cared to document the kinship ties that structured the many Indigenous societies of North America. Altogether the significance of Atkin's observations is how he obsessed over the four brothers, who we can then trace throughout the rest of the documentary record. Atkin thereby provided a means to piece together a Muscogee family's story in eighteenth-century America, a story that revolves around the intensely intimate and familial dimensions of the Muscogee world.

This is not to suggest that we can recover or even tell this family's entire narrative. All we have are fleeting glimpses of when individuals such as Sempoyaffee, Escotchaby, and Ufylegey acted in ways that attracted attention from Europeans such as Atkin, itself a testament to the colonial and fragmentary nature of the archives. As Joshua Piker reminds scholars, "we have a great deal of information about Creeks more generally," but when it comes to the individuals or even families, there are "inevitable weaknesses of the sources available" to us.[9] Given such difficulties, it is important to assemble whatever fragments we can find, no matter how seemingly insignificant or mundane. Fortunately, in the case of the four "vile" brothers, Europeans other than Atkin recorded their interactions with these individuals of Coweta, including Spanish officials in Havana and French agents in Louisiana. With that said, Europeans mainly wrote of Sempoyaffee and Escotchaby in particular, and it is ultimately through them—with the occasional voices of their kinsmen and women—that we can better understand and articulate the central importance of family and kinship in the lives of Muscogee peoples in early America.

Another important facet of focusing on a specific family is to illustrate how kinship was critical to how Muscogee peoples navigated the dramatic changes to their world wrought by European colonialism during the eighteenth century. While Muscogee peoples had interacted with the Spanish, French, and British for many decades by the time Sempoyaffee and Escotchaby came of age, the consequences of those interactions reached a climax during the mid to late eighteenth century due to the rapid commercialization of the deerskin trade and the more intense competition between European empires for the lands and resources of North America. Together Sempoyaffee and Escotchaby experienced paradigmatic shifts to the Muscogee world that forced them to respond in myriad ways, all in response to the intrusive forces unleashed by European colonialism. While difficult, this is exactly the type of history that Claudio Saunt challenged historians to write, to "integrate those broad historical forces with the lives of people in the Native South, neither diminishing the experience of Southern Indians nor overlooking the expansive imperial economic, social, and political networks that extended into the region" and beyond.[10]

This book is not the first, nor will it be the last, to interrogate the fundamental importance of family and kinship to the Indigenous Peoples of early America. It is inspired in part by other scholars who have blended historical analysis and biography to examine the intersections of the Indigenous and early American pasts, which include but are not limited to Tiya Miles, Angela Pulley Hudson, Emma Anderson, Ann M. Little, Rachel Hope Cleves, Jenny Hale Pulsipher, Michael Leroy Oberg, Joshua A. Piker, Steven C. Hahn, Elaine Foreman Crane, Timothy J. Shannon, and Theda Perdue. Similarly Helen Rountree's biography of Pocahontas, Powhatan, and Opechancanough is an inspiring work, given her ability to sideline Europeans for a much more authentic Powhatan history of early America. Finally, Erica Armstrong Dunbar does so much with so little in her exploration of the "interior lives" of Ona (Oney) Judge, a formerly enslaved woman in George Washington's household, who only "left the world just a bit of her voice."[11] With an array of historical, ethnographic, linguistic, archaeological, theoretical, and Indigenous sources, scholars have reconstructed the worlds in which certain individuals lived in order to flesh out their brief appearances in the archives.

There also exists a robust scholarship when it comes to the significant role that family—in all its manifestations—played in the lives of the many peoples of early America. From the seminal roundtable in the *William and Mary Quarterly* (2013) called "Centering Families in Atlantic History" to works by historians of slavery such as Jennifer L. Morgan, Jennifer L. Palmer, Joshua D. Rothman, Rebecca J. Scott and Jean M. Hebrard, and Annette Gordon-Reed, family is the critical component for understanding the lives of individuals in early America.[12] The same can be said of any history detailing European, African, Mediterranean, or Asiatic merchant networks, as illustrated by Francesca Trivellato, David Hancock, Rosalind Beiler, Lindsay O'Neill, Cathy Matson, and others.[13] Family also provided infrastructure for the empires of early America, as detailed by Susanah Shaw Romney, Ann Laura Stoler, Emma Rothschild, Durba Ghosh, Adele Perry, and Sarah Pearsall, among others.[14] This is not to mention the works focused on family in the European colonies and post-Revolutionary United States, such as those by Anne Hyde, John Demos, Jan Lewis, Albert L. Hurtado, Theodore Catton, Andrew Graybill, Rhys Isaac, and others.[15] And if you know how important family has been to Native American histories, you have likely read Rose Stremlau, Brenda J. Child, Dawn Peterson, Lisa Brooks, Natalie Inman, Mikaela Adams, Claudio Saunt, Jill Doerfler, Heidi Bohaker, Michael A. McDonnell, Andrew Frank, Susan Sleeper-Smith, Catherine Denial, and John Demos, among others.[16] This is only scratching the surface of the scholarship dedicated to illustrating how critical family was to the early American past.

With that said, there is still so much that historians do not fully understand about the familial dynamics of the Muscogee world and how kinship played out in the lives of Indigenous individuals such as Sempoyaffee and Escotchaby. As Piker describes it best, "Family was . . . a critical component of eighteenth-century Creek local life, particularly for structuring political relations within a community," but scholars only have "an abstract sense of what it [family] meant for particular people living in a particular community in the colonial era."[17] Therefore, it is important to understand that family proved incredibly complex and diffuse in Indigenous worlds. And specific to family and kinship in the Muscogee world, those concepts extended beyond the nuclear or immediate household to include all of one's relatives on the mother's side, as a matrilineal people. Therefore family and kinship also meant clan relationships and the *huti* (clan residence). Sempoyaffee and Escotchaby thereby shared kinship with a host of relatives inside and outside of Coweta due to extensive matrilineal connections, and they were shaped by

and responded to the interests and ambitions of their many relatives throughout their lives. We must assume, then, whenever Sempoyaffee and Escotchaby acted in the ways that they did, they often did so at the behest of their
relatives—or at the very least, with the good of their more expansive family
in mind. Altogether, one cannot write Sempoyaffee and Escotchaby's story
without reference to their broader kinship network.

The central premise of this book, then, is that family and kinship structured
the Muscogee world, and it examines how a particular family emerged out of
the historical shadows to shape the forces of empire, colonialism, and revolution that transformed the American South during the eighteenth century.
By exploring the many but still fleeting instances in which Europeans documented Sempoyaffee and Escotchaby and the ways these brothers acted in
tandem, we can move past the limitations of the archives to rearticulate the
familial dynamics of the eighteenth-century Muscogee world. In some cases
Sempoyaffee and Escotchaby moved mountains for family, especially in their
rapid ascent to positions of leadership in Coweta during the mid to late century. In other instances, though, they made poor decisions that ended disas-
trously for their family, such as their willingness to cede millions of acres of land
to the British Empir. Altogether Sempoyaffee and Escotchaby reveal the intimate negotiations, as well as the messy and contentious decisions, that a Muscogee family made to try and navigate the onset of empire in North America.

It cannot be overemphasized, though, how fraught and imprecise it is
to reconstruct the familial dimensions of the eighteenth-century Muscogee
world, which again speaks volumes to the colonial archives. As Kate Fullagar
reminds us, "one simple reason there have been so few biographies of eighteenth-century Indigenous personalities . . . is that the sources do not readily
suggest them. When it comes to Indigenous peoples, the sources seem so
compromised—so scant or so filtered by colonial bias."[18] Due to the many
dangers and difficulties of interpreting sources from a Eurocentric archives,
populated with documents written by those who rarely cared to understand
the intimate dynamics of Indigenous communities, tracking a specific family
is exceedingly tricky. It does not help matters that even though Sempoyaffee
and Escotchaby appear in the documentary record, the archives related to
Muscogee peoples in early America is itself a small source base. In addition,
the several instances involving the two brothers occurred mostly in the years
between 1756 and 1773 and abruptly ended in 1780. To make matters even
worse, Sempoyaffee and Escotchaby are the only well-documented individuals of their family, whereas most of their relatives remain obscured and forever
nameless to scholars. Despite that deeply unsettling truth, we can still privilege this family's story from the archival fragments we have, narrated through
the experiences of these two brothers.

Admittedly, this project is born of a troubled relationship with my previous book, *George Galphin's Intimate Empire,* which tells the story of an Indian trader and the intercultural, familial dimensions of empire and colonialism in eighteenth-century America. Sempoyaffee and Escotchaby featured prominently in that story, yet I treated them as peripheral actors. I convinced myself that it was not their story I was telling, although I never believed their story was not important to tell on its own. One might suggest that this book is a companion volume to the previous work. I would suggest the opposite: Galphin's narrative is subordinate to Sempoyaffee and Escotchaby's story. Galphin's "intimate empire" hinged upon his connections to Sempoyaffee, Escotchaby, and the many members of their *huti*; the same could not be said for Escotchaby and Sempoyaffee. While Galphin is a central actor in their story, he is not the be-all and end-all that Sempoyaffee and Escotchaby proved to be for him.

The story of Sempoyaffee, Escotchaby, and their family is also reflective of how concrete and intimate stories personalize the past in ways that other histories cannot. Over the course of my brief career as a teacher, at an institution in a region relatively removed from early America, students have tended to gravitate toward the stories of individuals who shaped and were shaped by the early American world. It is the manifold ways that individuals navigated the world around them, a chaotic world at that, that have resonated the most with students, which has been informative in how I think about, write, and teach early American history. Especially when talking about the entangled nature of European and Indigenous communities, nations, and empires over the course of three centuries, I find that stories like that of Sempoyaffee and Escotchaby make the subject all the more real for students. Stories also prove important when talking about how Indigenous groups confronted, negotiated, and subverted the imperial advance in North America over that three-hundred-year period, and stories give students a sense of how central the Indigenous Peoples of North America were to the existence—and in some cases the destruction—of empires in early America.

Naturally, such stories involved conflict and violence, and as Ned Blackhawk reminds scholars and students alike, the conflicts between Europeans and Indigenous Peoples produced a "violent transformation of Indian lands and lives" and created a legacy of "Indigenous trauma" that lives on today.[19] But stories like that of two brothers from Coweta reveal how violence was only one facet of the centuries-long relationship between Europeans and Indigenous Americans. And such stories not only matter in what they can teach us but also dramatically illustrate the central place of Indigenous Peoples in the grand narrative we call American history, being one and the same as they have always been and will always be. Finally, stories of individuals provide us with more than just a better way to understand the early American past; these two brothers demonstrate the resiliency, innovation, and vibrancy that has always characterized the Indigenous Peoples of North America and their histories and futures.

Yet being a non-Native person, let alone non-Muscogee, means that when I tell the story of Sempoyaffee and Escotchaby, I perpetuate a distinct form of violence or colonialism. In short, what does it mean to research and write a history of the Indigenous Peoples of North America, set in the early American past, as a non-Native? Ultimately, what are my responsibilities as a non-Native scholar to the peoples and communities who are descendants of Sempoyaffee and Escotchaby? First of all, I take seriously oral histories and Creation Stories, both of which can assist scholars in decolonizing the archives. Second, I try to read and understand every source from the perspective of a matrilineal people, who operated in the world according to their kinship connections to one another, other Indigenous groups, and at times Europeans, and thereby embrace seeing the world in different yet nonetheless valid ways. I am also honest by admitting my deficiencies as a non-Muscogee, non-Native person and committing myself to sharing this story. Because ultimately Sempoyaffee and Escotchaby's narrative is one of centering the irrevocable place of the Indigenous Peoples of North America to the entirety of US history. And it is also a story of healing, the healing of historical apathy and ignorance on the part of non-Native peoples in the United States that continues today.

This book should be thought of as a story in two parts. The first three chapters scaffold the Muscogee world that Sempoyaffee and Escotchaby inhabited in the early to mid-eighteenth century. Much of their story in part 1 relies on general sources and secondary literature related to Muscogee peoples during the early eighteenth century, which helps to contextualize the scattered appearances that the two men make in the archives during these early decades. Chapter 1 specifically details early eighteenth-century life in the *talwa* of Coweta and, with it, particularly related to what family life would have looked like in that community. From politics and trade, labor and gender roles, residence patterns and daily town activities, and religious ceremonies to entertainment pastimes and cultural taboos, it is wholly important to understand the world that Sempoyaffee and Escotchaby came of age within, from infancy to manhood. One of the other important elements of chapter 1 is to articulate the efforts by Muscogee peoples to live according to their ideals of a cosmic balance, which was central to how they understood the world around them. Within the eighteenth-century Muscogee world, there existed opposing forces in all things: peace and conflict, order and disorder, women and men, Upper and Lower *talwas,* red and white moieties, the Upper/Middle/ Lower Worlds, and so on. This worldview separated the Muscogee world into distinct halves constantly in tension with one another, and Muscogee peoples consistently sought to maintain a semblance of balance between these ideals in every aspect of their lives. This worldview is incredibly important, then, for understanding why individuals such as Sempoyaffee and Escotchaby responded to the forces of empire and colonialism in the ways that they did in the eighteenth century.

It is also important to note that in these early chapters, and especially chapter 1, I employ an ethnohistorical approach to reconstruct the vibrant Muscogee world in which the two brothers came of age, a world shaped by family and kinship, cultural practices, and cosmologies. Because no records exist for Sempoyaffee's and Escotchaby's early lives, chapter 1 is more about what the eighteenth-century Muscogee world would have looked like for young boys and young men. While Sempoyaffee and Escotchaby are rather absent in this chapter, it is important to flesh out the Muscogee world and worldviews that were vital parts of their lives. But to do so, the author utilizes written and oral sources from throughout the eighteenth and early nineteenth centuries, which poses the real danger of upstreaming and downsteaming when using the sources. While cognizant of such limitations—especially at the cost of understanding what elements of the Muscogee world changed and/or maintained consistency over the century—I attempt to walk a fine line between what could have been and what must have been in the early lives of Sempoyaffee and Escotchaby.

Chapter 2 explores Sempoyaffee's life in the 1730s–1750s, when he assumed the position of Coweta's *tustenogy* (or *tustunnuggee, tastanagi*). Sempoyaffee came of age during a period when Muscogee and European worlds became increasingly entangled. However, Muscogee peoples maintained the upper hand against the French and English by pitting those two empires against each other to the benefit of each *talwa,* at the same time preventing the English and French from fully encroaching upon their territories. It was in this context that Sempoyaffee emerged as Coweta's *tustenogy,* the head warrior, a position of great leadership and responsibility, particularly in times of conflict. As *tustenogy* he would have constantly endeavored to balance his role as the war leader and his influence among Coweta's young men with that of Coweta's civil leaders—the *micos*—whose primary function within the *talwa* was to maintain peace and trade. It was also at this time that Sempoyaffee's family broadened its kinship ties to Europeans, particularly with Coweta's resident trader, George Galphin, in order to represent and assert their own political interests within Coweta and in the *talwa's* relationship with Europeans and other Indigenous groups, which conflicted with the political ambitions of other families in Coweta such as that of Malatchi and Mary Bosomworth.

Chapter 3 focuses on the same period as the previous chapter but switches perspectives to Escotchaby and explores his time as Coweta's Cherokee king, an important role that embodies the intimate connections that existed between the different Indigenous groups in the eighteenth-century South. As the Cherokee king, Escotchaby acted as an official emissary of peace between Muscogee and Cherokee peoples, who were often at war with one another during the early to mid-eighteenth century. Escotchaby's position was unique at the time because it was the product of a mutual dialogue between Muscogee and Cherokee peoples and a role that situated Escotchaby as the counterbalancing force to his brother within the Muscogee world. Thus Escotchaby the Cherokee king was responsible for ensuring peace between Muscogee and Cherokee peoples, whereas Sempoyaffee the *tustenogy* waged war against the Cherokee. And in reaching such prominent positions in Coweta by midcentury, Sempoyaffee and Escotchaby embodied their family's ambitions and hopes for the future, to guide their family and *talwa* in a world increasingly beset by European empires and colonialism.

The final three chapters capitalize on a larger source base during the 1760s and 1770s and highlight Sempoyaffee's and Escotchaby's negotiations of empire in the mid to late eighteenth century. Chapter 4 details the Seven Years' War, a conflict in which Sempoyaffee transitioned from the *tustenogy* to a *mico,* one of Coweta's headmen whose goal was to ensure peace for his townspeople. Meanwhile Escotchaby succeeded his brother as Coweta's *tustenogy,* even though he still retained the role of Cherokee king. Together the two brothers navigated the imperial contest by playing the British off against the French and vice versa but always preserving neutrality for their family and *talwa.* At the same time, Sempoyaffee and Escotchaby contended with the other *micos* and young men of Coweta who sought to elevate their own influence within the *talwa* while trying to diminish the influence of Sempoyaffee and Escotchaby in the process. By the end of the Seven Years' War, though, Sempoyaffee and Escotchaby had successfully positioned themselves as two of the principal *micos* for Coweta, once again embodying their family's hopes and ambitions for the future.

Chapter 5 examines the critical decade between the Seven Years' War and the American Revolution to illustrate the profound transformations to the Muscogee world after 1763. It was at this point Escotchaby also transitioned from the *tustenogy* to a *mico* and, alongside Sempoyaffee, presided over one of the most turbulent periods of time in the Native South. With the expulsion of France and Spain from eastern North America, Indigenous groups no longer had the ability to play Europeans off against one another. This created a sense of unpredictability and anxiety for both Muscogee and British peoples. To make matters worse, a dramatic combination of settler encroachments upon Muscogee territories, the deregulation of the deerskin trade, several treaties that ceded Muscogee lands, and the growing resentment of the young men in Coweta and the other *talwas* all produced a sense of disorder that threatened to upend the precarious balance of the Muscogee world. Everything came to a head in 1773 with the Treaty of Augusta, which ceded more than two million acres of land, a treaty that was engineered in part by Sempoyaffee and Escotchaby to try and reign in the chaos of the previous decade. When the treaty failed to create peace, though, the two brothers joined the rest of their townsmen in a violent conflict—what I call the Coweta Conflict (1773–83)—to try and put a stop to the incessant encroachments by the English colonies. This decade of crisis represented a pivotal moment within the eighteenth-century Muscogee world, as Sempoyaffee, Escotchaby, and the people of Coweta pursued alternative strategies to prevent the inroads of empire.

The final chapter reveals how the Coweta Conflict persisted into and throughout the broader Revolutionary War, as Sempoyaffee and Escotchaby continued to combat the colonies' encroachments upon Muscogee territories. Whereas scholars have argued that Muscogee peoples and the majority of other Indigenous groups sought to remain neutral in the early years of the war, the people of Coweta—led in part by Sempoyaffee and Escotchaby— violently resisted the intrusions on their lands by the American revolution-aries from the very beginning. When not protecting Muscogee territories, Sempoyaffee and Escotchaby solicited support from Spanish Havana and combated the efforts of the other *talwas* to remain neutral during the war. However, it was also during the revolution that Sempoyaffee and Escotchaby faced an internal crisis of their own, in which a faction of young men from Coweta, bitter and frustrated with the decades of violence and encroach-ment, sought to supplant the influence of the two brothers and convince their townspeople to remove them from their positions of leadership within the *talwa*.

And with that, the American Revolution brings an unceremonious end to Sempoyaffee and Escotchaby's story. Their experiences in the Revolution are brief and incomplete and represent a more insidious trend of how Americans erased the Indigenous Peoples of North America from their narratives during and after the war. One of the reasons that Sempoyaffee and Escotchaby's story ends in 1780 is because they disappear altogether from the archives. While some may attribute this to the nature of those who were the "winners" and "losers" of the Revolutionary War, this significantly detracts from the real violence that Indigenous people such as Sempoyaffee and Escotchaby experienced by being written out of the archives by the so-called winners. The Indigenous Peoples of North America were not just obstacles to US independence, but the diversity of their choices during the revolution presents a counternarrative that troubles the more nationalistic narratives of the founding of the United States. In this sense Sempoyaffee and Escotchaby are inconvenient actors with their own motives and interests—and those of their immediate and extended family members—that conflicted with the revolutionaries. As Kathleen DuVal puts it so beautifully, the Revolutionary experiences of Indigenous Peoples "is a story without minutemen, without founding fathers, without rebels [and] reveals a different war with unexpected participants, forgotten outcomes, and surprising winners and losers," a narrative of those who "tried, in dramatic and innovative ways, to use the war to forward their own ambitions for themselves, their families, and their nations."[20]

It should be noted, though, that Escotchaby and Sempoyaffee hailed from a particular family (huti), talwa (Coweta), region (Lower Muscogee), and people (Muscogee), but this should not detract from the larger importance of their story and what it can tell us about how Indigenous Peoples strategically navigated the forces of empire and colonialism in the eighteenth century: as a family. They are also reflective of the broader intersections of Indigenous and imperial worlds in early America: the compromises, exchanges, and negotiations that defined Indigenous-European interactions over three centuries. And even though the mid to late eighteenth century represented a break from what came before, Sempoyaffee and Escotchaby's story is hardly unique to the broader breakdown of Indigenous-European interactions in eastern North America after 1763. In fact, one might argue that Sempoyaffee and Escotchaby's story is a quintessentially American story, a testament to the intimate entanglement of Indigenous and European peoples in early America.

One

The Muscogee World, 1700–1730

In June 1735 a delegation of Lower and Upper *micos* journeyed along the Creek Path, destined for Savannah, the infant settlement of the newly established Georgia colony. Led by Chigelli, a *mico* of Coweta and one of the preeminent leaders among the Lower *talwas* during the early to mid-eighteenth century, the group was greeted by James Oglethorpe and British authorities, who hosted the *micos* in Savannah for the next three days. Chigelli and the other *micos* descended upon Savannah for one purpose: to forge a formal relationship and an alliance of peace and trade with the new colony. During the visit, it was Chigelli who related one of his peoples' Creation Stories—the Cusseta Migration Story—to signify a new beginning with the British, which was afterward "written on a Buffaloe Skin" and sent to London, where it was to be preserved as a testament to their new friendship.[1]

The Cusseta Migration Story has been utilized by scholars of the Native South in myriad ways. One of the most compelling interpretations has been Steven C. Hahn's argument that Chigelli performed a very particular version of that story in 1735. As narrator Chigelli not only asserted his influence among the other *micos* at the conference but also made the case for the importance of his *talwa*, Coweta, in any future negotiations with the British. It is hardly a coincidence that at the end of the story, Chigelli declared, "I am of the Eldest Town and was chosen to rule after the death of the Emperour Brims. I have a Strong Mouth and will Declare this Resolution to the rest of the Nations." As Hahn asserts, the story represented "Coweta's own vision of the Creek Nation and its privileged role in leading it." But even if Chigelli told his own variation of that Creation Story in 1735, this does not diminish the cultural elements and traditions that were embedded within it. The very nature of Creation Stories is that they are malleable and fluid, changing over the course of generations but retaining cultural truths about the people. In

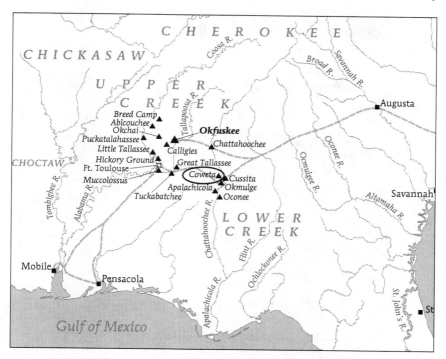

Map of the Creek Path (dashed line) between British North America & Creek Country (Coweta circled). (OKFUSKEE: A CREEK INDIAN TOWN IN COLONIAL AMERICA by Joshua Piker, Cambridge, Mass.: Harvard University Press, copyright © 2004 by the President and Fellows of Harvard College)

other words there is "no single hegemonic narrative" when it comes to Creation Stories, and for Muscogee peoples their stories were an amalgamation of several different Indigenous groups that coalesced in the seventeenth and eighteenth centuries.[2] However, these Creation Stories all have thematic similarities that speak to what Muscogee peoples believed about themselves and the world around them. The fact that Chigelli employed the Cusseta Migration Story can tell us a lot about what mattered to Muscogee peoples and what they valued about themselves in 1735, which is critical for understanding the broader world that Sempoyaffee and Escotchaby came of age within during the early eighteenth century.[3]

As the story begins, the Cussetas emerged out of the ground and followed the "Setting of the Sun" in search of the "white path." After much suffering, they settled upon the "red blood river," where they lived for several years, until they encountered a thunderous hill—the King of Hills—with "a great fire." The Cussetas then took "Fire from the Hill" and joined "the people of three Different Nations": the Abeka, Alabama, and Chickasaw. Together they performed the Busk, an annual fast and offering of the first fruits, where the "Women make Fire by themselves and learned to be separate at Certain times from the Men." However, all the different peoples disputed who was older and "Should have the Rule," and it is here that Chigelli likely told his own version of the story. According to him, the first to cover a red stick from the "Root upwards with Scalps of Enemys . . . should be the eldest," which just so happened to be the Cussetas. It was also at this time that the King of Birds appeared and started to kill the people. To confuse the Eagle, the Cussetas made a "Figure of a Woman," and with advice from a red rat, they killed the Eagle. But in reverence, Muscogee peoples afterward carried eagle feathers with them, that were painted "red for Warr and White for peace and if an Enemy comes with White Feathers and a White Mouth and makes a Noise like an Eagle they cannot kill him." The people continued to travel in search of the white path and later met the Coosas upon the Caloosahatchee River, who asked the Cussetas to save them from the Man Eater, a lion. The Cussetas dug a pit and "took a motherless Child and throw'd it into the Lyons way," and the lion fell into the pit and died. Once again Muscogee peoples, in remembrance of that part of the story, "take Physick and fast six days and the next day they go to Warr."[4]

After four years, Chigelli's ancestors left the Coosa and crossed several rivers still in search of the white path. They first came upon a High Hill and found people there. To learn if the people were good, the Cussetas shot white arrows, but the Hill people seized the "White Arrows and made them Red." The Cussetas left the Hill people alone, traveled until they met the Flat Heads, and again shot white arrows, which were returned red once more. The Cussetas, out of anger, killed all the Flat Heads except two and pursued them "till they came to the White Path again." Then the Cussetas stumbled upon the Pallachaculla or "white" path people, who convinced them to drink *cassina* (black drink), and "told them their Hearts were [now] White." It was there that Chigelli's ancestors remained, on the Chattahoochee River that separates present-day Georgia and Alabama. Once again Chigelli transitioned into his variation of the story, as the Cussetas settled two *talwas* on the Chattahoochee—Cusseta and Coweta—which were "allowed to be the Head Towns of the Upper and Lower Creeks." Even though Cusseta and Coweta were "Bloody Towns" and possessed "Red Hearts," they were still determined to follow the white path. Chigelli then turned to Oglethorpe and concluded that "the coming of the English to this place is for good to them and their Children," and he pledged to be at peace with the colony.[5]

While the biggest takeaway for British authorities was the offer of friendship and alliance, the Cusseta Migration Story encapsulates much about the Muscogee world in the early eighteenth century. The importance of kinship is constant throughout the story, such as when Chigelli's ancestors sacrificed a motherless child to the Man Eater to save their people. In a matrilineal society in which kinship was reckoned by female descent, the abnormal absence of kinship ties to a woman made one "motherless" and thereby expendable. Similarly, the story explains how Muscogee peoples came to be as one community by the early eighteenth century, being descended from a heterogenous mix of language groups held together by kinship ties. The migration story also illustrates Muscogee ideals or understandings of the cosmic order, in which opposing forces were constantly at play in the world and in one's life. For instance the Cussetas constantly searched for the white path "for their good"— that was signified by eagle feathers and white arrows, metaphors for white mouths and hearts—but consistently acted with red hearts, as when they attacked the Flat Heads with red arrows or "Bloody Tomihawks." Also telling is the fact that Muscogee women, the life-givers within the Muscogee world, removed themselves from the presence of the men, the life-takers, at several points in the story, and thereby men and women "learned to be separate" from each other. This dynamic between two forces—red and white, women and men—governed much of how Muscogee peoples understood the world in the early eighteenth century, as a balance between those forces throughout one's life. Yet there were traditions and practices to help them mediate these opposing forces, by performing rituals such as the annual Busk or drinking *cassina* to "whiten" one's heart and restore one's walk along the white path. Thus it was into this vibrant world of family and kinship, Creation Stories and cosmology, ritual and ceremony that Sempoyaffee and Escotchaby came of age during the early eighteenth century, immersed in the beliefs and practices of their people handed down over the millennia.

Early Years: Family and Kinship, the *Huti,* and Creation Stories

The early eighteenth-century Muscogee world revolved around family and kinship. We do not know when Sempoyaffee and Escotchaby were born, and we know even less about their immediate and extended relatives, but it is not impossible to reconstruct a semblance of their familial environs by using what little information they provided about themselves and our basic understandings of how kinship functioned for the Muscogee. The two brothers were born in the Lower *talwa* of Coweta around the time of the Yamasee War (1715–17), given that both identified themselves as "Old men" and were distinguished as *micos* in 1768. They were also close in age, for even though Escotchaby was the eldest of his siblings, Sempoyaffee preceded Escotchaby in their many accomplishments as hunters, warriors, and *micos*. They had two other brothers, Ufylegey and the Second Man of Coweta, both of whom served as "ruling [men] in their Absence."[6] Meanwhile, it was well-known that Sempoyaffee and Escotchaby hailed from a family that "has more to do in Land Affairs, than any other Indians of the Lower Creeks," meaning the two were born into an important lineage. The most important member of the family would have been their mother, being a matrilineal people and all kinship ties reckoned through the matron.[7] Their mother maintained a constant presence in their lives, as late as 1763 accompanying Escotchaby to visit the Spanish in East Florida.[8]

In addition to family, Sempoyaffee and Escotchaby were part of a specific clan, which was considered the "most important social entity to which a person belonged" in the Muscogee world. As a matrilineal society, clan membership was determined along the mother's lineage, meaning Sempoyaffee and Escotchaby were also linked to their mother's clan relatives and were part of a collective matrilineage.[9] Regrettably, we do not know the clan that Sempoyaffee and Escotchaby belonged to, although it may have been one of the more influential ones.[10] There is extenuating evidence that suggests they were part of the Tiger clan, being one of the "principal Families" and "most numerably of any in the Nation."[11] However, there is also evidence that points to their being of the Bear clan, another influential clan in the Muscogee world.[12] In any event Sempoyaffee and Escotchaby belonged to an expansive family via blood and clan ties.[13]

Clan membership was critically important in the early eighteenth-century Muscogee world. Belonging to a clan provided a Muscogee person with a sense of identity and determined what one's responsibilities were to other peoples within the Muscogee world. In particular all the members of a clan abided by certain taboos, and one of the most significant was refraining from sex or marriage with a kinswoman or a woman of the same clan, to ensure group identity was not broken or violated. When a male member of the clan was to be wed, it was the women who consulted the other clan's female members and the "brothers and uncles on the maternal side." One of the other important functions of a clan was related to policing behavior. In the event of a clan member committing adultery, the individuals were punished by the clan, some of whom would "[go] to the house of the woman, the remainder to the family house of the adulterer . . . and then crop them."[14] In the case of murder, the clan "alone have the right of taking satisfaction," and even the *micos* "have nothing to do or to say in the business." As members of the same clan as the murderer, clan members were obligated to put the murderer to death, although there were instances in which the family of the deceased accepted gifts as compensation for the killing of a loved one. It was also common for clan members to accompany one another to important visits and negotiations: when Escotchaby, for example, ventured to St. Augustine in 1763, he "brought with him his Youth, his Mother, and other Caciques," some of whom were his clan relations.[15]

Due to kinship and clan connections, Muscogee peoples lived together in what was called the *huti*.[16] The *huti* "consisted of a cluster of nearby house compounds occupied by members of a residential matrilineage," where family and clan members shared the land and their labor with one another. In fact each *talwa* such as Coweta consisted of around "four to ten lineages" and *hutis*, and "each block of houses in the town . . . consisted of a household comprising a matrilineage." Thus the spatial dimensions of every *talwa* reinforced how clan membership "was more important than membership in anything else" in the Muscogee world. In addition to the many houses of a *huti*, the matrilineage maintained a cook-room, summer and winter-lodging houses, a warehouse to store deerskins, a granary, a kitchen garden, and cow pens. To reinforce further the matrilineal nature of the Muscogee world, all these buildings belonged to the female members of the matrilineage.[17]

Surrounded by family and clan in the *huti*, young boys would have learned early and often about their Creation Stories. As Gregory Smithers reminds scholars, Creation Stories evoke great "meaning and purpose," "connected people to a place and a community," and were critical to an individual's identity.[18] Although many variations of Creation Stories exist that provide "different ways of accounting for the beginning of time and the creation of earth and the people," these stories were all passed down orally and firmly established how the Muscogee world was structured in the past and present.[19] The stories also embodied conceptions of sacred time, where despite millennia between creation and the present, Muscogee peoples reenacted and reexperienced creation with rituals and ceremonies such as the Busk. This is why Europeans could not fathom or credit Creation Stories as real or authentic, even when confronted with oral histories such as that of Chigelli in 1735, which firmly rooted how Muscogee peoples migrated to the Chattahoochee River "about Ten Thousand Years ago." To transmit such knowledge, it was often maternal uncles who taught children the stories that explained how they came to be as a people and imparted certain values or morals to children.[20]

In several Creation Stories, the Muscogee world existed in three parts—the Upper, Lower, and Middle Worlds[21]—and the people lived upon the Middle World. All three worlds were governed by the Great Being Above, also named at various times as the Giver of Breath, Master of the Breath, Master of Life, Giver and Taker of Breath, and Master of All, who made all things and "gave this Land to us." Even though humans lived on the Middle World, they shared relationships with the animate and inanimate beings of the Upper and Lower Worlds. For example Muscogee peoples still communed with their ancestors who no longer resided in the Middle World, from whom they acquired knowledge such as the "Ancient Custom[s] of their Nation."[22] The relationships between living and nonliving family members were often mediated in dreams and visions, where the ancestors urged the living—in the words of Stump Finger, a *mico* of Coweta—to "not forget the Bones of our People." One's ancestors also took the shape of things, such as town or ceremonial fires referred to as Grandfather, who continued to reach out to and teach their descendants. Similarly Muscogee peoples were in relationship with the creatures and things of all three worlds, such as eagles, who traveled back and forth between the Middle and Upper Worlds as messengers or heralds. They also refused to harm snakes for "fear of receiving injury" from otherworldly forces, as serpents were one of the most powerful beings of the Lower World. This is why Upper and Lower *micos* valued certain things such as eagle wings, which "is the Same as our Bodies." There were also dances like the *tcula obnga* (fox dance) or *suli obnga* (buzzard dance), clan totems of "some Bird or Beast," and medicines[23] that signified Muscogee peoples' relationships with the many beings and objects of all three worlds.[24]

However, the Middle World existed in a precarious balance with the Upper and Lower Worlds, all of which were "permeated with different and opposing forces." As Chigelli cautioned in 1735, "He that is above, knows what he made us for, we know nothing, we are in the Dark." Living upon the Middle World, then, Muscogee peoples could commune with or call on the beings and energies of the Upper and Lower Worlds while never permitting the two to come into contact with one another. This cosmic balance between Upper and Lower Worlds was maintained on the Middle World, for if the forces or beings of the Upper World ever overwhelmed the forces or beings of the Lower World, or vice versa, the imbalance threatened to sow disorder in the Middle World. This is why Muscogee peoples performed a series of annual ceremonies and rituals, including preparations for war and celebrating the first fruits of the harvest, as well as mourning the loss of a loved one and, in the case of women, separating themselves when menstruating, all to maintain a semblance of balance between the worlds.[25]

The early eighteenth-century Muscogee world, then, revolved around ideals of a cosmic balance that consistently needed to be maintained and manifested in all manners of life. This is why there existed Upper and Lower *talwas*,[26] who hosted "separate councils, claimed separate territories, and very often pursued different foreign policies" from one another. As several Upper *micos* remarked to British authorities in 1767, "we look upon the lower Creeks to be a different nation from us" and "cannot intermeddle with them." This cosmic balance likewise extended to the *talwas,* in which one town, such as Coweta, was paired with another town, such as Cusseta, as "sister towns." The *talwas* were further distinguished by a moiety system that organized *talwas* as either "red" (Coweta) or "white" (Cusseta). While the red *talwas* assumed preeminence in times of conflict, whereas the white *talwas* did so in times of peace, the two concurrently existed as forces in tension with one another.[27] Even within the *talwas* themselves, leadership varied between the *micos* and the *tustenogy* depending on whether the *talwa* was at peace or in conflict. Even clans reflected the cosmic balance, being "separated into two divisions, one called *Hathagalgi,* 'People of the Whites,' and the other *Tcilokogalga* . . . [the] fighters, blood, red."[28]

The cosmic equilibrium evoked in Creation Stories extended to a separation of the sexes within the Muscogee world. Women possessed generative or life-giving power that was nowhere more evident than in the act of giving life to a child or producing food that nourished one's family. In contrast hunting and warfare were central to a man's identity, and such responsibilities entailed violence and destruction, the opposite powers of women. Therefore the separation of women and men was instilled in Muscogee peoples from the beginning of their lives through their Creation Stories. The many stories about Corn Woman exhibited the "overwhelming power of female fertility," to which her sons witnessed and were "terrified by the capacity of women to create living things from their own bodies." In every variation Corn Woman— or Corn Mother—sacrificed herself to feed her family and community.[29] This is why women were known as *hompita haya* (food makers), who gave of themselves through their labors in cultivating corn and making *sofki* (corn gruel) to feed their people; why *micos* consistently referred to the lands on which they lived as "our Mother"; and why the most important *talwas* were considered "Mother Towns" and all peoples "were nursed by the Breast of the Same Mother." When women's life-producing powers manifested in the Middle World, such as when menstruating or when giving birth, women sequestered themselves away from the men so as not to upset the balance and thereby endanger the community.[30]

In the Muscogee world, women were primarily responsible for child rearing, food cultivation, and the general care of the community, whereas men supported such activities in very specific ways. Much of a Muscogee woman's time was spent tending to the *huti*'s fields and gardens, cooking the day's meals, collecting wild fruits, nuts, and medicinal herbs, or hauling wood and water back and forth. Women also fashioned homespun blankets and shoes as well as pottery, dishware, and baskets, all a testament to their creative power. Meanwhile, men cleared the fields before and after the women planted, hunted for the meat that the women cooked or the furs that were processed by the women for the deerskin trade, erected the buildings and other infrastructure for the *huti,* and trained to defend their families and *talwas.* Such gender-specific labors were complementary in nature yet also segregated women from men, thus reflecting the idyllic balance imparted to Muscogee peoples by their Creation Stories.[31]

However, Muscogee peoples constantly struggled to lead a life of peace—or to walk the white path—because of everyday disagreements and violence. While Muscogee women and men believed the "earth is white" and "everything on its face is peaceful," the potential for spilling blood on the land and staining it red was real and thus required vigilance to prevent conflict or to restore peace in the event of violence. In many cases when talking to Europeans, *micos* substituted the metaphor of the white path for its opposite, the red path or "red road," to convey a sense of how the cosmic balance played out in their daily lives.[32] Although conflict inevitably took place and interrupted the idyllic balance, often denoted by symbols such as black and red wampum beads and other emblems, peace could be restored and was signified by the giving of white beads and chalk, tobacco, and other items. These were reminders that everyone "is the Same as the Earth . . . which is white."[33]

One of the most important ways that Muscogee peoples renewed the cosmic balance and returned the Middle World to a state of peace was by celebrating the annual Busk, also called the Green Corn Ceremony. The Busk—a corruption of the Muscogee word for fasting (*poskita*)—occurred annually during the summer months (usually July or August) when the corn ripened, and it represented a time of annual renewal and reconciliation as Muscogee peoples forgave all quarrels and conflicts from the previous year and thus provided a "turning point" in the new year.[34] According to Benjamin Hawkins, he was told by several Muscogee peoples in the late eighteenth century that it was the Great Being Above who "impressed it on them to follow and adhere to . . . the Boosketau." As several scholars have likewise demonstrated, the Green Corn Ceremony was descended from Muscogee peoples' Mississippian ancestors, who placed great emphasis on that ritual practice. Because of the Busk's importance within the Muscogee world, all usual activities within the *talwa* ceased, which Europeans such as John Stuart frustratingly noted when trying to contact several *micos* and instead "found the Religious Ceremony of the Green Corn Feast a temporary insuperable difficulty."[35]

Even though the Busk looked different in each *talwa* and evolved over time, the practice both reinforced and epitomized Muscogee worldviews.

For instance, women and men remained separate throughout the ceremony. Women were responsible for food preparation and forbidden from entering the town square where all the men assembled. During this time men could not touch any woman, and it was "a rule that when the men wanted to refer to women, they were not to use the word which meant 'woman.'" At the start of the Busk, the women retreated to the *huti,* where each would "extinguish all the old fires—throw out all the brands and ashes and cleanse her whole house and all her household furniture." The men then "cleanse[d] the council house and the sacred square in every part" and "white-washed anew the white seats and such other parts as were kept white." Men and women remained apart in separate quarters at night, and any woman who was menstruating was forbidden from doing any work at the time of the Busk. When it came time to "make new fire" and thereby signal the start of a new year,[36] the *tustenogy* "rehearsed briefly the traditional history of the people, emphasized the importance of the festival they were observing, and informed them that it had existed from immemorial times" before he reiterated the rituals and rules governing their world. Afterward the women—still not yet allowed into the town square—would send young boys to the men, who brought back the new fire to the women. The women then rekindled the fires in their *hutis.* Women and men also cleansed themselves separately and, for the next several days, did not intermingle, although they danced to celebrate the newly ripened corn.[37] Toward the end of the Busk, several appointed women "brought the new corn, cooked and set it down near the sacred square," and after another round of cleansing, the entire *talwa* gathered to eat and begin the festivities, everyone "being now considered clean from all impurities." The Busk, then, was a time unlike any other in the Muscogee calendar: a time of great importance and the celebration of creation, an experience that reinforced Muscogee understandings of the cosmic order.[38]

Therefore, Sempoyaffee and Escotchaby's childhood would have been largely spent among their mother's people in the *huti.* As the sources of both identity and education, family and clan members within the *huti* played significant roles in the early lives of children. One of the most important responsibilities of one's relatives was to orient children toward the ways of seeing and understanding the world around them, from the Creation Stories that imparted cultural truths and lessons to the rituals and ceremonies designed to maintain the cosmic order that was so central to Muscogee worldviews. And as Sempoyaffee and Escotchaby transitioned from childhood to adulthood, they would have continued to experience how family and kinship, their peoples' Creation Stories, and the cosmic balance manifested visibly in their daily lives.

From Boys to Men: Becoming Young Men
in the Muscogee World

Like other young boys growing up among their mothers' people in the *huti*, immersed in a world of kinship and creation, Sempoyaffee and Escotchaby would have been put to work for the good of the *huti*. During the planting season—the spring, summer, and fall months—boys helped in communal work such as planting the *talwa*'s common fields and maybe those of the *huti*, serving as messengers between *talwas* or as guides for visitors, assisting family and clan members or other townsmen in erecting buildings, and retrieving runaway cattle, chickens, and livestock. Children also fished along the Chattahoochee River, where they used scoop nets to catch the fish that they brought back to the women who cooked for the *huti*. Young boys thus provided labor for a mixed, integrated economy that combined both "multi-cropping and intercropping" agriculture with recreational and commercial hunting, gathering, and fishing.[39]

Naturally children found ways to break up the routine of work. For instance young boys and girls were not prohibited from taking part in certain dances, particularly the nightly social dances, which also conveyed knowledge and ritual to youth. Some children may have also practiced with instruments, such as the tambour rattle or drums, to help "keep exact time" with the dancers. Young children played games to pass the time, such as chunkey in the designated yard of the town square. Players "rolled a stone disk and then attempted to estimate where the stone would stop rolling," followed by a competition to "see who could land their stick or spear closest to the place the chunkey stone stopped." Some games exposed young boys to their first experiences of what manhood would bring later, like the ball game, which was meant to simulate warfare. The ball game involved members of a single *talwa*—at times in competition with other *talwas*[40]—who formed two teams and wielded a racquet nearly three feet long, the object being to "[carry] off the ball from the opposite party, after being hurled into the air, midway between two high pillars, which are the goals, and the party who bears off to the ball to their pillar wins."[41]

As young boys grew older, they would have joined the other men in hunting to provide food and to secure deerskins for trade.[42] Beyond the material importance of feeding the members of one's *huti*, hunting provided a means for men to distinguish themselves from one another and to prove themselves as providers who might one day ascend to a position of leadership within the *talwa* based upon their skills as hunters and, later, warriors. As several *micos* articulated to Henry Ellis in 1760, Muscogee men "take great Pains in hunting" in order to prove to themselves, their families, and their *talwas* that they could "supply our Families with Cloathing" and food, one of the most important attributes of one's manhood. Muscogee Creation Stories reinforced how men were tasked with hunting by the Great Being Above to provide for the subsistence of their people. For example, in the Coweta Origin Migration Story, it was the Cowetas—instead of the Cussetas—who traveled far and wide in search for "where the hunting was good." It was also expected that men show proper respect and ritual when hunting, such as sacrificing a part of their first kill to give thanks for their success and out of acknowledgement for the animal's sacrifice to feed one's family.[43]

Hunting was also a family affair. During the hunting season—the fall and winter months—a hunter and his immediate family left the *huti* in search of game and deerskins. Each family hunted in areas specifically designated by their *huti* or *talwa,* places they called their "Beloved hunting Grounds." For Sempoyaffee and Escotchaby, these were lands east and north of Coweta "all the way to the Ogeechee and Oconee Rivers" and lands south of Coweta toward Pensacola and the Tensaw River, where they set up temporary winter camps for the season. The women who joined the hunting party provided the complementary labors to process the meat and the deerskins that the men brought in from the hunt.[44] The other members of the *huti,* such as elders, matrons, young children, and those unable to hunt or assist in such labors, stayed behind at the *huti* and awaited the return of their relatives in the spring.[45]

Hunting provided young men with an opportunity to expand their knowledge of the paths, riverways, and territories of the American South. Hunters from Coweta ventured as far south as Pensacola and as far east and north as the Cherokee and Chickasaw territories, whose hunting grounds overlapped in certain areas with Muscogee lands. In doing so Sempoyaffee and Escotchaby would have traversed a "world of paths" that connected the peoples and lands of the South to one another.[46] In addition to navigating the paths that linked the *talwas* together and the Creek Path that led to the English colonies, hunters from Coweta traveled along various hunting paths to the south, east, and north of the *talwa,* which intersected with other hunting paths from other *talwas.* And being so close to the Cherokee and Chickasaw, Coweta's hunters trekked along the larger Chickasaw Path and Cherokee Path that linked their peoples to each other. There were also the waterways such as the Chattahoochee, Tallapoosa, and Coosa Rivers—connected to the Ogeechee and Oconee Rivers—that similarly tied Coweta and the other *talwas* to their hunting grounds. As hunters, then, young men would have collected extensive knowledge about the paths and "waterways that crisscrossed Creek Country" and the broader South.[47]

Warfare was the other important function of being a young man in the early eighteenth-century Muscogee world. In fact one's masculinity and the claims to lead others was entirely "dependent on his accomplishments in warfare." As several *micos* articulated to John Stuart in 1764, no one "can attain any Rank in the community except by some Warlike Exploits." Thus Sempoyaffee and Escotchaby would have been like any other young men who sought "opportunity of signalizing themselves by Warlike Exploits, by which they can only obtain War Names, and bear any rank" in the community. If successful in battle, a young man first achieved the rank of *tasikayalgi*, which was followed by the *imathla labotke* (or little *imathla*) and then *imathla thlako* (or big *imathla*) if one found further military success. Ultimately a Muscogee man's rank culminated in the title of *tastanagalgi*, a veteran warrior or war leader. But a select few men—including Sempoyaffee and Escotchaby later in life—proved themselves so capable as leaders in battle that they ascended to the role of the *tastanagi* or *tastanagi thlako* (big warrior), also known as the *tustenogy* or *tustunnuggee* (war king). While the prestige or reputation that accompanied such exploits was a motivation for many young men, their primary responsibility remained tied to protecting their *huti* and the *talwa*. Therefore, even before young men set out to war, family members and community leaders made sure that the *hutis* and *talwa* were defensible and had "a sufficient Quantity of Corn," and if they did not, the young men had to remain behind and "content themselves."[48]

If Sempoyaffee and Escotchaby followed the path that most young men did, they would have sought—and struggled—to live out the idyllic cosmic balance that was central to the early eighteenth-century Muscogee world. Due to the use of violence, young men turned the peaceful state of the Middle World "bloody" and thereby evoked the red path, unlike their elders and *micos,* who sought to maintain peace upon the earth. Together the younger and older generations enacted the precarious balancing act between the opposing forces of peace and conflict that was at the heart of Muscogee worldviews. As the *mico* Emistisiguo of Little Tallassee best described to his British audience in 1774, "their young people were become unruly" as of late and therefore "will not be governed by their headmen as usual," which threatened to disrupt the principles that the "earth is white, and everything on its face is peaceful." In some cases *micos* struggled to "restrain their young men" and feared the men "would be Glad of Plunging their Nation into a War." But again, such tensions between the two generations were a product of the cosmic balance that structured the Muscogee world, in which young men sought to prove their manhood through red acts that were mediated by *micos* and elders who sought to maintain the white paths to and from Muscogee communities. In the event that violence reached a point of excess and threatened such imbalance, *micos* implored the young men to think of the greater good for their *hutis* and *talwa* and thereby join the *micos* in whitening their "Black Heart."[49]

Before joining their first war party around the time of puberty, young men on the cusp of manhood would have performed the same rituals as older, more experienced men before leaving the *talwa*. They purified themselves over several days and engaged in little or no contact with women. They sat and sweated in a hothouse, where they drank *cassina*, both fasting and purging one's self. At some point they ingested "war-physic" (Sous-watch-cau) made of button snakeroot, which was believed to enhance a man's strength. Before leaving the *talwa*, the young men joined a "war dance in the Town house," in which seasoned veterans recounted their past exploits and danced the eagle dance. The party would have been led by a *tastanagalgi* (veteran) or even the *tustenogy* himself, and the young men understood if they or "any of Our Young Men Will be So head Strong as not to follow orders" of the leader, the offender "loses his Reputation." Although there were some instances when Muscogee peoples engaged in prolonged warfare, as they did in the late 1740s and early 1750s against the Cherokee, war parties tended to target small groups or settlements. In these encounters young men had the chance to prove themselves by either capturing prisoners or killing another man, then taking a trophy. In some cases, the leader or the *tustenogy* may have been instructed by the *micos* to leave a sign for their rivals and/or enemies after the attack, effectively to give notice that satisfaction had been taken for a previous attack or that war now existed between them.[50]

Upon arriving back in their *talwa*, the young men would have produced their trophies in the town square before their family and community, which heralded their ceremonious passage from boyhood to manhood. According to Muscogee customs, every man who claimed a trophy was bestowed with a war name (Tus-se-ki-o-chis-co). As the Okfuskee Captain explained to John Stuart in 1764, when "a Warrior gets a Name, it always remains with him," and each name was accorded a "certain degree of Respect & Influence." While we do not know if the returning men received the name then and there, since there is speculation that the name was bestowed more formally at the Busk, the gaining of such an honor was a big affair. Over the course of several days, the privileged young men would have secluded themselves in a house and fasted the entire time, occasionally eating some *humpetuh hutke* (boiled grits). They also endured several sweats and drank emetics such as Sou-watch-cau to induce visions, and at the end they bathed themselves to complete their passage into manhood. In Sempoyaffee and Escotchaby's case, it seems they may have distinguished themselves in combat as young men, for the names and scars that they received reflected prowess on the battlefield. Escotchaby was known as the Young Lieutenant, meaning that he likely distinguished himself at an early age, and Sempoyaffee was described as having only "one eye" after his several exploits in past skirmishes.[51]

As men Sempoyaffee and Escotchaby would have assumed new responsibilities from both their *huti* and *talwa*. They now permanently joined Coweta's raids against their rivals and protected their *huti* and *talwa* in the event of an attack, and when ordered to wage war by the *tustenogy*, they were prepared to leave for an extended time. Sempoyaffee and Escotchaby also could now take a female partner, which came with its own expectations and responsibilities that pulled them away from their *huti* toward their wives' relatives instead of their own. Yet the two brothers retained their kinship connections to their mother and her people rather than their wives' relatives, although their offspring were considered a part of their mothers' clan. There were also new rules or protocols to follow as young men in the Muscogee world, such as learning the rituals associated with taking part in the councils and ceremonies in the town square.[52] Particular to the Busk, Sempoyaffee and Escotchaby could now be involved in the many purification rituals at the same time that they learned new men's dances such as the E-ne-hou-bun-gau and abstained from any sexual contact with women.[53]

Altogether Sempoyaffee and Escotchaby came of age as men in Coweta at a pivotal time in the early eighteenth century. The two brothers would have learned and abided by a series of responsibilities to both their *huti* and *talwa* that only increased with age. Their lives were also governed by an understanding of the world that was consistently fluid and influenced by peoples' actions and reactions, a precarious balance of opposing forces that required ritual and ceremony and a way of living that was instilled into them by their peoples' Creation Stories. Thus Sempoyaffee and Escotchaby started to walk a fine line between peace and conflict in their daily lives, as men and as members of a specific *huti* and *talwa*. They also started to learn how truly entangled their lives were with the white people to the east, west, and south of Coweta.

Two

The *Tustenogy's* World, 1730–1756

It was fall 1750, and Sempoyaffee watched grimly from the town square as Mary Bosomworth—a half-Muscogee, half-English woman with kinship ties to the people of Coweta—implored Coweta's *micos* to sign an "instrument of writing" that would cede the islands of St. Catherine's, Sapelo, and Ossabaw to her. Even though the Busk has been recently performed and the new year started, already Bosomworth and Malatchi, one of Coweta's most influential *micos* and self-proclaimed "Emperor of the Creeks," threatened to embroil Coweta in a conflict with the English colonies. Not only had Bosomworth demanded that Coweta's *micos* cede some of their lands to her, a dangerous precedent for the future, but she and Malatchi also had met with "three French Officers and . . . 4 private Men" who came to the *talwa* earlier in the year. Malatchi and Bosomworth's intrigues thereby incensed British authorities and endangered the trade alliance between the colonies and the *talwa*.[1]

Standing off to the side was Coweta's resident trader, George Galphin, who shared "some Convercation" with Sempoyaffee about Mary's performance in the town square. Galphin was also wary of Bosomworth, after she tried to force him to sign the cession as a witness. When Galphin refused, Bosomworth threatened to get "her relations privately to do me a mistchef." Fortunately for Galphin, he also shared kinship ties with the people of Coweta, through his relationship with Metawney. Metawney just so happened to be a kinswoman to Sempoyaffee, both of whom were part of the same *huti*. Therefore when Sempoyaffee shared "some Convercation" with Galphin, he confided in a European man who—in a sense—had recently married into the family. And as Sempoyaffee and Galphin talked, they debated about what to do when it came to Bosomworth's proposal and how to put a stop to Malatchi's negotiations with the French. As Sempoyaffee promised Galphin, the lands in question "could not be given away without all the nattion willing," and there were other *micos* who seemed similarly unhappy with what was happening in Coweta in fall 1750.[2]

The significance of Sempoyaffee and Galphin's conversation is that this is Sempoyaffee's first documented appearance in the archival record and one that identified him as the "head war king of the Cowetaws," or *tustenogy* (*tustennuggee, tastanagi*). One could make an educated guess that during the 1740s Sempoyaffee repeatedly proved himself in combat and established an impeccable reputation that earned him the honor of becoming the *talwa's* leader in times of conflict. This role not only propelled him to a position of leadership in Coweta but also elevated him to an office that carried influence with the other *talwas*. Naturally this leadership role came with new responsibilities, the most important of which was striking a delicate balance between the "warriors and young people" who wanted to prove their manhood in combat and Coweta's *micos,* who attempted to dissuade the young men from attacking their rivals and neighbors. As *tustenogy* Sempoyaffee bore the burden of maintaining the precarious balance of peace and conflict that was so important to the eighteenth-century Muscogee world. This is not to mention the fact that Sempoyaffee contended with the ambitions of his *huti,* who wished to project a voice equal to that of Malatchi and Bosomworth in the *talwa's* affairs. So when Sempoyaffee and Galphin conversed in fall 1750, their exchange represented the broader convergences of family, kinship, and politics within Coweta, a *talwa* that was becoming increasingly entangled with the European empires around it by mid-century.[3]

Coweta the *Talwa,* Sempoyaffee the *Tustenogy*

Within the eighteenth-century Muscogee world, each *talwa* such as Coweta existed as an autonomous entity "with its own political hierarchies and [was] free to make independent political decisions." This is why European authorities such as James Grant, the governor of East Florida, observed that the Muscogee consisted of "so many Different Republicks which form one State" and that each *talwa* "has separate Views and Interests" that led them to have "frequent Disputes amongst themselves, and are all Jealous" of each other. Because each *talwa* consisted of several different matrilineages, there existed "so many Headmen in every Town contending for power" that it was simply impossible to "claim a Superiority over the Others."[4] In short, every family and *huti* competed with one another to lead, a constant back-and-forth between the many *micos* within every *talwa.*[5]

During the early to mid-eighteenth century, Coweta was regarded as a "leading Town" among the Lower *talwas*. Despite its origins as a community of migrants who ascended to political relevance among the more established

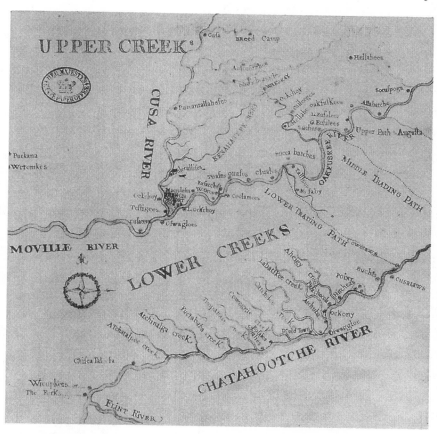

William Bonar's "A Draught of the Creek Nation"—the Creek Path and Coweta
(Image Courtesy of the National Archives (Kew), CO700/Carolina21)

talwas during the late seventeenth century, Coweta distinguished itself as
"Tall Coweta" and was honored as a "foundation town" alongside older *talwas*
such as Okfuskee and Tuckabatchee. Coweta's prominence is also reflected in
Creation Stories such as that of the Tuckabatchee-Coweta Alliance. In this
account Muscogee peoples "came pouring out of the earth like ants" and "laid
down the *towaka* (logs) about the stomp ground." After arranging the *towaka*
as the foundation for a town, "up came the Tall Coweta," whose people told
the people of Tuckabatchee, "Here is my medicine; let us combine the two."
Tuckabatchee and Coweta thereby cemented an enduring connection, a relationship that continued well into the eighteenth century.[6]

The reasons for Coweta's eminence among the other *talwas* were many.
Coweta enjoyed a strategic location alongside the Creek Path leading to

Augusta and Charleston. By the early eighteenth century, it had effectively monopolized access and trade to the colonies, as the "Cowetas were the first who opened the path" and had the power to "shut up the path" and "stop the trade." Coweta was also uniquely positioned on the Chattahoochee River— which Europeans considered a "inlett to all the Indian Nations"—which further contributed to its influence in the deerskin trade and the Muscogee-British alliance. Yet another reason for Coweta's authority was that one of its *micos,* Brims, had "made the law" for all *talwas* to observe neutrality in their dealings with Europeans, which Steven C. Hahn has called the Coweta Resolution of 1718. This strategy established a precedent for Muscogee autonomy in the eighteenth century, and it was Coweta's *micos* who deserve credit as "the first to offer the vision of a Creek Nation." It should be noted that even though Coweta was considered a principal *talwa* among the Lower *talwas,* its *micos* "cou'd say nothing with regard to [the] Upper Creeks" because the Upper *talwas* "look[ed] upon the lower Creeks to be a different nation" and vice versa.[7]

Coweta was also a diverse and cosmopolitan community that reflected the broader intercultural realities of the eighteenth-century American South. As European observers marveled about *talwas* such as Coweta, "the habitations of the people are placed with considerable regularity in streets or ranges" like a grid, and the *talwa* was home to a range of peoples that included Savannah, Yuchi, Shawnee, Natchez, Cherokee, Apalachee, and Chickasaw peoples, among others, as well as runaway enslaved fugitives from the colonies and "many Englishmen."[8] This is why the Muscogee "language [was] understood by many Nations" throughout the South, and why Muscogee peoples likewise circulated along the same Natchez, Cherokee, and Chickasaw paths that connected their *talwas* to the other peoples and places of the South. As Robbie Ethridge describes, the Muscogee world "was not a purely Indian world, nor had it been for almost three hundred years" and the various peoples who lived in and frequented Coweta shared "interwoven lives."[9]

Another significant characteristic of Coweta was that it was a red *talwa* or "bloody town" (*kiyapa, kipayalgi*). Within the Muscogee moiety system, each *talwa* was designated as either a red or white town, which structured "everything from international diplomacy and warfare to the attendance at key religious ceremonies and participation in ball games." Red was the hallmark of younger men and symbolized the state of conflict and violence as well as passion or youth (i.e., inexperience), whereas the color white denoted peace, resolution, and the wisdom of elders (i.e., experience). Therefore Coweta was one of the Lower *talwas* "where the *micos,* chiefs, and warriors assemble when a general war is proposed" in addition to having one of the leading voices when it came to military affairs. It enjoyed a power to wage war and "shut up the path," as well as to put to death accused murderers or captives that were taken in war. To balance out red *talwas* such as Coweta, white *talwas* such as Cusseta were "sacred to peace" and ideally immune to violence. In contrast to Coweta, then, Cusseta assumed the responsibility of negotiation led by "civil instead of military officials," and "when a general peace is proposed, deputies from all the towns . . . assemble . . . to deliberate upon a subject of so high importance."[10] Just like the delicate balance at the heart of Muscogee world-views,[11] the influence between red and white *talwas* swung back and forth on an ever-changing basis.[12]

As Coweta's *tustenogy* and the leader of a "bloody town," Sempoyaffee played a critical role within the *talwa*.[13] Having likely accumulated several war names in battle, he was appointed Coweta's Great Warrior, the highest war rank in Muscogee society, and "there was only one in every town." When Sempoyaffee joined any dance in the town square where men boasted of their accomplishments, his feats likely "exceeded that of his peers." We might safely assume, then, that Sempoyaffee brought honor to his *huti* and *talwa,* given that red *talwas* "foster the warlike spirit" against their enemies. The title of *tustenogy* not only came with great respect and influence but also "Followers and Adherents [that] increased in proportion to the Eloquence & other Abilities of the Bearer."[14]

As *tustenogy* Sempoyaffee inherited a host of responsibilities that revolved around the young men of Coweta. For instance, in the event of an impending attack or if Coweta stood on a war footing, the *tustenogy* sent out scouts to patrol around Coweta until called back. Similarly, when Coweta was on the offensive, the *tustenogy* decided who to send to war and planned when an attack was to be made and why. In some instances the reasons for war simply involved providing an outlet for the young men to "show themselves so" and an avenue for the youngest men to be given the opportunity to pass into manhood. At other times the *tustenogy* may have sought satisfaction for the loss of a townsperson at the hands of their rivals such as the Cherokee or Choctaw. The decision to wage war was made in conjunction with Coweta's *micos*. In this case the *micos* "called the Head Warrior to the War Cabin" to "consult with the beloved men" whether to attack or not. If the *tustenogy* and the *micos* agreed they should, they sent the "war whoop through all the Town" and the young men prepared themselves for battle. But at any point, the *micos* could "stop it and proceed to adjust the [matter] by negotiation."[15]

In the event of an impending assault, the *tustenogy* took several precautions before letting the war party leave. First and most important, he ensured that the *talwa* had enough defenders and food in case of an attack while the men were out, which is why Coweta and other *talwas* refused to go to war in 1740 unless "the corn was about Three-foot long" and ready to harvest. The *tustenogy* may also have sent word to Europeans that there were "several of his people out at Warr," so as not to scare away the British or French traders in the colonies or in any *talwas,* which might disrupt the deerskin trade. The *tustenogy* also met with the headmen of the war party and instructed them to gather the town's medicine bundle, which "contained objects that were of spiritual significance" and "exude power." Before the bundle could be taken into battle, the *tustenogy* conversed with whoever would handle a thing "so sacred and power laden." In some cases one of Coweta's *hobaya* or *hills haya* (healers, ceremonial specialists) joined the party to care for the bundle and performed rituals to empower the young men. Sempoyaffee also decided whether or not the party leader should leave a sign that war existed between them and their targets, what was called the "marks about the dead." Such declarations of intent took many forms, such as "a painted War Club left upon a Body," or was etched into the landscape itself, like "several trees blazed . . . [with] an M with two strokes."[16]

In some cases the *tustenogy* accompanied the men on their expedition. Like the other men, he would have painted his body and equipped himself with the implements of war in addition to any other ritual preparations. When finished, the party left Coweta, oftentimes traveling along one of the war paths by either horse, foot, or canoe.[17] Once they reached their destination, the fighting varied upon the occasion: whether or not the party consisted largely of young men seeking to earn war names, to extract retribution for a previous act of violence, or to carry on a prolonged "war of conquest" that required more manpower, resources, and strategy. If a small raid, the party aimed for the element of surprise and conducted a quick surgical strike, either by ambush or attacking with superior numbers with the intent of taking captives and "Enemies Scalps." In contrast, when at war with the Cherokee in the 1740s and 1750s, Muscogee parties instead "burn't to the Ground two Towns of the Cherokees [and] killed many of the Inhabitants upon the Spot," and at times numbered more than "400 [who] went against the Cherokees and killed between 30 and 40." In such cases Muscogee peoples waged a war by which they claimed Cherokee lands "as their Property." Upon returning to Coweta, the party recounted their deeds in song, with any captives and trophies in tow. Finally the Muscogee men purified themselves by "Physicking," and if anybody had been killed, they started the ritual "mourning days."[18]

Besides matters of war, the *tustenogy*'s other important function was to police or monitor the behavior of Coweta's young men and thereby maintain the idyllic cosmic balance.[19] By mid-century the deerskin trade demanded a near constant supply of deerskins, so the hunting season grew progressively longer, and as deer populations thinned out, Muscogee hunters increasingly encroached on their neighbors' hunting grounds, which precipitated greater violence between Muscogee peoples and their neighbors. It was not uncommon for "mischief being done by rash people on either side" to threaten a war that no one wanted. This is where it was the *tustenogy*'s responsibility to put a stop to it "before any mischief happened." As one *tustenogy* described in 1753, "I have kept my Warriors at Home, notwithstanding we have lost [some] of our Friends," which did not always prove to be a popular decision among the young men, and indeed the decision earned this particular *tustenogy* the "ill will" of the young people. In the event of violence, the *tustenogy* was the one who investigated and questioned the accusers and/or the accused as to the events that provoked violence and he tried to devise some sort of resolution. And if ever the *tustenogy* proved unable to corral the young men, he could always shame them, for "if any of Our Young Men Will be So head Strong as not to follow orders and will Committ any Hostilletys," they would bear a stain on their reputation.[20]

The *tustenogy* also represented the young men in the *talwa*'s councils and in the negotiations with other *talwas*, Native groups, and even Europeans. Each council consisted of the *micos*, the *tustenogy*, and representatives from each clan, during which the *tustenogy* addressed everyone on behalf of the young men and provided counsel regarding any decision that might impact them. Meanwhile whenever their rivals, such as the Cherokee or Haudenosaunee, visited the *talwa*, the *tustenogy* again represented his men, especially if it came down to giving satisfaction for those killed in combat. In one memorable instance in the history of Coweta's *tustenogy*, the head warrior "went into the Chickasaw Town, and told them That they must make Satisfaction, And if they did not, They the Creeks Would Stop the Path" to them. Reciprocally the *tustenogy* traveled to other communities, such as the Cherokee town of Chote, as an emissary of peace and added his name to any talk that Coweta's *micos* sent to their rivals. This is exactly what Sempoyaffee did throughout the 1740s and 1750s, when he sent a "talk" to the Haudenosaunee with an "Eagle-Tail & Rattle Trap," both tokens of friendship. When dealing with Europeans, the *tustenogy* was the young men's voice, especially when it involved their frustrations with the encroachments upon their hunting grounds and the individuals who "traded in the woods to their great prejudice." In some cases, to make a point to Europeans, a *tustenogy* threatened to act on his own accord, just as Sempoyaffee did when he warned British officials that he intended to expel the "white people . . . [who] hunt in their lands."[21] The *tustenogy* might go so far as to walk out of a council with Europeans to make a statement on behalf of his young men. This is exactly what the Okfuskee Captain did when he "went out of the Room" when talking with the governor of South Carolina, followed by "several of the other Warriors and young men," who all left "without taking any of the Presents with them."[22]

Some of the other responsibilities of a *tustenogy* were related to matters of ceremony and ritual, land allotments, and ensuring a steady supply of weapons and goods from Europeans. For example during the Busk, he presided over the town square and "rehearsed briefly the traditional history of the people, emphasized the importance of the festival they were observing, and informed them that it had existed from immemorial times." He thus reinforced the importance of ritual, the ideals of a cosmic balance, and the other rules that "tended to preserve their health and prolong their lives." The *tustenogy* also acted alongside the *micos* to "measure a certain proportion of Land to each Family" within the *talwa,* lands that became the basis for a *huti.* And whenever a family removed itself from the *talwa,* their former property returned to the *talwa* and was parceled out in a similar fashion. Finally, as the voice of the *talwa*'s young men, the *tustenogy* consistently implored Europeans for the "guns, ammunition, &c . . . to go to war they could [not] make" themselves, in exchange for promises to protect any "white people among them." Altogether Sempoyaffee inherited extensive responsibilities as Coweta's *tustenogy.*[23]

Sempoyaffee also grappled with the generational tensions that existed between Coweta's *micos* and its young men, yet another manifestation of the cosmic balance that characterized the Muscogee world. Although such tensions had long existed in Muscogee society and revolved around the efforts of young men to assert their manhood, which could at times produce unnecessary violence, such tensions confounded European authorities, who sought to limit the violence that at times targeted European people and property. As Tobias Fitch tried to censure Okfuskee's *micos* and *tustenogy* in 1725, "you pretend To Excuse Rogue Action . . . By Saying it was Don Rashly by the young people, But that Excuse will not do With our King for you are [men] in years and ought To know better and Since you was the head of them People you Should have prevented their . . . proceedings." Over time, though, Europeans gradually recognized that authority and leadership in the Muscogee world were consensual in nature, meaning that the *micos* and *tustenogy* were beholden to their townspeople, and if they ever displeased or failed to heed the people of their *talwa,* these leaders risked losing credibility if not authority altogether. Therefore Sempoyaffee needed to strike a delicate balance between allowing the "rage of the young men to acquire War-Names" and restraining the young men who wanted to "gain reputation and the name of warrior by not consenting to make peace."[24]

Throughout his tenure as Coweta's *tustenogy,* Sempoyaffee spent the better part of his days mediating the conflicts between the young men and the *micos.* Amid the on-and-off wars between Muscogee and Cherokee peoples during the 1740s and 1750s, it was Sempoyaffee who at times stopped several parties of young men from attacking the Cherokee, instead asking them to wait, because he soon "expected some of the Cherokees to come to the Cowetas before long." In this case he promised that if peace were made with the Cherokee, the young men could instead "go out and kill the Norward Indians." In a similar case, Sempoyaffee competed against Coweta's young men, who had been solicited by the Long Warrior of another *talwa* to go out and kill any Cherokee they might find and "set up the Creek marks about the dead." If not for Sempoyaffee, who "restrained the Warriors" in this instance, Coweta's young men might have dragged their *talwa*—if not Muscogee peoples in general—into a broader conflict with the Cherokee. In the event that violence occurred despite the *tustenogy*'s efforts, Sempoyaffee communicated with their rivals and "acknowledge[d] that our young men do many things that they ought not to do, and very often act like Madmen" and hoped "our whole nation will not be blamed for the fault of a few madmen."[25]

When it came to the young men's complaints about European encroachments upon Muscogee lands, things proved equally if not more difficult for the *tustenogy*. Throughout the eighteenth century, *micos* such as Emistisiguo of Little Tallassee repeatedly told Europeans that the younger generations believed the "white people wanted to take away their lands . . . and were all around them." It did not help matters that several Europeans hunted upon Muscogee territories or that their livestock trampled over Muscogee lands, destroyed their foodstuffs, and disrupted deer hunting patterns, all of which produced "ill blood [with] their young men." In most cases the *tustenogy* brought complaints to European authorities in hopes they might prevent such intrusions, repeating the "Great Difficulty our Head men and Warriors" have had in trying to "restrain their young men from Going into your Nation." In the instances when words failed, the *tustenogy* may have chosen to take matters into his own hands. As Emistisiguo told John Stuart in 1770, he once witnessed Sempoyaffee march into a nearby settlement and threaten the white people to stop hunting on their lands, telling them that if they continued it would "spoil" the path between them. While Sempoyaffee's actions bordered on the hostile, he knowingly risked conflict to make a statement that any further encroachments on Muscogee lands would not be tolerated.[26]

Sempoyaffee's actions in this case reflected how his specific role as *tustenogy* was connected to the cosmic balance that structured the eighteenth-century Muscogee world, as he navigated between matters of peace and violence.[27] As a number of Muscogee *micos* articulated time and again during the eighteenth century, "our ancestors were wise men and knew that war is very destructive to all parties" and counseled them to "avoid and prevent quarreling and going to war upon any mischief being done by rash mad people." Thus any violence committed by young men prompted the *tustenogy* to join with the *micos* of a given *talwa* in rebuking such actions, and they "unanimously agreed" in the town square, in front of the entire community, to give satisfaction and restore peace. Coweta's *micos* and *tustenogy* were always mindful of what violence might mean for the people of their *talwa,* knowing how "sometimes a small spark, if not attended to, will kindle a great fire." The *tustenogy* thereby presided over the rituals and ceremonies of peace alongside the *micos,* and he "readily complied with every Thing" so that "the path may be white and clean again and the blood which has been spilt may be washed away." The *tustenogy,* then, had as much interest in peace as he did conflict.[28]

Sempoyaffee and the Politics of *Talwas* and Empires

As Coweta's *tustenogy* during the 1740s and 1750s, Sempoyaffee confronted the tumultuous transformations introduced by European empires that threatened to reshape the Muscogee world at mid-century.[29] By the 1740s Muscogee peoples had effectively established a confederacy of *talwas* founded on the principles of neutrality and diplomacy, with the British to the east, the French the west, and the Spanish to the south.[30] As imperial authorities on all sides noted with frustration, the Muscogee *talwas* "are Situated now in the Midway between us, the French, and the Spaniard and deals with those that give them most, Affecting a Neutrallity & making their Advantages of the Differences happening between the European Nations." If you asked *micos* like the Young Tallassee King, though, they framed the geopolitical situation as being "friends with the Mothers, the English, French, and Spaniards, and . . . hold[ing] them there fast by the hand." The founding of the Georgia colony, however, forced Muscogee peoples to pay closer attention to their relationship with the British, given the close proximity of that colony.[31] The shift in priorities was observed with great anxiety by French officials such as Diron d'Artaguette, who wrote to the Count de Maurepas in Paris that the "Kawitas . . . are completely devoted to the English," and he redoubled his efforts to organize a meeting with Coweta's *micos* at Fort Toulouse.[32] The Spanish in Florida, on the other hand, attempted to wipe out the British altogether and sought to lure Muscogee peoples to join them in the War of Jenkins' Ear (1739–48). But as Upper and Lower *micos* consistently remarked to British agents, "Our Ancestors have Taught us to have great regard for our friends the English . . . who supply us with Cloathing for our selves, Women and Children."[33]

These sentiments further reflected the profound changes introduced into the Muscogee world by the commercial deerskin trade. By the 1740s Georgia and South Carolina emerged as the "seat of the Indian trade" with Charleston and Augusta enjoying privileged access to the Creek Path, a commercial connection that led to Coweta and the other *talwas.* As Muscogee hunters increasingly harvested the *itchu* (white-tailed deer) to meet European demand while consuming the influx of goods that Europeans imported back into the Muscogee world, the deerskin trade effectively remade a Muscogee "self-sufficient subsistence economy to one based on commercial hunting and trade." As British authorities stated in council with several *micos* in November 1765, "your Profession is hunting . . . but it is Your Interest to have Your Brothers the English near you, as they only can supply You in Exchange for Your Skins" with the "Things which You cannot make for Yourselves." This is not to suggest Muscogee peoples were wholly dependent upon the British, given that trade was a thoroughly mediated affair that the *talwas* shaped as much as the English. But it is nonetheless important to recognize that the Muscogee world that Sempoyaffee inhabited had changed remarkably by mid-century, a product of sustained interactions with European empires and a deepening involvement in the deerskin trade.[34]

It was in this deeply entangled world of politics and trade that Sempoyaffee served as Coweta's *tustenogy,* but he also acted as a member of a specific family and *huti* within Coweta. Because each *talwa* consisted of several different *hutis,* the members of each *huti* competed with one another for a voice in the affairs of the *talwa.* This is why the *micos* of any given *talwa* did not always share the same interests or pursue the same goals in their dealings with one another, with the other *talwas,* or with other Indigenous groups and Europeans. As James Grant observed with remarkable clarity in 1764, there existed so many different *micos* with varying interests "in every Town contending for power, that it would be very difficult to prevail upon them to put their Affairs into the hands of One Man." There was only one *tustenogy* in each *talwa,* though, which afforded Sempoyaffee and his family with opportunities to manipulate the affairs of the *talwa,* no matter how small or big those opportunities might be. Sempoyaffee, then, was not only the representative of Coweta's young men, but he also harbored an even more intimate attachment to his family and clan and thereby represented their interests in his position within Coweta. His tenure as *tustenogy* was an example of how his *huti* hoped to project its voice into the politics of the *talwa.* He was the first of the "4 vile Brothers" who would later "overrule all when on the Spot" in Coweta.[35]

At the same time, though, Sempoyaffee was limited in what he could accomplish in the interest of his *huti.* He was the *tustenogy,* not a *mico.* Coweta's *micos* were the ones who made the most important decisions for the *talwa* and negotiated with Europeans and their Indigenous neighbors. Due to the "consensual nature of Creek society," the *micos* were selected by the broader community—based on their previous accomplishments that demonstrated leadership capabilities—and they were valued as the collective wisdom of the *talwa*.[36] However, a *mico's* authority hinged on the continual support of his *huti* and his townspeople, meaning that each *mico* had to find ways to bring favor upon his family and clan as well as his *talwa,* and in competition with Coweta's other *micos.* More often than not, the *micos* cultivated favor by ensuring a steady supply of goods into Coweta or by judiciously redistributing among family members and the broader community the gifts that they received from Europeans. In addition these individuals devoted themselves to the "white path of peace" and to "never shed human blood." As peacemakers, then, *micos* continually held the *talwa* in check, striving to maintain the idyllic balance that was so central to eighteenth-century Muscogee worldviews. In short, being a *mico* meant juggling the "support of his clan and townspeople" in terms of both favor and conflicting interests, not to mention the competing ambitions of the other *micos.*[37]

During the 1740s and 1750s, one of the preeminent *micos* of Coweta was Malatchi. Historians have characterized him as the "most powerful Creek of his generation," and his contemporaries averred that "when Malatchi is here there needs no other." As the son of Brims, who had pioneered the political system of neutrality for the *talwas* in their negotiations with Europeans, Malatchi navigated back and forth between the British, Spanish, and French throughout his life.[38] This is why British authorities believed he had been a "French friend from his Childhood," while the French considered him "to be in the Interest of the English." Malatchi went so far as to proclaim himself the "Emperor of the Creek Nation" in his hopes to usher in an unprecedent revolution within the Muscogee world: a single, unified nation of *talwas* under a central leader who was above the politics of the *talwa.* At times he was assisted by Mary Bosomworth, who shared kinship ties to his *huti.*[39] Bosomworth had long served as a deerskin trader and intermediary with the British, having been present when Oglethorpe first negotiated with Muscogee peoples. But she had grown disillusioned with the colonies since then, and her relationship with Malatchi was a means to protect her home and stores on the islands of Ossabaw, Sapelo, and St. Catherine's.[40]

Naturally Malatchi's efforts to build a unified nation was either supported or contested by the many *micos* of Coweta and the other Upper and Lower *talwas,* and it was into the political contest that Sempoyaffee—as Coweta's *tustenogy*—maneuvered in the interests of his *huti.*[41] At first Sempoyaffee joined a handful of *micos* from Coweta and other Lower *talwas* who took the extraordinary step of acknowledging Malatchi as "our Rightful and Natural Prince" who "has full Power and Authority . . . to Transact all Affairs relating to our Nation." This declaration was signed and delivered to the British in the name of "Simpeyofy, War King of the Cowetas." However, this document should not be understood as demonstrating overwhelming support for Malatchi but instead was a deliberate assertion of sovereignty—both politically and territorially—as the Georgia colony sought several islands that the Lower *talwas* determined were theirs. This is why in fall 1750, when Sempoyaffee conversed with Galphin, he was taken aback when he learned how the lands in question were to be given to Bosomworth, which prompted Sempoyaffee to remark to Galphin how the land "could not be given away without all the nation willing." Thereafter Sempoyaffee "did not Seem to be well pleased" with Malatchi or Bosomworth. This conversation tells us much. Sempoyaffee believed not only that the lands in question were Muscogee lands but that Malatchi's pretended authority as emperor was all smoke and mirrors, because he could not do anything "without all the nation [being] willing." As Steven C. Hahn and Joshua Piker have described, there were limits to a single *mico*'s authority, even one as influential as Malatchi, since *micos* were beholden to the restrictive "traditions regarding chiefly authority and coercive force."[42]

As Sempoyaffee started to distance himself from Malatchi and Bosomworth in fall 1750, he and his *huti* increasingly counted on the support of George Galphin. Galphin, a trader from Ireland who first set foot in Coweta in the early 1740s, had been fatefully matched with a Muscogee woman by the name of Metawney, who just so happened to be a "sister" to both Sempoyaffee and Escotchaby.[43] Metawney was not Sempoyaffee's sister by blood, though; instead they were related by clan ties, meaning Metawney's mother and Sempoyaffee's mother descended from the same clan matron. While not brother and sister in the literal sense, then, Metawney and Sempoyaffee were still considered kin.[44] Thus, based on his "connexion with one of their women," Galphin was accorded a temporary place in the Muscogee world as a quasi-member of Metawney's extended family, which included Sempoyaffee and Escotchaby. Even though Galphin was not a part of the clan per se (whereas his children with Metawney were), he was for all intents and purposes "looked upon as an Indian." Naturally Galphin owed much to his wife's people, particularly their protection of his trade, which went hand-in-hand with Metawney's relatives assuming responsibility for Galphin's actions within the *talwa*.[45] Galphin emerged as one of Sempoyaffee's closest confidants, and they consistently addressed and treated one another as "friend" and "brother." The intimate relationship between the two men continued for decades.[46]

More specifically Galphin provided Sempoyaffee and his *huti* with both political and economic advantages that other matrilineages in Coweta did not benefit from. The most tangible advantage was the lifeline of trade between Coweta and the colonies, which heavily favored Sempoyaffee's *huti* and explains why Sempoyaffee and other members of the *huti* frequented Galphin's plantation at Silver Bluff, where they received many gifts and goods and always "went away very well Satisfied." As Galphin accumulated his own prestige and wealth in the deerskin trade in the 1740s–50s, enough to establish his own firm, some of his most lucrative traders were tied to Sempoyaffee's family, such as the White Boy of Coweta. This individual trafficked in as much as "1186 lbs. Raw Skins" at a single time, which he exchanged for goods worth thousands of pounds sterling and sometimes more. Another advantage to having relations with Galphin was the fact that he emerged as a valued intermediary between Muscogee peoples and the colonies, who facilitated dialogue between imperial authorities and Coweta's *micos*. In a sense Galphin offered Sempoyaffee's *huti* a direct line of communication to the colonies, as in September 1750 when he went to Coweta with talks from the governor of South Carolina or when he transmitted a talk from Sempoyaffee's *huti* to Thomas Boone, the governor of North Carolina, in May 1762.[47] Thus Galphin was an outlet for Sempoyaffee's *huti* to voice their complaints and grievances directly to the colonies, such as the many encroachments upon their *huti*'s hunting grounds that threatened to "bring on a war." Galphin, in a sense, provided Sempoyaffee and his *huti* with an insurance policy in the event of a major conflict with the British. He was obligated by kinship ties so long as his interests remained inseparable from that of the *huti*.[48]

Therefore what unfolded in Coweta during the late 1740s and early 1750s was a clash between rival families—those of Sempoyaffee and Malatchi—that occurred behind the scenes of a broader crisis known as the Bosomworth Controversy. In December 1746 Malatchi heard from Queen Senaukey of the Yamacraw that British authorities had claimed that Muscogee peoples ceded the "islands upon the seacoast known by the names of Ossabah, St. Catherines, & Sappala." Malatchi went immediately into the town square and demanded that Galphin, as Coweta's resident trader, interpret the treaty they had made with Georgia in 1739. Accordingly Galphin stated that "the talk that was in that Paper [is] that [they] had Given Away All our Lands," which surprised Malatchi. Yet this controversy presented him with a perfect opportunity to move forward with his aspirations to lead for all the *talwas* and create a unified nation. And in reaching out to Bosomworth, whose own home and stores happened to be on those islands, Malatchi desired to assert Muscogee sovereignty over the three islands that Georgia now claimed as its own.[49] The Bosomworth Controversy, then, was about nascent Muscogee nationhood and sovereignty in the face of European colonialism.[50]

By December 1747, only a year removed from the revelations in Coweta's town square, Malatchi stood before British officials at Frederica in Georgia, where he proclaimed, "I am *now* Emperor of the Creek Nation, that I Have 2000 fighting Men under my Command as well as the Care of their

Wives & Children and therefore think myself obliged to speak every thing for their Good." Even though he emphasized how Muscogee and British peoples "lived together as Brothers for some time," he protested that "no white people should hold any Lands or claim any Rights to the territories encompassing the three islands." Malatchi also informed British agents that they had mistreated Bosomworth, who stood accused of trying to incite several *talwas* to attack the colony. To protect Bosomworth and their mutual concerns,[51] Malatchi warned that "all these bad Talks put me in mind of the Words of My Father, that the English were come from the East, to settle upon our Lands" and "make Slaves of your Wives and Children." With that Malatchi reasserted his title as emperor and effectively put the British on notice that the islands in question were Muscogee in every sense of the word and to suggest otherwise risked violence.[52]

Matters took an even more dramatic turn in the summer of 1750, when Malatchi entertained a party of French officers, who presented him with "French Colours" that were "Hoisted up in the [town] Square." This was not the first nor the last time that Malatchi hosted French agents in Coweta or visited the nearby Fort Toulouse. On several occasions he had threatened to British officials that "as long as he lived he would neither permit us to take that Fort or to build one of our own there, if he could prevent it," and at one point he retreated to Fort Toulouse and informed French authorities about what had transpired in the colonies. Like every other *mico*, Malatchi sought to exploit the rivalries between England, France, and Spain, and in this case he escalated matters further in his efforts to project a Muscogee sovereignty that risked the outbreak of war in the South. As Governor James Glen exaggerated after the French visit to Coweta in 1750, Coweta was a *talwa* "where never Frenchman had been before," but they were now "received by them with open Arms." To make matters worse, after the French left, Bosomworth arrived in Coweta and stayed for a month while she and Malatchi devised a deed that ceded the islands in question to her, signed by Malatchi and "four or five" other *micos.* Malatchi and Bosomworth had seemingly executed their plan masterfully.[53]

In the wake of the French visit in fall 1750, Sempoyaffee and Galphin started to mobilize against Malatchi and Bosomworth. It was at this point that Sempoyaffee "had some Convercation" with Galphin about Mary's "Business" and "what was in the writing that had been signed." But before that, as early as 1747, word had been leaked to British officials that the French had sent weapons and ammunition to several of the Lower and Upper *talwas* and that Malatchi specifically "received a Gun that day" with a friendly talk from the French. The leak from Coweta was traced back to the "English Linguist by two of the *beloved Men* of the Creeks," a term often ascribed to men in positions of leadership within the *talwa*. The "linguist" was likely Galphin, and we might assume that the source of the leak may have been Sempoyaffee. Whatever the case, Galphin proved to be a readily available source of intelligence for British authorities between 1747 and 1750, especially as it related to Malatchi and Bosomworth. It may be safe to say that Sempoyaffee fed the British information to counteract Malatchi's overtures to the French and his pretended claims to be emperor of the *talwas*.[54]

Sempoyaffee's support likely emboldened Galphin to act in the ways that he did after the French visit in 1750. Galphin not only "had a good many Words with some of [the] Head Men and left the Square shortly after," but also, when pressed by Malatchi and several other *micos* to send a talk to the colonies, he refused to do so. As he put it, "I would not go and sit under French Colours to write a Talk down to my King." After further conversation Coweta's *micos* lifted the English colors back up in the town square, despite Malatchi's wishes. Meanwhile Bosomworth tried to downplay Galphin's actions by framing him as inept for having been denied "admittance into the Square" when the French were in town, which the Cowetas "never before had refused him." Fortunately for Galphin, another trader by the name of Daniel Clark verified Galphin's story. Shortly after Clark witnessed Malatchi and several other *micos* going to "Mr. Galphin's Store" to try and salvage the situation. Altogether it was Galphin who acted on behalf of Sempoyaffee and his *huti*, while Sempoyaffee organized dissent from within the *talwa*.[55]

However, Malatchi and Bosomworth responded to Galphin's actions with a vengeance. As Galphin recounted to a fuming Georgia Assembly later in 1750, Bosomworth had "sent hur husbands brothers to me . . . [and] requested of me to sign as a witness" to another deed for the islands. When Galphin declined, Bosomworth "strongly pressd me for to Witness it," and Galphin believed that "if I refused hur she might look upon me as an Enemy to hur and might get some of hur relasions privately to do me a mistchef." In other words Bosomworth threatened Galphin with a visit from the members of her *huti*, so he relented and witnessed the deed that would cede the islands to her. As Galphin confessed, he signed the deed out of "apprehension that I might be in Danger one day or another if I Refusd it." Bosomworth then left Coweta with the deed in land, determined to make a statement to the Georgia colony.[56]

Soon after Sempoyaffee assumed a more active role in the Bosomworth Controversy. After further conversation between Galphin and Sempoyaffee, Galphin confidently wrote to the Georgia Assembly that "if you will send me an Instrument of writing to Disanoll what [Bosomworth] had got done I am Shuer I Can have it Signd by more head men then She had to Sign hurs." It may be safe to assume that Sempoyaffee was one of the headmen that Galphin referred to. In fact while Malatchi and Bosomworth turned their attentions to England to try and legitimize the deed, Galphin and Sempoyaffee spread word to the other *talwas* about Malatchi's efforts to cede the islands to Bosomworth. In particular they planted what John Juricek calls a "story of Mary's deceit," that she had strong-armed the other Lower *micos* into signing the deed. Therefore when British officials sent one of their agents, Patrick Graham, to disavow the Bosomworth deed in favor of an English one, Galphin served as interpreter and witness to the Graham deed, which was signed by a number of Lower and Upper *micos*. When Malatchi rejected the legitimacy of the Graham deed and Bosomworth tried to convince Upper *micos* to sign a "repudiation" of it, Galphin provided an alternative to the situation. As he told the *micos* who had originally signed Bosomworth's deed, "they had been duped . . . [and] gulled into signing it, and therefore were blameless" in the whole affair. This meant that Galphin offered Malatchi a potential out to the entire situation, which must have appealed to Malatchi for some reason, because he afterward "declared they had *all* been in the Dark, for they had never signed such a deed '*that they know of.*'"[57]

However, Sempoyaffee and Galphin did not stop in their efforts to minimize Malatchi's influence in Coweta between 1753 and 1756. Even though Malatchi changed his tune toward the colonies and "profest the Same Friendship & attachment to the English whom he Called his friends & Brethren," he remained hostile toward the encroachments on their hunting grounds. He even threatened publicly that he would "send the English a Summons to leave those Settlements and if they did not remove, the War Whoop should drive them" away. Galphin again stepped in to mediate. He interpreted a favorable letter to Coweta's *micos* from Governor Glen, who "all approve much of it," which forced Malatchi to similarly "agree to your Talk." At one point Galphin reported that Malatchi was so "well pleased" with the English that everything in Coweta was "Peace and Quietness." While this was largely true, Sempoyaffee had his own confrontation with Malatchi that effectively put the *mico* in his place. During the 1750s Muscogee and Cherokee peoples waged a large-scale war against one another, and it was a conflict that Malatchi himself helped ignite. But as the violence started to wind down, Malatchi overstepped his authority when he stopped "two gangs of Indians going out against the Cherokees." This he had no authority to do, since it was part of Sempoyaffee's role as *tustenogy*. As Sempoyaffee made it abundantly clear to Malatchi, Malatchi could no longer bend the rules of leadership in the Muscogee world as he had by proclaiming himself emperor of all the *talwas*, conspiring with Bosomworth over land, and now presuming to usurp the authority of the *tustenogy*. By early 1756 Malatchi had fallen ill, followed soon after by his death.[58]

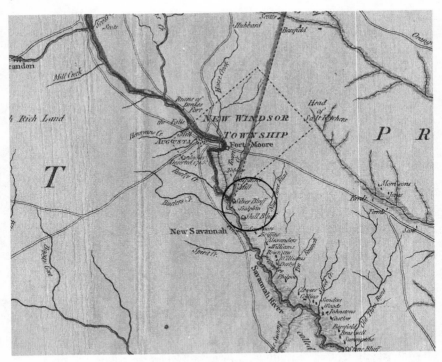

Map of Silver Bluff (circled) and the Savannah River. (Image Courtesy of Hargrett Rare Book and Manuscript Library, University of Georgia Libraries)

After Malatchi's passing Sempoyaffee ascended to even greater prominence in Coweta. It is no coincidence that it was Sempoyaffee who spoke on behalf of the Lower *talwas* when they met with British authorities in October 1756. As he declared, "We, the Lower Creeks . . . have always continued our Friendship with the English and as we know the Benefit of our Friendship, we design not to be led astray by bad Councils" like Malatchi had in years past. But Sempoyaffee reiterated some of what Malatchi championed in his lifetime, namely the "desire that you will stop all out-Stores, and let none of your People . . . incroach any Ways on our Land, for we are resolved not to sell any of our Lands, nor let the White People settle any nigher us." After 1756, Sempoyaffee started to cultivate a reputation as a "man of great weight in the Nation and well affected to the British Interest," thereby establishing the credentials for what would later be his transition from *tustenogy* to *mico*. It was also at this time Sempoyaffee coupled with a Muscogee woman and had children.[59]

As for Galphin, his wealth and influence continued to grow on account of his connection to Sempoyaffee and his *huti.* For instance, he convinced the governors of South Carolina and Georgia as well as the superintendent of Indian affairs to let "no other person . . . have a License from this Government to trade" at Coweta. While not unprecedented to have one trader per *talwa,* this feat essentially gifted Sempoyaffee's *huti* with a monopoly over the trade to and from Coweta. Therefore, when European observers noted that Galphin was a man "who possessed the most extensive trade, connexions, and influence . . . particularly with the Creeks," they inadvertently meant his ties to that one specific family of Coweta. And over the course of the 1750s, Galphin carved out his own little kingdom at his Silver Bluff plantation, where he built one of the most profitable firms in the deerskin trade. However, Sempoyaffee and the members of his *huti* considered Silver Bluff to be as much theirs as it was Galphin's, because whenever Sempoyaffee, Escotchaby, and other family members spent time away from Muscogee territories, it was usually at Silver Bluff, and their visits ranged anywhere from a few days to weeks on end.[60]

Altogether Sempoyaffee's experiences as *tustenogy* in the 1740s and 1750s embodied the complex and interdependent relationships that existed between the Muscogee *talwas* and European empires and how a particular *huti* of Coweta mediated such relationships. Naturally the hopes and ambitions of Sempoyaffee and his family clashed with those of the other *hutis* in the *talwa,* most visibly in the case of Malatchi and Bosomworth. Meanwhile Sempoyaffee's brother Escotchaby started to emerge in his own right as another influential figure of their *huti* within Coweta, and together the brothers—as the vehicles of their *huti*—negotiated the transformative changes that reshaped the Muscogee world at mid-century.

Three

The Cherokee King's World,
1730–1756

With the corn starting to ripen in August 1753—which would herald the coming of the Busk and the time of forgiving the past year's transgressions— Escotchaby waited patiently in the town square for a Cherokee delegation that intended to "Confirm a Peace" with Coweta's *micos*. Ever since the Yamasee War, when several *micos* had been assassinated in the Lower Cherokee town of Tugaloo in 1715, Muscogee and Cherokee peoples had been at war on and off with one another. Their incessant conflict had grown more expansive in the 1740s and early 1750s, incited in part by Malatchi and the Cowetas, who remained hell-bent on revenge for the Tugaloo killings.[1] As the Cherokee headman Saluy revealed more than a decade later, Coweta's *micos* still harbored "an old Grudge" for the "14 of their head Men having been killed in Toogola." What made August 1753 so important was that Escotchaby now waited for the arrival of the Cherokees, who promised to come into the public square of their bitterest rival in hopes of putting the violence behind them.[2]

It was no coincidence that Escotchaby was among those who greeted the Cherokee headmen at Coweta in late 1753 or early 1754. The Cherokee delegation was specifically visiting only two of the *talwas* to formalize the peace between their two peoples: Okfuskee among the Upper *talwas* and Coweta for the Lower *talwas*. As part of that peace, the Cherokee delegation also intended to endow certain individuals within the Muscogee world with a newly invented role, and the responsibilities, of being their Cherokee king, an official emissary of peace between the two sides. These Cherokee kings would represent and care for Cherokee interests within the Muscogee world, while their counterparts—known as Coweta kings, Okfuskee kings, etc.—within the Cherokee world would do the same for the Muscogee. It just so happened that Escotchaby was nominated and then appointed Coweta's first Cherokee king.[3]

The documentation related to the Cherokee kings is negligible. With that said, there exists oral traditions handed down by Cherokees in the early nineteenth century that provide some history and context for understanding why these individuals existed and played such an important role in Muscogee and Cherokee societies. These oral traditions describe the practice of nominating Cherokee kings among the Muscogee—and in Cherokee society designating individuals with titles of certain *talwas* like the Coweta king—as "ancient usages" and customs that continued into the nineteenth century. In fact it was Coweta's *micos* despite their grudge against Tugaloo who were the "principal actors" in reestablishing peace through these individuals. Therefore Escotchaby was the living embodiment of the "friendly intercourse that existed between the Cherokees . . . [and] Coweta" and represented a "brotherly, family friendship" between the two sides. As the Cherokee king, he spent a considerable time in the Cherokee world, where he met and coupled with one of their women, learned the Cherokee (Iroquoian) language, acclimated to Cherokee ceremony and ritual, and so on, so much so that he stated how he "looks upon the Cherokees as [his] people." Reciprocally the Cherokee considered Escotchaby to be their "brother" and one "connected with [their] Nation." For all intents and purposes, Escotchaby bridged two Indigenous worlds and was responsible for brokering a peace that had long eluded both sides.[4]

Individuals such as Escotchaby reveal the relationships that the Indigenous Peoples of North America forged with one another in the eighteenth century. As scholars have not yet fully articulated,[5] the Cherokee king provides a way to understand how Indigenous groups approached their relationships with each other, negotiated their differences and conflicts, and incorporated one another into their worlds, despite sharing a mutual antagonism toward each other. There is another reason why Escotchaby and such intra-Indigenous connections are so compelling, for Muscogee peoples are linguistically, culturally, and ceremonially *Muscogee* as opposed to the Cherokee, who are *Iroquoian*. Such differences accentuated the conflicts between the two peoples throughout the seventeenth and eighteenth centuries. Yet despite this fact, both groups found ways to bridge such difference and acclimate to one another, although this process proved uneven at times. What is important to recognize, though, is that Escotchaby embodied the various intra-Indigenous connections that defined the everyday lives of the Indigenous Peoples of North America during the eighteenth century.

In addition, like Sempoyaffee, Escotchaby represented the ambitions and hopes of his *huti* for the future. By assuming a prominent role in the frequent

conflicts and negotiations between Muscogee and Cherokee peoples, Escotchaby cultivated considerable influence on both sides, which ultimately prepared him for a future leadership role within the *talwa*. Naturally he always
had the members of his *huti* in mind. And ironically enough, the *huti* now
had two brothers in important positions of influence within the *talwa*, one
related to matters of war and the other, peace. Escotchaby thereby presented
his *huti* with a unique opportunity to forge connections with the Cherokee,
connections that also reflected the intra-Indigenous realities of early America.

The Cherokee King: The Intersection of Muscogee and Cherokee Worlds

It should come as no surprise that the Muscogee and Cherokee worlds intersected in such intimate ways, and it all started at the most fundamental level:
kinship. Simply put, Muscogee peoples lived with Cherokees and Cherokees
lived in Muscogee communities, whether it was the number of Muscogee
men who partnered with Cherokee women or the "Cherokee men, women,
and Children" who resided in Muscogee *talwas*. As Oconostota, a beloved
man of Chote and a Cherokee *skiagusta* (head warrior), best described such
kinship: "we are here mixed like Brothers." As a testament to such intimacy,
Muscogee *micos* and Cherokee leaders interchangeably designated one another as "younger brothers" and "older brothers" in their councils with each
other. In some cases they established joint communities, such as the towns
of Coosawhatchie and Old Night-assay, which straddled the boundaries
between Muscogee and Cherokee territories. Both peoples also appointed
specific towns such as Ettuca, Chote, Okchai, and Coweta as the places of
"rendezvous" to better "Manage the Affairs" of their two peoples. Muscogee
and Cherokee peoples thus maintained an intimacy as much as they shared
animosity toward one another.[6]

　　Muscogee and Cherokee peoples also communicated with one another
on a frequent basis. It was not unusual to see "messengers of peace" going
back and forth between Muscogee and Cherokee communities, often in one
another's company. Muscogee *micos* and Cherokee headmen also invited one
another's townspeople to their towns, like the Cherokee leaders who hosted
"a grand meeting at Chote" with Lower and Upper *micos* in summer of 1773.
Quite often Muscogee-Cherokee conversations usually concerned Europeans,
like the message that Chote received from the Cowetas who presented Chote's
headmen with "some Tobacco, which they Said came from the Spaniards and
. . . informed them . . . that the Carolina people had not Such a Regard as
they pretended to have for the Cherokees." Muscogee and Cherokee peoples
similarly shared with each other their resentments toward Europeans, such as

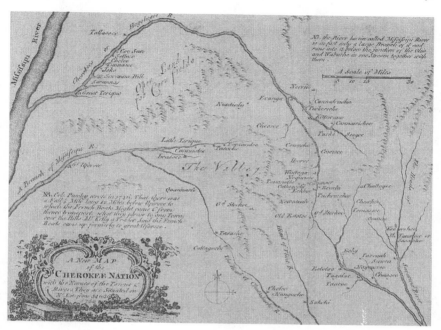

Thomas Kitchin's "A New Map of the Cherokee Nation: With the Names of the Towns & Rivers They Are Situated on No. lat from 34 to 36." (Image Courtesy of American Antiquarian Society, Maps, Georgia 1760 001 Boxed.)

the *micos* who confided to British authorities that "we are informed by the Cherokees, that the white people have Sent Cattle to the Head of the Coosa River, We hope that they have not." When their frustrations with Europeans festered to the point of ill intention, Muscogee and Cherokee leaders sent messengers to each other with a potential "confederacy in view." In extreme cases Muscogee and Cherokee peoples debated war against Europeans, as, for example, when the Cowetas "sent in a Runner with a String of White Beads with Three Red Beads on it" to Keowee, an invitation to attack the English colonies. Muscogee and Cherokee peoples conversed with one another on an everyday basis about a host of matters that demonstrate the intimate intersections of their two worlds.[7]

Muscogee and Cherokee peoples similarly shared their hunting grounds and exchanged goods and labors.[8] Particularly with the onset of a commercial deerskin trade at the turn of the eighteenth century, Lower Muscogee and Lower Cherokee hunters often joined in company with one another when hunting the *itchu* in the territories between their communities. Escotchaby did exactly that in February 1760 when he met a Cherokee headman known as the Pidgeon, who had been "hunting that way all this Winter." They also established shared communities on the hunting paths, which is where Cherokee peoples fled in October 1776 when they "went to the Highwassey river, where there is a Town on the path to the Creeks." Frequent intimacy also stemmed from the fact that Cherokees often had to travel through Muscogee territories if taking their deerskins to Charleston or Augusta or to the stores along the Creek Path, "wherein Goods were deposited for the Trade." Muscogee and Cherokee peoples also traded their skins in one another's towns, which frustrated British authorities, who complained of the Muscogee hunters who "come into . . . [Cherokee] Towns to Trade" and thereby deprived the resident traders of that product. This is not to mention the exchange of foodstuffs, baskets, clothing, and other domestically produced goods that Muscogee and Cherokee peoples bartered for with their deerskins. It should be noted that such intimate contacts extended to ceremony and ritual. For instance the Busk was practiced by both Muscogee and Cherokee peoples, despite the many differences between them, which hints at some of the religious exchanges taking place among them.[9]

Needless to say, such frequent intimacy also bred disagreement and conflict. As early as 1674, Europeans observed that the "Cowatoe and Chorake Indians . . . are at continual warrs" with one another. As Tyler Boulware reminds us, the violence "did not represent a sharp break with the past," because both sides' "ancestors had a long history of unstable relations dating back many centuries" when the Cherokee had moved beyond the Appalachian Mountains into Muscogee territories.[10] As a number of *micos* from the Lower *talwas* asserted, the Lower Cherokee town of Chote was actually "their property,"[11] as well as the Cherokee towns on the lower Little Tennessee Valley. Naturally, Cherokee headmen rejected such claims and declared that "the Land is ours, and not the Creeks; they know it well." Further, with the onset of the commercial deerskin trade, Muscogee and Cherokee peoples increasingly competed for the diminishing supply of *itchu* by encroaching onto each other's territories. As Cherokee headmen recalled in 1826, Muscogee peoples by the "extension of their hunting grounds . . . for the sake of obtaining skins" had incited the "frequent murders" of Cherokee hunters that devolved into "frequent quarrels and war." However, according to Coweta's *micos,* it was instead their people who met some Cherokees in their hunting grounds and had "7 of our People" killed that prompted the violence. It should be noted that Muscogee-Cherokee violence also revolved around the efforts of the young people on both sides to prove their manhood and attain war names.[12] In this case conflict served a function in both Muscogee and Cherokee worlds, tied to the young men who "will be So head Strong" and "Committ Hostilleys" against one another.[13]

But the warfare between Muscogee and Cherokee communities took a darker turn in the 1740s and early 1750s as the violence became more widespread and destructive. As Cherokee leaders again reflected in 1826, their communities had faced an unprecedented "invasion by the Creeks in larger bodies than the usual custom," which forced their "outmost towns [to] evacuate after the loss of many lives, and [flee] to other towns."[14] Even Europeans observed the intensity with which Muscogee peoples attacked the Cherokee who "seem to be in a distressed Condition." The new level of violence was largely attributed to the Lower *talwas* who decimated Lower Cherokee communities along the Tugaloo River in a bid to reclaim former territories. In several cases the Lower *talwas* razed entire towns, including Estatoe and Echoi. In response Cherokee leaders such as Tasattee of Hiwassee pleaded with Europeans to broker peace on their behalf with the Lower *talwas,* who seemed "determined to destroy our Towns." In May 1752, it was even reported "all the Lower Cherokee Towns were broke up and removed further up into the Nation" out of fear for being "cutt off and destroyed by the Creeks." This did not include the men, women, and children who were captured amid the violence or, in the case of nine Cherokee men captured in 1750, were burned alive in the *talwa* of Tallauhassee.[15] While the violence was not as palpable for Muscogee peoples as it was for the Cherokee, they still experienced "a great many of their People killed by the Cherokees."[16]

From the outset of the conflict, it was specifically Malatchi and the people of Coweta who produced "much Blood-shed" against the Cherokee. In April 1750 Malatchi reportedly incited hundreds of Lower Muscogee men to commit "great Cruelties" against the Cherokee by "destroying Man, Woman, and Child; burning two of the Towns to Ashes, and even setting Fire to the Trader's House." While Malatchi's "name became a Terror" to the Cherokee, it also earned him the approbation of the young men of Coweta and the other Lower *talwas,* who increasingly viewed him as the "greatest Leader they ever had," thereby bolstering his claims to be emperor for all the *talwas.* According to Malatchi, his reasons for a prolonged conflict were part of his efforts to reacquire hunting grounds that once belonged to Muscogee peoples but had since been occupied by the Cherokee.[17]

On account of the ceaseless violence, Cherokee leaders reached out to British authorities in hopes of brokering a peace with the Muscogee, but Malatchi time and again rejected such efforts. In May 1753, when Governor Glen proposed to mediate between the two sides, Malatchi dominated the proceedings and declared to Glen that despite "all the Trouble you have taken, we fear it will prove ineffectual." He not only blamed the conflict on the Cherokee who "always broke the Peace" but also chided Cherokee headmen for not even attending the conference in the first place, which he believed was because the

Cherokee were "afraid" of him. Of course, it remained in Malatchi's best interest to prolong the war, which added to his prestige along with the "conquest" of Cherokee lands. So he only added fuel to the fire when articulating how the "Cherokees encourage the Northern Indians to come through their Towns to make War upon us" and that "I do not at present know what Damage they are doing in our Nation, I cannot therefore be answerable that it will be a firm Peace till I return." Malatchi had even prevented peace the previous year when he and other *micos* met at Fort Moore, "where we expected to have met the Cherokees, and found that they were not come."[18] When a Cherokee delegate did show up, he and Malatchi shared "a good deal of Conversation" about how "most of the Cherokees were inclined to a Peace." But Malatchi dismissed that meeting a year later to Glen, saying, "I do not think it is much to be regarded" and "would be in vain to make a Peace." He thereby continually derailed the talks of peace, despite reports that the Cherokee town of Keowee sent emissaries to spread word that "they were now in Peace with your Nation."[19]

In contrast to Malatchi and the Cowetas, the Upper *talwas* desired an end to the incessant conflict, and led by the *micos* of Okfuskee—Coweta's inveterate rival among the Upper *talwas*—sought to intervene and stop the violence.[20] Within the Muscogee world, it was traditionally the Okfuskees who mediated with the Cherokee in order to restore the peaceful intimacy between their peoples.[21] As Joshua Piker describes, before then the "Cowetas and Cherokees fought; Okfuskees and Cherokees negotiated." This is why at the same conference that Malatchi tried to sabotage a potential peace with the Cherokee in May 1753, the *tustenogy* of Okfuskee declared that his *micos* "readily complied" with Governor Glen's efforts to negotiate with the Cherokee. As the Okfuskee head warrior stated, "I never shall be the Man that will stand out against any good Talk," a sharp and deliberate rebuke of Malatchi. In particular the Okfuskees were furious that Malatchi had targeted the Cherokee town of Estatoe, which shared a privileged connection with Okfuskee. In addition, Malatchi had blamed the assassination of a Cherokee delegation in Charleston in 1752, known as the Acorn Whistler Crisis, on the Upper *talwas* despite the killings having been committed by the Lower *talwas* and likely at Malatchi's instigation. This is undoubtedly why the headmen of the Overhill Cherokee towns sent word to British authorities that they were at "war with the Cowetas" but not the Upper *talwas,* who "we look upon as Friends, according to the Peace."[22]

When Malatchi refused to entertain further talks with the Cherokee, Okfuskee's *micos* and *tustenogy* stepped up their efforts to force Malatchi into a peace. In yet another meeting with British administrators, the Okfuskees again reprimanded Malatchi in front of Governor Glen and stated that "since the Peace with the Cherokees was proposed," they had kept their "Warriors at Home." Then up stood the Captain of Okfuskee, who delivered an unmistakable message to Malatchi, resigning his "commission" from the British and walking out of the room, followed by "many of the Warriors" who were all "seemingly displeased." Malatchi tried to downplay the significance of the event by chastising the Okfuskees and apologizing to Glen "that some of our People who call themselves Head Men and Warriours, should behave so like Children . . . They in a very rude and abrupt Manner broke in upon my Discourse without any Power or Commission from me or the Nation." Contrary to what Malatchi claimed, though, the Okfuskees demonstrated the limits of his authority, especially as it pertained to continuing the war against the Cherokee on behalf of all the *talwas*. That, combined with Okfuskee's incessant pressure after the conference, forced Malatchi to concede and promise the Cherokee that the *talwas* would "not go to War for three Months." When Malatchi proved true to his word, Muscogee *micos* and Cherokee headmen agreed to formalize a peace, embodied by the Cherokee delegation that visited Okfuskee and Coweta in late 1753 or early 1754, followed by the Muscogee delegation that accompanied the Cherokee back to their territories.[23]

In addition to the Okfuskees, it seems that individuals from Coweta (at least those not-named-Malatchi) had also been critical to carving out peace between Muscogee and Cherokee peoples in the early 1750s. As Cherokee leaders recalled in 1826, the Cowetas "were the principal actors in re-establishing . . . peace" despite Malatchi's efforts to prolong the conflict. As those Cherokee headmen related the story of the peace, when a group of Cherokee from Tugaloo came down to attack Coweta in presumably 1753, among them was a "Creek man" called the Pidgeon, who "had been either taken as prisoner or had come in this nation in time of peace, when quite a youth, who became attached to this nation by marriage." After reaching the Oconee River, the Pidgeon spied ahead and stumbled upon two Muscogee men, one of whom may have been Escotchaby.[24] The Pidgeon asked them what they were doing, and they identified themselves as "messengers of peace" from Coweta. The three men agreed to meet the following day in hopes of "establishing firm peace between the respective nations." In fact the three men eventually resolved that their "Kings and Chiefs should have a meeting of the two nations." Accordingly, Muscogee *micos* and Cherokee headmen agreed to stop hostilities upon the condition that the Oconee River should serve as the "boundary to be observed by the hunting parties." As Cherokee leaders later reminisced, "the peace which was there re-established at this last meeting has ever since remained firm between the two nations." Because of the role that these Coweta townsmen played in this peace, its *micos* were granted the "right of nominating a beloved mediating chief" among the Cherokee who was generally called the Coweta king, while the Cherokee appointed a Coweta man as a Cherokee king.[25]

Therefore, the Cherokee delegation that arrived among the *talwas* in late 1753 or early 1754 had the dual purpose of formalizing peace between the two sides and installing the individuals who would serve as their Cherokee kings. Although the Cherokee were again forced to cede hunting grounds on the south side of the Savannah River near Augusta, both sides confirmed that the "daily killing and Destroying each other" was over. Together Muscogee and Cherokee leaders conceded that "if any of their people should be found killed in the Woods," neither side would be "suspected or accused of it." Instead the offended party would "send and Complain of the Injury" to the other in hopes of securing satisfaction. In Coweta, at the conclusion of the peace, the two sides exchanged emblems and words to denote the newfound peace between their peoples and proceeded to talk about who would serve as the Cherokee king.[26] The nomination or appointment process started as a dialogue between Coweta's *micos* and the Cherokee headmen, who exchanged two twists of tobacco, "one wrapped up in a white belt of wampum and the other with a string of black and white common beads." After eliminating several candidates for the position, the two sides eventually settled upon Escotchaby, likely on account of his interactions with the Pidgeon earlier in 1753. After calling Escotchaby into the town square, Coweta's *micos* and the Cherokee delegates invested Escotchaby with the "honor" of becoming the Cherokee king. After much ceremony, Escotchaby was presented to both sides and "looked upon by them as conservator of their rights and protector of their persons" in their respective councils. Escotchaby was now considered —in the words of Cherokee leaders—a Cherokee man, one "welcomed among them as a brother" and known by the epithet "Beloved Brother," and a "Cherokee Chief" now "connected with this nation." Escotchaby then accompanied the Cherokee delegation back to their communities, in company with several of Coweta's *micos*, where he would be presented to the Cherokee towns and—in consultation with Cherokee leaders—help the *micos* appoint their Coweta king among the Cherokee.[27]

This act of installing Cherokee kings (for Muscogee peoples) and Coweta kings (for Cherokee peoples) thus cemented the "brotherly relationship" between the two peoples that persisted well into the nineteenth-century and brought an end to the Muscogee-Cherokee conflicts. This practice was not entirely new to the Indigenous groups of the American South; Thomas Nairne wrote as early as 1708 that the "people of these parts have one pretty rationable Esteablishment," in which two groups chose a "protector in the other" whose sole purpose "is to make up all Breaches between the two nations."[28] Thus if violence ever erupted between Muscogee and Cherokee peoples in the future, instead of first seeking retribution, both sides turned to their Cherokee kings and Coweta kings to mediate. Over time the selection of Coweta kings and Cherokee kings evolved to include other individuals such as the Mortar of Okchai (or the Chote King), the Old Coweta King and Young Coweta King of Tugaloo, Little Turkey (or the Young Turkey), the Coosa King of the Upper Creeks, and others not readily identifiable in the record. All these individuals not only served as the "channels" of peace but also as a bridge between their communities. For instance the Mortar maintained a connection between his *talwa*, Okchai, with the Cherokee town of Chote.[29] Similarly individuals from the Upper *talwa* of Okfuskee and the Cherokee community of Hiwassee exchanged places and roles in their respective societies. Some Muscogee and Cherokee communities even traded names, such as the Overhill Cherokee town of Tallassee, named after that Muscogee *talwa*.[30] Where Escotchaby differed from his counterparts, though, was that he acted as intermediary with several Cherokee towns, including Keowee, Toxaway, Estatoe, and Tugaloo. In fact the Coweta-Tugaloo connection was critically important because of the "old Grudge" that existed between the two communities since 1715.[31]

As a Cherokee king, Escotchaby would have left behind his *huti* in Coweta and took up residence among the Cherokee for a time, most likely in Tugaloo. In the early to mid 1750s, he coupled with a Cherokee woman[32] from whom he likely learned the Iroquoian language if he did not speak it already, as well as the Cherokees' most important cultural customs, ceremonial protocols and rituals and overall acclimated himself as to what it meant to be a Cherokee man. The Cherokee headman Tiftoy, when attending a congress at Augusta in November 1768, thus addressed Escotchaby as his "brother" who "was once in the Cherokee Nation and we know you." When Escotchaby mediated for Muscogee and Cherokee peoples, he acted as the interpreter for both sides, since he spoke the language "as well as a Native." Even after he returned to Coweta, he remained a brother to the Cherokee, and whenever he trekked into Tugaloo or another town, he joined the headmen and "stay'd all night in the town house." Escotchaby thereby occupied a prominent position in both Muscogee and Cherokee worlds then, and bestowed great distinction upon his *huti*.[33]

The most important labor that Escotchaby performed was to ensure peace by any means possible. Like Sempoyaffee, he bore a responsibility to sustain the cosmic balance of the Muscogee (and in this case also Cherokee) world. Whereas eighteenth-century Muscogee peoples would have termed Escotchaby's new role as walking the "white path," eighteenth-century Cherokees considered it to be sitting on the "White Bench." Escotchaby thereby attended the Cherokee councils "sometimes as a guest, sometimes to examine into complaints of aggressions from his own nation," while appearing in Coweta's councils, where he similarly represented the "Rights of the Cherokees." He acted as Muscogee when in council with Cherokee headmen but as Cherokee when in the councils of his own people. While the presence of the Cherokee king could be requested by either Muscogee *micos* or Cherokee leaders, Escotchaby also possessed the power to "summon people of all the Nation to be present at a Talk." In addition to such impromptu congresses, he made periodic visits to Cherokee towns, such as his trip to Tugaloo in February 1760 in company with the Pidgeon.[34]

Escotchaby would have remained in continual contact with Cherokee leaders and often communicated with his counterparts such as the Old Coweta King and Young Coweta King. For instance when rumors threatened to embroil Muscogee and Cherokee peoples in conflict with each other, they sought advice from "one of our Nation who has been some Years amongst the Cherokees" and who gave a different account of the Cherokee being "inclinable to a peace." In the event Escotchaby was unable to persuade the *tustenogy* or young men of Coweta to refrain from harassing the Cherokee, he sent word to the Coweta kings "to provide for their own safety" and the safety of their people. And when violence seemed close at hand, Cherokee headmen like the Little Turkey, Tiftoy, and the Bag of Toxaway sent messengers to Escotchaby and asked for his help, to convince Muscogee peoples "not to bring any darkness over us, nor to Stop our Trading Path" and "if they are for War . . . not to come near our Towns."[35]

When talks could only do so much, Escotchaby either welcomed Cherokee leaders into Coweta or led a delegation of the Lower *micos* to Cherokee Country. For example, in the years after the peace, Cherokee headmen traveled among the Upper and Lower *talwas,* being "commissioned by their Nation to Confirm and Strengthen the Peace in their Way." During one of those visits, Escotchaby greeted the Cherokee dignitaries in Coweta when they spent a "considerable time in the Creek Nation and were well Entertained there." When it was time to return home, Escotchaby likely accompanied the Cherokee delegation in the company of "Ten Creek Warriours" if not some of Coweta's *micos*.[36] Upon reaching Cherokee territories, the two sides hosted several conferences to affirm the peace, where Cherokee leaders described they "not only heard their Mouth But had Seen their Hearts." At one point Escotchaby presented gifts to the Cherokee leaders, including conch shells and white beads, as well as corn and watermelon seeds that could be planted so that when he next came to the Cherokee towns he "may Eat with them and be as Brothers." Escotchaby and his party then returned to Coweta and related how they were "received by the Cherokees like Brothers" and "entertain'd in the most kind and Affectionate manner."[37]

Escotchaby also turned Coweta into a place of refuge for Cherokee peoples in times of need. In summer 1757, when Cherokee leaders feared attack from the English colonies, they sent to Coweta and "demanded assistance from the Creeks, and a place of Safety for their Wives and Children." While such pleas for asylum were often temporary, there were instances in which refuge proved permanent, like in 1761 when the Cherokee went to war against the colonies, and the Lower *talwas* offered the Cherokee both provisions and protection if they "will remove to the Creek Towns." At the same time, if "the English will march an Army against the Cherokees," the *micos* promised to assist the Cherokee. Lower Cherokees specifically responded in the affirmative. Again in 1776 Coweta harbored Lower Cherokee refugees after the Americans sent several armed expeditions into Cherokee territories. As British agents reported a year later, the Lower Cherokee were all "preparing to leave the lower Creeks, that many of them had left fine Fields of Corn almost ripe" in Coweta. The Cherokee returned the favor for Muscogee peoples in 1838, when Muscogee refugees fled to Cherokee towns "for protection" when threatened with removal to Indian Territory by the US government.[38]

Another important function of being Cherokee king was to monitor the many peoples who moved between Muscogee and Cherokee territories. When in the company of the Pidgeon in February 1760, Escotchaby inquired about "two Large gangs of Cherokee" who were out and about and learned that "another Party are gone out about Saluda and a very Large gang gone to the Northward." Similarly, when Tiftoy met with Escotchaby in 1768 and complained of "your People who we consider as outlaws and renegados who are constantly in our towns," Escotchaby promised Tiftoy that "we shall send for our people and endeavour to prevail on them to return home," and if they did not, Escotchaby gave Tiftoy permission to drive them out. Such policing included the young men on both sides who at times threatened to upend the peace. For instance amid the Cherokee war against the English colonies, British authorities attempted to solicit the support of the *talwas* with "considerable rewards." However, Escotchaby prevented Muscogee men from taking the bait and persuaded Coweta's *micos* to send a talk "to Governor Ellis against his continuing to take such Steps." Escotchaby also contended with the Cherokee, who sought the support of the *talwas* against the colonies, such as the "Cherokee fellow and three women" who arrived at Coweta, bearing a "war-spear having 300 notches on it, denoting so many of the white people [that] have been killed by them."[39]

When violence invariably erupted, it was still Escotchaby's responsibility to repair the damage. In the aftermath of any violent event, the first seven days were known as the "broken days,"[40] during which the *micos* deliberated on "whether to continue [with] War, or make up the Breach."[41] During the

broken days Escotchaby emerged as an important voice for peace, repre-
senting Cherokee interests in his peoples' councils at the same time that he
traveled to Cherokee territories to voice Muscogee concerns, all the while
delivering talks, messages, and emblems of peace. At other times Escotchaby
escorted Muscogee *micos* and Cherokee headmen back and forth from their
communities to present their own grievances or to offer condolences in person. Similar to what occurred during the broken days in October 1788, several *micos* stated that despite their peoples' penchant for violence, they "had
always advised them to look forward to the hour of peace." And when it was
time for the Busk, Escotchaby invited the Cherokee with "as many or as few
as they please" to attend, so that the year's past offenses might be forgiven.[42]

It was within this context that Escotchaby undoubtedly worked alongside
his brother, Coweta's *tustenogy,* given Sempoyaffee directed and surveilled the
young men of their *talwa*. Once again the young men of the Lower *talwas*
depended upon conflict with their Indigenous neighbors like the Cherokee
as a means of attaining war names, or for the youngest men, as a way to prog-
ress from young adulthood to manhood. As British authorities took stock
of the situation, "No Indian can attain any Rank in the Community except
by some Warlike Exploits," which "is the Source of perpetual Bloodshed." It
did not help matters that a number of young men had professed that "when
they heard that their Relations were gone out against the Cherokees," they
vowed that if any of their relatives were killed they would kill the Cherokee
in response. As Escotchaby confessed, the "young Creeks itched to fall upon
the Cherokees, and for the Purpose many of them kept out of Way of their
Headmen," which made keeping peace all the more difficult. Together Sempoyaffee and Escotchaby managed to keep the young men of Coweta idle at
several points after peace had been established, in one instance reporting how
"no Mischief has been done" as of late.[43]

Escotchaby's responsibilities as peacekeeper even extended to Muscogee
and Cherokee territories and boundaries. For instance he attempted to ensure "there was no intrusion" on Cherokee territories by Muscogee peoples
and vice versa, and if any of their peoples violated such an agreement, they
would be removed off the "lands of the other."[44] The territorial dimensions of
being a Cherokee king originated at the first peace in the early 1750s, when
the Coweta king and Cherokee king had designated that "the marked tree
on the high shoal of the Appalatchees" was the boundary line between their
peoples' hunting grounds.[45] Thus Cherokee kings possessed extensive knowledge about both peoples' territories and boundaries in order to maintain
peace, particularly when it involved hunting grounds. It is also one of the reasons that Escotchaby joined the surveying parties that "mark out and run the
Boundary-Line between their Hunting Grounds and Georgia" in 1763, 1765,

and 1768, to ensure the integrity of Muscogee-Cherokee boundaries when land was ceded to the Georgia colony. As a territorial authority, Escotchaby was within his rights in 1772 when he sent two young men to the Cherokee in order to "bring two of their headmen" to Coweta, so that he "might Enquire of them whether they had given the Land above Little River to the white people or not," lands that belonged to the Muscogee.[46]

As the Cherokee king, then, Escotchaby fulfilled an important function within the Muscogee and Cherokee worlds, and that is why it is somewhat surprising that he inherited the office of *tustenogy* from his brother in the mid-1750s. In doing so Escotchaby became both a mediator of peace as well as an arbitrator for war. While one might be skeptical that he retained his title as Cherokee king while serving as *tustenogy*, he was identified simultaneously in 1759 and 1760 as both a Cherokee king, as "Head Warrior of the Cowetaw Town," and as one who "gains ground among the young people, who are fond of getting war names." Again it might seem wholly unusual that he could act in both capacities, but this might explain why British authorities found that "nothing could be done effectually without this Scochaby." Also, the role of the *tustenogy* was as much about restraining Coweta's young men and preserving peace as it was going to war. And in the wake of a decades-long conflict, to have Escotchaby bear the titles of both Cherokee king and *tustenogy* may have been a very calculated decision by Coweta's *micos*, for it is no coincidence that peace—in the words of Cherokee leaders in 1826—"ever since remained firm between the two nations."[47]

In the end things were looking up for Sempoyaffee, Escotchaby, and the members of their *huti* by 1756, given how the two brothers each attained positions of great influence within the *talwa* and in Coweta's relationships with both the Cherokee and Europeans. However, that influence was about to be tested with the outbreak of the Seven Years' War in North America. Yet it was within the crucible of war that Sempoyaffee and Escotchaby emerged as the "eldest of the 4 vile Brothers, Owners of the Town Ground & who over rules all when on the Spot," a testament to the ways in which they steered their *huti* and *talwa* through a global conflict that threatened to upend the Muscogee world.[48]

Four

The Muscogee World
and Imperial Crisis, 1756–1763

In October 1759 Sempoyaffee and other Lower *micos* ventured to Savannah to reaffirm their neutrality during the Seven Years' War, despite French efforts to incite the *talwas* against the British. During the conference between the two sides, Sempoyaffee stated that "there have been many lying Talks given out concerning us," and he now hoped that the "constant and uniform Friendship our Nation has shown to the English even before we were born, and ever since would have sufficiently secured Us from any Suspicion of that Kind." Although Sempoyaffee admitted that "the French have also given Us many bad Talks," he promised British agents that "we shall return to our Nation with glad Hearts and a lasting Friendship will be established." Sempoyaffee expected the English to reciprocate their pledge of neutrality and friendship with gifts that the *micos* would redistribute to their *hutis* and *talwas*, a key component of maintaining one's status as a *mico*. And to remind the governor of Georgia, Henry Ellis, of such obligations, he added, "We Indians have nothing to depend upon for the Support of ourselves and Families but the Game in the Woods, while the white People have many Ways of obtaining Necessaries," a familiar refrain to the many imperial authorities who interacted with Indigenous groups in early America.[1]

Sempoyaffee, though, entertained ulterior motives during the proceedings. Identified as the "uncle" to Togulki—the son of Malatchi—he seized the opportunity and declared that while "this young Man (pointing to Togulki) is the Head of our Nation, you see he is young and unexperienced in public Affairs." Instead "I being his Uncle am deputed to speak for him and all the rest present who are the head Men of two of the principal Towns in our

Nation." In this case Sempoyaffee made a bold claim to be one of the leading voices within Coweta as well as among the other Lower *talwas*, at least under the guise of speaking for Togulki, who was only a "Minor" and in no way the "Head of our Nation." To bolster his claims and at the same time appease the British, Sempoyaffee vowed that "we are not so blind as not to distinguish the superior Happiness of our present Situation in Comparison with that of the French Indians whom we frequently see almost without a Flap to cover their Nakedness."[2]

Despite being one of Coweta's newest *micos*, and as a measure of his audacity to speak for all the *micos* in that moment, Sempoyaffee rearticulated his peoples' grievances to British officials, a not-so-subtle reminder that the friendship between Muscogee and British peoples was a two-way street and could take a turn for the worse at a moment's notice. Sempoyaffee did not hold back when it came to the encroachments on Muscogee lands, for there were a "great many Virginia people settled high up in the Countrey, in our hunting grounds." This was not to mention the settlers who trekked "all over the Woods destroying our Game, which is now become so scarce that we cannot kill sufficient to supply our Necessities" or deerskins for trade. While Sempoyaffee did not explicitly say that the resulting trouble might produce violence, imperial authorities well understood what he implied when he demanded that they should order the encroaching settlers to "remove off from our Hunting Grounds, and that we may have a Paper given us to show those People that it must be done." At this juncture British agents noted how the assembled *micos* agreed with what Sempoyaffee said and "strenuously urged" imperial officials to do as asked. As Ellis replied, "he would consider of the Matter untill to Morrow when he would see them again and endeavour to remove their Complaint."[3]

Sempoyaffee was not finished, though, and turned to another pressing issue: reports that the *talwas* intended to join the Cherokee who were currently at war with the English colonies. While he admitted it was true that the "Cherokees have strongly solicited Us to join and break out war with the English," he reiterated that the reason the Cherokee were at war with the colonies was because the "English wanted to take away their lands." This was Sempoyaffee's way of articulating once again a subtle threat to imperial authorities that if they did not attend to his complaints about the "Virginia people" sooner rather than later, they could expect the *talwas* to join the Cherokee. But Sempoyaffee reassured Ellis that so long as the encroachments stopped, Muscogee peoples would "not heed the Talk" or tolerate any of their peoples being "concerned with the Cherokees." Ellis remained rather skeptical of Sempoyaffee's promises and warned him that if the Cherokee conflict exploded in Georgia, he could not control the settlers, who might blame Muscogee peoples rather than the Cherokee for any person that may be killed, for "how can we distinguish between the Indians of the one Nation, and of the other, at a Distance in the Woods?" After trading such veiled threats, Ellis implored Sempoyaffee to intervene with the Cherokee, "for there is no Time to be lost, nor any other Way to preserve Peace . . . You are too wise not to see the Goodness of my Councels."[4]

Little did Ellis know that this is exactly what Escotchaby was doing at that very moment. While Sempoyaffee met with British officials in October 1759, Escotchaby made his way back and forth between Muscogee and Cherokee communities in the hopes of preventing further violence. Although he was undoubtedly sympathetic to Cherokee reasons for going to war,[5] he nonetheless tried to defuse the tensions between them and the colonies, at the same time—as *tustenogy*—restrain the young men of Coweta from joining the war. And while British authorities reported that Escotchaby and "other Head Men of the Creeks" set out for Cherokee territories with ill intentions, they gravely misunderstood his mission. The only reason British agents could report a few months later that the "Creeks are not at present very warm in the Cause of the Cherokees" was the fact that Escotchaby succeeded in convincing other *micos* to stay out of the conflict, although he had to contend with the same British officials who sought "to prevail if possible upon a party of their young men" to attack the Cherokee. Throughout the war, Escotchaby also received Cherokee talks (like the messenger from Estatoe who brought black and white beads) and delegations (one of which included the Mankiller of Estatoe) that attempted to draw Coweta and the other *talwas* into the war.[6]

Together Sempoyaffee and Escotchaby wielded their positions of newfound influence to mediate the imperial conflict on behalf of their *huti* and *talwa*. As North America descended into war that threatened to embroil the *talwas*, Sempoyaffee and Escotchaby—alongside Coweta's other *micos*—continued to abide by the politics of playing off the European empires against one another. In doing so they maneuvered Coweta into an advantageous position by extracting the promises of trade as well as gifts from both the English and French, which only accentuated the influence and authority of Coweta's *micos*. Part of the balancing act this time, though, was the fact that they had to contend with the Cherokee—their neighbors/kinsmen, rivals/friends—who sought to eradicate the colonies and thereby undo much of what Sempoyaffee and Escotchaby's *huti* and *talwa* had accomplished up to that point. While the two brothers emerged from the war as "owners of the Town Ground & who overrules all when on the Spot," that was hardly a foregone conclusion in October 1759.[7]

The Politics of the *Huti* and *Talwa* during the Seven Years' War

With Malatchi's death at the start of the war, Sempoyaffee and Escotchaby continued to ascend as two of the principal leaders of Coweta. The first plans they set into motion for their *huti* involved setting themselves up as the "uncles" or "guardians" of Togulki, Malatchi's son and intended successor to his father. As the brothers described their roles, they "governed for the not-of-age Emperor," although Togulki had no real power or title like his father had. And while scholars have long identified Togulki's uncle/guardian as Old Stumpe, another Coweta *mico*, this individual at best shared custody with Sempoyaffee and Escotchaby. In fact British and French agents recognized Escotchaby as Togulki's "Unkle who is his Guardian from the Cherokees," meaning that Escotchaby likely exploited his position as Cherokee king to situate himself and his brother as Togulki's stewards. It is also no coincidence that newspaper accounts in the summer of 1759 described Sempoyaffee as "Togulki's Uncle, the principal Headman of the Cowetas," who also accompanied Togulki to the Cherokee towns and then on to Augusta, where they were greeted by British officials.[8]

It was at one of these congresses in October 1759 that Sempoyaffee dragged Togulki in front of British authorities and undermined any pretensions that Malatchi, Togulki, or their *huti* may have had for Togulki's political future. At one point he dramatically pointed to Togulki and stated how young and inexperienced Togulki was to make any claims to lead Coweta as his father had, and that being Togulki's "Uncle" it was Sempoyaffee's responsibility to "speak for him and all the rest present who are the head Men of two of the principal Towns in our Nation." Sempoyaffee's rebuke was not only a humiliating experience for Togulki but also a deliberate ploy to rein in the young upstart. At the very start of the war, rumors placed Togulki at Fort Toulouse, where he was wined and dined by the French and "seemed very pleased with the honor." Impressed with the French, he pledged that Coweta would join them in their war against the English. What became known as the Young-Twin's Conspiracy enraged Sempoyaffee and Escotchaby and set the stage for what occurred in October 1759. Despite such humiliation, though, Togulki attempted to persuade the young men of Coweta to attack the colonies in May 1760, once again with French support. After learning that his "nephew had rebelled against him" again, Sempoyaffee stood up to speak at a conference in the Lower *talwa* of Chehaw, where he angrily stated to Muscogee and British leaders that "his nephew [had] behaved ill and [was] not worthy of a

Commission" and that "he intend[ed] to carry him down to Savannah and deliver up his Commission and from there to Charles Town where he will do the same."[9] Sempoyaffee and Escotchaby made sure that Togulki, and thereby the memory of Malatchi, was suppressed throughout the war.[10]

Turning his attentions to the war itself, Sempoyaffee joined the rest of Coweta's *micos* in maintaining their time-tested strategy of playing European powers against one another, despite incessant pressure from the many sides to join the conflict. As Governor William Henry Lyttleton put it best, Coweta's *micos* "hold us in one hand & the French in the other. And it looks as if they meant to play between us and the French in order to trade with & get presents from both." Like Coweta's other *micos*, Sempoyaffee wanted to ensure that the trade to Charleston and Augusta remained open for his *huti* and *talwa*, balanced with trade to Fort Toulouse. Throughout the war he and Coweta's other *micos* continually approached French and British authorities and demanded that "unless they were more plentifully supplied, it would be impossible to preserve or extend the influence of our party." Governor James Glen grew so concerned about maintaining the relationship with Coweta and the other *talwas* that he asked the traders to sell their various goods in exchange for deerskins at "reduced prices" to better ensure Muscogee peoples remained allies. Tellingly, when British officials asked Sempoyaffee what it would take to affirm a neutrality with the colonies in September 1759, he assured them that even though they maintained a "good understanding with the English, French, and Spaniards," it was the English colonies "who are the chief support of our nation."[11]

Yet Coweta and other *talwas* were hard-pressed to maintain such neutrality even in the first year of the war. As early as September 1756, Upper and Lower *micos* loudly complained about the many settlers living upon the Ogeechee River who "[spoil] our hunting Grounds and [frighten] away the Deer." To make matters worse, when several Muscogee hunters stumbled on one of these illegal settlements on the Ogeechee, they were fired upon, and two of the hunters were killed and another wounded. While the Upper *micos*—led in part by the Gun Merchant of Okchai—used the Ogeechee incident to make certain demands of British officials, Sempoyaffee and other Lower *micos* distanced themselves from their counterparts, since they believed the Upper *talwas* pushed too far and threatened to plunge the *talwas* "in a Cruel war" with the colonies.[12]

To try and salvage the situation, Sempoyaffee turned to George Galphin. Now identified as one of the "six principal traders" within the deerskin trade, Galphin worked tirelessly with Sempoyaffee to make sure trade continued to flow between Coweta and the colonies. The two men spent a majority of their time between 1756 and 1763 in each other's company and continually

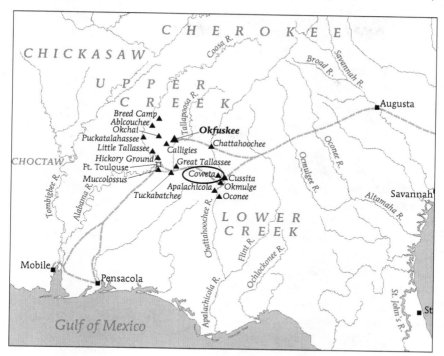

Map of the Creek Path (dashed line) between British North America & Creek Country (Coweta circled). (OKFUSKEE: A CREEK INDIAN TOWN IN COLONIAL AMERICA by Joshua Piker, Cambridge, Mass.: Harvard University Press, copyright © 2004 by the President and Fellows of Harvard College)

throughout the war brought Muscogee and British leaders together. They put together one of the largest gatherings of the *talwas* during the conflict—twenty-one in number—in October 1757, where it was decided that despite the Ogeechee incident the previous year, "peace and good friendship is hereby renew'd & establish'd." Similarly, due to his relationship with Sempoyaffee, Galphin confidently reported to imperial authorities in April 1759 that "I satisfied *my Interest* in the Coweta party to serve the Contrey" and that the "French interest be gote out of the Towns."[13]

This did not mean that Sempoyaffee and Escotchaby did not reach out to the French to exploit the situation for their *huti* and *talwa*. While Coweta's *micos* might exhibit "Disdain and Contempt" toward the French when in the English colonies, they also took the opportunity in the early years of the war to accept offers of trade and presents from Fort Toulouse. For example, the French approached the Lower and Upper *talwas* with an opportunity to negotiate a peace with the neighbors and rivals the Choctaw, which proved "an Affair of the greatest Importance" to many of the *talwas*. In other cases Sempoyaffee and Escotchaby joined the delegations that went to Fort Toulouse, although they afterward informed British agents of their activities and told them their reason for going was to keep an eye on Togulki. Therefore the brothers accompanied Togulki to the fort in March 1759, where the French commandment asked them to join an assault on Fort Loudon. Although Togulki showed great interest in the matter, Sempoyaffee and Escotchaby reportedly forced him to "not attempt to propose this matter in publick" so as not to "stir up his Countrymen." While we do not know if Sempoyaffee and Escotchaby were true to their word, we do know they went to Fort Toulouse to secure presents and the continued promises of trade and afterward kept a wary eye on Togulki. In addition their two other brothers, Ufylegey and the Second Man of Coweta, accompanied Togulki back to the French fort in June 1759 and from there to Mobile and New Orleans. When the party returned to Coweta, Ufylegey leaked word to the English colonies that when in New Orleans, the French governor promised to send to Muscogee and Cherokee communities a shipment of "Guns & Tomahawks, & Cutlasses & Knives." This was followed by the Second Man of Coweta, who traveled in company with Togulki to Fort Toulouse a second time, although the details of that visit are lost. Once again the constant presence of the "4 vile Brothers" around Togulki might have raised red flags for some as it did for Superintendent Edmond Atkin, but it was all smoke and mirrors, part of a decades-long practice of negotiating back and forth between European empires, and it just so happened that Togulki provided Sempoyaffee and Escotchaby with the perfect cover to do so.[14]

Whereas Sempoyaffee spent much of his time negotiating with the British and French, Escotchaby emerged as an intermediary with the Spanish in nearby Florida and Havana.[15] Once again it was Togulki who drew the interest of Europeans, as Spanish officials dispatched a letter addressed to the "Emperor of Cabeta"—Togulki—inviting him to talk at St. Augustine. But when Spanish agents arrived, it was instead Escotchaby who met them and "brought with him his Youth, his Mother and other Caciques." Like Sempoyaffee, Escotchaby wasted no time in dismissing Togulki's presence in front of the Spanish and accepting the gifts they presented to him. He then talked with the Spanish and afterward sent "messengers" into the *talwas* to inform everyone that peace now existed between them and Spain. Unfortunately for the Spanish, they believed Escotchaby had "come to unite with the Spaniards" against the English colonies, but all he did was play the Spanish like he and his brother did the French and British. With that said, in late 1762 rumors had it that the Lower *talwas* had "resolved to go to war against the

Spaniards at St. Augustine," although it was later reported the "young Lieutenant" (Escotchaby)—in his capacity as *tustenogy*—had "dissuaded them
from their purpose." In such ways Sempoyaffee and Escotchaby continued to
preserve Muscogee neutrality on all fronts.[16]

One might even say that everything was going according to plan until the
outbreak of the war between the Cherokee and the English colonies in 1758.
While the origins of that conflict stemmed from the encroachments upon
Cherokee territories, the French also enflamed Cherokee resentments toward
the English. As early as 1756 and as late as 1759, Cherokee headmen met at
Fort Toulouse and in New Orleans, where they exchanged talks and a "large
belt of Wampum that was Strong," in which the black beads represented
"the bad Intentions [of] the white people" toward the Cherokee. Together
Cherokee frustrations and French agitations sparked violence between the
Cherokee and the English colonies.[17] And despite the efforts of certain headmen such as the Little Carpenter who tried to prevent any further bloodshed,
other leaders such as the Old Hop "[were] no way disposed to Give Satisfaction for the Mischief they [had] done."[18]

Naturally the Cherokee reached out to their Muscogee neighbors for assistance against the colonies, which put Escotchaby in quite the unenviable
position as both Cherokee King and *tustenogy*. As early as summer 1756, the
Cherokee sent the "Warr Hoop" into Coweta and tried to convince Coweta's
micos and the young men that "if there is not a Stop put to the settling of
Ogatechy it will prove the ruin of the Whole Country." This report so alarmed
the people of Coweta that Escotchaby sent out scouts to the Ogeechee River,
who returned "very much Dissatisfyed concerning some Bad usage they met"
with from a group of settlers who resided there, and illegally so. Even though
Escotchaby calmed the young men, the seeds of resentment had been effectively planted. And once the Cherokee conflict started, Cherokee headmen continually reached out to Coweta for support. In one instance it was
a Cherokee elder and three women in the company of "some Creek fellows"
who ventured to Coweta, bearing a message for none other than Escotchaby.
The talk was from one of the Coweta kings explaining how he had been
imprisoned by the English and now feared for his life, thereby pleading with
Escotchaby to help free him. This message was followed by the news that the
Cherokee had seized the English fort at Keowee and "invited the Creeks to
come and share the plunder with them." Escotchaby also later learned that
several young men from Coweta did not heed his orders and left the *talwa* to
join the Cherokee and killed several of the settlers, after which they paraded
around "a bloody stick or hatchet."[19]

Rather than convincing the Cowetas to join them as Cherokee leaders
hoped, all these developments encouraged Coweta's Cherokee king and

tustenogy to keep his townspeople out of the conflict. For example when Escotchaby first heard reports of the Cherokee attacks, he ordered all the young men from Coweta who were out in "hunting gangs" on the Savannah River to return home immediately. Then it was Sempoyaffee (identified in the records in this instance by his pseudonym Fool Harry) and Escotchaby (as the Young Lieutenant) who scouted along the river in search of any straggling hunters out of fears that the settlers might mistakenly seek revenge upon their townspeople or that their young men might do the same. Shortly after Cherokee leaders arrived in Coweta with a "large Strap of Wampum" like the one they gave to the French at Fort Toulouse. They informed Escotchaby and Coweta's *micos* that the "Nottoweagas," or Northern Indians, had agreed to join them, and thus they renewed their demands that the *talwas* do the same. Contrary to Cherokee hopes, though, Coweta's *micos* berated them and declared that "they would take no talks from the Cherokees against the English." Governor Ellis breathed a huge sigh of relief when writing to his superiors, that "I find that the Creeks are not at present very warm in the Cause of the Cherokees," and he hoped to convince groups of their "young men" to harass Cherokee communities.[20]

As the Cherokee conflict dragged into 1760 and grew progressively worse for the Cherokee, they continued to send messengers to Escotchaby that betrayed a desperate plea for Coweta to join the war.[21] In early 1760 Cherokee men and women from the town of Estatoe arrived at Coweta with a "war-spear" and demanded that Coweta unite with the Cherokee and enjoy the "goods they had at Fort Prince-George." However, Escotchaby remained adamant that he and his *talwa* "would not deviate from their neutrality" or "suffer their paths to be spoiled or stained with blood." A few months later, the Cherokee tried again by sending two men with war tokens into Coweta, but they were quickly turned back around. A year after that, the Young Warrior of Estatoe came to solicit Coweta's support, but like every effort before it, Escotchaby refused to allow his *huti* and *talwa* to become involved in the conflict. Afterward Escotchaby with Sempoyaffee and "70 Creek Indians" went to Galphin's Silver Bluff, where they told British agents what had transpired.[22]

Meanwhile Escotchaby sent his own messages to Cherokee communities in hopes of preventing further conflict with the colonies that threatened to embroil the *talwas*. This included the two "Warriours" he sent to Chote, where they met with the Old Hop and presented "two pieces of tobacco . . . wrapped in a white belt of wampum" that were sent "to clear up the bad talks the Creeks had heard of the Cherokees." Escotchaby also reached out to the Pidgeon of Tugaloo in February 1760, one of his counterparts among the Cherokee, who informed Escotchaby about the "large gangs of Cherokees" that had joined the siege of Fort Prince George and Fort Loudon. The violence hit particularly close to home for Escotchaby and the Pidgeon when they learned that a Coweta king and a Cusseta king were among the Cherokee who were "shut up in the Fort by the Governor of Carolina." Both men could do little, though, particularly when Hoyahney—a *mico* of Chehaw—told Escotchaby that the Cherokee had no one to blame but themselves for their situation. As Hoyahney stated to Escotchaby, "he had not forgot the bullets that had been shot at him by the Cherokees." Therefore, despite Escotchaby's best efforts, the Cherokee conflict raged on.[23]

To make matters more difficult, Escotchaby competed against the influence of the Mortar of Okchai, a rival Cherokee king, who sought to involve the *talwas* in the Cherokee conflict. The Mortar, also a *mico* of an Upper *talwa*, had long tried to unite Muscogee and Cherokee peoples against the colonies, and the Seven Years' War provided him with a perfect opportunity to do so. As early as 1756, the Mortar arranged a meeting of the Upper *talwas* at Fort Toulouse, where they received a talk from the Cherokee.[24] It was there that the Mortar declared "the English has now a Mind to make Slaves of them all, for they have already filled their Nation with English Forts and great Guns . . . and Cattle." Scholars have argued that the majority of the Upper and Lower *micos* did not share the Mortar's political views or goals, but the English anxiously sought to discover what occurred at the "constant Meetings" between the Mortar and the Cherokee.[25] At several points during the war, the Mortar traveled to Tellico and Chote and, in the presence of their headmen, "asked them why they Suffer there People to go to war for the White people as the Return gives them Nothing," citing the example of when several Cherokee men had assisted the Virginia colony in 1758 but were later killed by those same colonists on their return home. Later that night Moytoy of Settico and other headmen "stay'd all night in the town house with the Mortar" and shut out the Little Carpenter, who often sided with the English. Afterward the Mortar and the Cherokee headmen agreed to settle several mixed communities—like Coosawhatchie and Ettuca—that were "halfway between the two Nations" and nearby Fort Toulouse. This exchange took place right before the Cherokees' next attacks upon the colonies in 1759, led by Moytoy himself. Some British agents even suspected that the Mortar was the one who planted the "stratagem" with the Cherokee of first targeting Fort Loudon.[26]

Escotchaby combated the Mortar's efforts to drive the *talwas* into the arms of the Cherokee and French. As early as the summer 1757, he and the Red Coat King confronted the Mortar and several Cherokee headmen in Okfuskee. There the Mortar denounced the English colonies for "overrunning their Lands with white People, which they could not or would any longer endure." When Escotchaby and the Red Coat King attempted to delay the Mortar, he instead retreated with the Cherokee dignitaries to Fort Toulouse, where the French "advised them by all means to assault and destroy the Forts and drive all the white People out of their Nation."[27] That same summer Escotchaby dispatched scouts along the path between the Upper *talwas* and Upper Cherokee towns to keep a close eye on the Mortar, and the scouts later reported seeing the Mortar going to Chote in company with several Cherokee. With the Cherokee conflict in full swing by the summer of 1760, the Mortar was so brazen as to send his brother to Coweta with a talk from the Cherokee, "telling them that he expected they had not forgot the engagements they entered into when they received a bloody hatchet and string of red and black beads from the Cherokees last summer." But Escotchaby recognized the Mortar's play for what it was, an effort to turn Escotchaby's reception of Cherokee envoys in 1759—who brought scalps into the town square and presented them to the *tustenogy*—into a pledge of support for the Cherokee. The Mortar failed in this instance to provoke Coweta's *micos,* who instead listened to their Cherokee king and *tustenogy.* Again in early 1761 the Mortar pressed Coweta's *micos* to assist the Cherokee, going so far as to travel to Coweta in person. While no details survive for what transpired in the town square when the Mortar arrived, we might assume he returned to Okchai empty-handed, for Escotchaby and Sempoyaffee afterward traveled to Galphin's Silver Bluff and "sent a good talk" to the colonies.[28]

At the same time Escotchaby contended with the Mortar, he also faced pressure from British officials who demanded the *talwas* intervene on their behalf against the Cherokee. Whether meeting with Superintendent Atkin or the governors of the southern colonies, Escotchaby promised time and again "that the Nation was not to become a Party in the present War." In one instance he chided British authorities, because if it had not been for him and other *micos* being "in the Way" of the Cherokee, they "would have got [English] scalps." Nonetheless Escotchaby performed his due diligence to ensure his *talwa* and others remained detached from the Cherokee conflict. In the summer of 1757, he and other Lower *micos* alerted the colonies to impending Cherokee attacks, including efforts "to cut off the Garrison of Fort Loudon." This was not the first nor the last time that Escotchaby warned the colonies about the threats toward Fort Loudon.[29] When the Cherokee conflict started, he continued to feed information to British agents concerning Cherokee designs upon the colonies. He not only told the English that the "Cherokees were in a ferment and much disturb'd" but also tried to communicate to British authorities in March 1760 that "a great number of Cherokees will be down upon us, early next month." Escotchaby at times took it upon himself to learn more about Cherokee plans, as in April 1760 when he left Coweta to "make what Discoveries [he] could about the Cherokees." He even protected settlers from Cherokee attacks and had in one case been "the means of preserving the Lives of several people, women, & Children, who had fled & lost 'em selves" until found by Escotchaby, who then escorted them back to Augusta. And he also worked alongside Galphin to turn Silver Bluff into a haven for refugees who were also protected by a group of young men from Coweta.[30]

Escotchaby also dealt with the moments when the war intruded into Muscogee territories or claimed Muscogee lives. In April 1758 he learned that several Cherokee from the town of Settico had slain two Muscogee hunters. In retaliation a small party of men had attacked Cherokee peoples from Little Estatoe, killing two. This violence prompted Escotchaby to communicate with the Cherokee headmen of Estatoe and Little Estatoe, who sent their Mankiller to Coweta to try and defuse the situation. And while it seems that violence did not occur between Muscogee and Cherokee peoples any more in 1759, the years 1760 and 1761 were a different story. In early 1760 a party of Muscogee men, having been "fitted out for war against the Cherokees" by the English traders, arrived in Savannah with three Cherokee trophies.[31] The following year it was the Yuchis who skirmished with the Cherokee "a little above Augusta" and during the battle lost one of their leaders, Istichiago. Thus, despite Escotchaby's efforts, the Cherokee conflict at times involved Muscogee peoples.[32]

Escotchaby's sobering experiences only grew more difficult with a second British invasion of Cherokee territories in 1761. If the Cherokee did not resent the *talwas* for being so unwilling to join the conflict against the colonies, they now "look[ed] with an Eye of Envy on the Prosperity of the Creeks & would gladly see them humbled." This undoubtedly explains why Escotchaby's efforts to reach out to Lower Cherokee headmen in 1761 failed, and why when he invited Cherokee refugees to Coweta and other Lower *talwas* "to be protected," only a few accepted his invitation. This did not stop him, though, from continuing to supply the Cherokee with corn and other foodstuffs while repeating his offer for them "to remove to [his] Towns" for "Provisions and Protection." However, in the wake of several British invasions of Cherokee territories, more of the young men from the *talwas* including Coweta sensed blood in the water and raided Cherokee communities, tempted by "considerable rewards" from the colonial governors. In response to the English bribing the young men of Coweta to attack the Cherokee despite Escotchaby's wishes as *tustenogy,* he escalated his "endeavours" to prevent the young men from leaving Coweta. Together with Sempoyaffee and other Lower *micos,* Escotchaby confronted the governors and warned them not to employ "any of their people against the Cherokees" anymore. When imperial authorities ignored the *micos* and continued to incite the young men to attack the Cherokee, which resulted in a group of Muscogee and Chickasaw men burning Estatoe and Keowee to the ground, Escotchaby and other Lower *micos* cut off communication with the colonies altogether and forbid the young men from any more "hostilities against the Cherokees."[33]

Escotchaby thereby scrambled to keep his *huti* and *talwa* out of the expanding conflict while continually interposing himself among the Cherokee to try and prevent further violence, albeit unsuccessfully so. For instance even though he and another *mico* by the name of Saletchi sent a talk to the Cherokee on behalf of the colonies and received a favorable reply in October 1760, talks quickly broke down when Cherokee headmen refused to comply with the more extreme demands of the colonial governors. The same situation occurred in December 1760 when Escotchaby and Sempoyaffee were set to meet with Cherokee leaders in the hopes of ending hostilities. But that meeting likewise failed to happen. In fact, regardless of Escotchaby's efforts, it was Cherokee headmen led by the Little Carpenter and Old Caesar who instead approached imperial authorities in the Virginia colony in September 1761. Arriving in Charleston a year later, the two Cherokee leaders agreed to sacrifice four of their number as retribution for the violence, to abandon Fort Loudon and return the prisoners of war, to expel any Frenchmen living in the Cherokee territories, and to allow the English traders to return to Cherokee communities. The war was over, no thanks to Coweta's Cherokee King.[34]

Meanwhile the killing of British traders in Okfuskee in May 1760 also threatened to plunge the *talwas* into war with the colonies, and it was even rumored to have been instigated by "Fool Harry" (Sempoyaffee) and the "Young Lieutenant" (Escotchaby). Despite all their proofs to the contrary during the war, Sempoyaffee and Escotchaby were still viewed by British agents with a mixture of anxiety and fear, another sobering reminder for the two brothers. Nonetheless they joined the other Lower *micos* in distancing themselves from Okfuskee and the Upper *talwas*. In particular English officials breathed easier when they learned that Coweta's *micos* were "strongly against" the killings and that Sempoyaffee and Escotchaby agreed that their *talwa* remained at peace with the colonies "notwithstanding the mischiefs done by a few mad people." Eventually the Lower and Upper *micos* met with British authorities and "unanimously agreed" to be at peace, and together the *micos* expressed a "strong disposition" to resume their neutrality in the war between France and England.[35]

Just when Sempoyaffee and Escotchaby might have thought that the dangers to their *huti* and *talwa* were coming to an end, they received the "bad News" that two of their townsmen had killed a resident of Augusta in the summer of 1761. Coweta's *micos* immediately sent word to the Georgia governor that they were "very sorry" for the death and promised—particularly in light of the previous year's killings in Okfuskee—"you need be under no

Concern for the Traders amongst Us for they shall be safe." Naturally Coweta's *micos* had one thing in mind, maintaining the deerskin trade with the colonies that was vital to both their *hutis* and *talwa* as well as Coweta's broader influence among the other *talwas*. This is likely why Sempoyaffee worked with Galphin to mediate for the two sides, traveling back and forth from Coweta to Georgia to try and defuse the situation. As Sempoyaffee and other Lower *micos* reassured British agents, "the Day should never come that the Coweta's would throw away the white People's Talk."[36]

As the Seven Years' War and the Cherokee conflict started to wind down by mid-1762, Sempoyaffee, Escotchaby, and the members of their *huti* and *talwa* started to come to terms with what Britain's victory would mean for the future. It is quite telling that in March 1762, British officials grew overly concerned when they learned that Escotchaby "has been under some uneasiness at a piece of intelligence that he received from two white men." The two traders had told Escotchaby that the colonies "were on the point of sending a large army" into Muscogee territories. Although Escotchaby told English authorities he did not give much "credit to this wicked and infamous story," he could not have ignored the fact that the *talwas* had nearly come to blows with the colonies on several occasions during the war. He also likely had the sobering realization that Britain's victory meant a profound transformation to the Muscogee world as they knew it, with the potential removal of France and Spain from their holdings in North America, thus leaving only the English colonies, whose leaders proved consistently unable to restrain their settlers from threatening Muscogee territories. This was likely the context in which Escotchaby and Sempoyaffee sent a talk with Galphin to the colonial governors in May 1762, in which they exaggerated that "there has been no bad Talks here for a long time" despite evidence to the contrary. But as Escotchaby and Sempoyaffee articulated the sentiments of their *huti* and *talwa,* the brothers were determined not to "throw the white people away," for it "is a thing we cannot do, for we cannot do without them." Even though the Seven Years' War and Cherokee conflict were coming to an end, both those events had changed everything in the South, and it was into this dramatically different world that Sempoyaffee and Escotchaby would try and lead for their *huti* and *talwa.*[37]

The Treaty of Augusta, 1763

One of the first hurdles that Sempoyaffee, Escotchaby, and the other *micos* and *talwas* faced in the immediate aftermath of the war was joining the many other Indigenous groups of the South in confirming a peace with the British Empire. Throughout the summer and fall of 1763, Sempoyaffee and

Escotchaby along with the other Lower and Upper *micos* made plans to meet with British officials at Augusta, where John Stuart, the new superintendent of Indian affairs, invited the most influential groups in the South to a treaty conference.[38] Everyone involved, including Sempoyaffee and Escotchaby, knew this was a pivotal moment, if not a turning point, for their peoples. For decades Muscogee peoples thrived in a "climate of imperial rivalry and not one of British encirclement" that had allowed the *talwas* to carve out their own autonomy among one another as well as throughout the broader South. But that all threatened to unravel at Augusta in November 1763.[39]

At the same time, though, Sempoyaffee and Escotchaby recognized that they—as the representatives of their *huti*, Coweta, and Muscogee peoples more generally—had to strike some kind of balance at Augusta between their many and competing interests and that of the British Empire as well as the other Indigenous groups of the South. This is undoubtedly why Sempoyaffee, Escotchaby, and "a few [*micos*] from the lower towns" were among the first to arrive at Augusta, where they stayed at Silver Bluff and likely strategized with Galphin for what was about to be a game-changing event. Escotchaby also contended with the fact that the Cherokee had spread rumors on the eve of the conference that "the Creeks have bad intentions." Therefore when the Augusta congress convened in November, the stage was set for a volatile confrontation that could potentially reshape the Muscogee world—and the broader South—for the future.[40]

While the Augusta congress involved a plethora of peoples—Muscogee, Cherokee, Catawba, Chickasaw, and Choctaw, among others—and issues such as trade prices, encroachments, the need for new boundary lines, and giving satisfaction for the war's violence, it was the Lower *micos* and Lower Cherokee headmen who "dominated the proceedings" since they had the most to lose, given the proximity of their territories to the colonies. Whereas the Lower Cherokee faced an uphill battle in their negotiations because of their involvement in the conflict against the colonies, the Lower *talwas* had more to work with. This is why some of the choices that the Lower *micos* made during the Augusta conference, particularly their decision to cede some of their most "extensive and valuable land," might seem so puzzling at first glance. In the end Lower *micos* gave up a lot to the British Empire despite remaining neutral for the most part in the war. Naturally this raises the question of why. As John Juricek describes, the decision by Lower *micos* to make a large cession of lands to the colonies was part of a strategic gamble to put distance between their *talwas* and the colonies while at the same time buying some goodwill with the dominant—now only—European power in the South, despite losing a portion of their valuable hunting grounds.[41]

Among the many Lower *micos* who negotiated the Treaty of Augusta, Sempoyaffee and Escotchaby were intimately involved from beginning to end. The primary reason for their participation was the fact they were members of a *huti* that has "more to do in Land Affairs, than any other Indian of the Lower Creeks being a privilege annexed to [their] Family."[42] It is again important to note that Sempoyaffee and Escotchaby had arrived early in Augusta, where they conversed with Galphin for several days before the start of the conference. Scholars have long interpreted Galphin's involvement in the negotiations as being one of the empire's proxies or as having been tasked by the new Georgia governor, James Wright, with putting the Lower *micos* in a more "cheerful frame of mind about the congress." As historians conclude, Galphin's involvement made the *micos* more "willing to make a land cession in return for the forgiveness of past offenses."[43] In this interpretation the cession is understood as Lower *micos* falling upon their sword for the Upper *talwas*, particularly for the Okfuskee killings in 1760 and the Mortar's intrigues with the Cherokee. Historians also situate the cession in the context of trying to "eliminate the recent causes of friction" between them and the colonies by sacrificing some of their hunting territories to buy goodwill again and to put distance between the two sides.[44]

What if, though, Sempoyaffee, Escotchaby, and Galphin had helped orchestrate the cession of lands, motivated somewhat by their concerns to appease the English but more so to protect the future of their *huti*, *talwa*, and Muscogee peoples as best they thought they could? By wielding their *huti*'s influence in matters of land—which accorded them a prominent role in the negotiations—Sempoyaffee and Escotchaby helped dictate where the new boundary line between Muscogee territories and the colonies would be located and in doing so they sought to distill the threat of colonial expansion. This cession of land would also gift the Lower and Upper *talwas* with some time to process and acclimate themselves to the seismic transformations occurring in 1763. Further it is no coincidence that the western part of the new boundary line passed right through Galphin's lands. Therefore what if the Lower *micos*, led in part by Sempoyaffee and Escotchaby, sacrificed some of their hunting grounds in the hopes of corralling the violence for the future and pinned their hopes on their abilities and Galphin's ability to mediate for the two sides moving forward? And while Stuart suspected as much, that "the Indians [were] privately tampered with . . . by the traders" and he specifically named Galphin, again, what if the reverse was true: that Galphin did not so much tamper with the *micos* as collude with Sempoyaffee and Escotchaby to convince both sides where to place the new boundary line? To articulate the need for a strict boundary line where he and Escotchaby intended it to be, and without betraying their intrigues, Sempoyaffee stood up in the middle of the Augusta conference to talk, even though he had not been appointed as one of the two speakers for the Lower and Upper *talwas*. After listing several grievances that were a testament to the need for a new boundary line, Sempoyaffee concluded to the governors that if they did "not forwarn the white people" from settling on Muscogee lands, "he will take all they have from them, and ask them if they are French or Spaniards." It is important to realize that Sempoyaffee interjected himself into the conversation about a need for a new boundary line that would be enforced by both sides to make a point to everyone. As Sempoyaffee later concluded near the end of the congress, the boundary line was intended to "prevent any future disturbances." To top it off, Sempoyaffee and Escotchaby likely counted on the fact that Galphin would continue to provide trade goods for the members of their *huti* and *talwa*, a blessing that was reinforced when the governors determined the official repository for the "distribution of presents to the Indians at the Congress" was Galphin's Silver Bluff plantation. In short Sempoyaffee and Escotchaby were hard at work behind the scenes at Augusta, trying to engineer an outcome somewhat favorable to their *huti* and *talwa* while at the same time placating the British.[45]

In the wake of the Augusta congress, and likely out of recognition for their central roles in the treaty negotiations, Sempoyaffee and Escotchaby were identified by the British on several different occasions as Coweta's two "Principal Head-men" "who govern[ed]" and possessed the "most influence" of any *mico* in Coweta. On the one hand, British observers exaggerated the importance of the two brothers, given that one—or even two—*micos* could not govern any *talwa* in the Muscogee world. With that said, such observations reflect a sense of how influential Sempoyaffee and Escotchaby had become by 1763 on account of their prominence during the war and now at Augusta. It was also at this time that Escotchaby, like his brother before him, relinquished the role of the *tustenogy* to become another one of Coweta's *micos*. Together the two brothers continued to represent the interests of their *huti* in Coweta's town councils and for the perceived good of their *talwa* for the future.[46]

Sempoyaffee and Escotchaby—like every other *mico*—recognized how the Muscogee world had changed considerably during and after the Seven Years' War, but they reacted proactively rather than reactively. The absence of France and Spain was the obvious and most dramatic transformation to the South, which threatened to destabilize the political integrity of the *talwas* and undermine Muscogee autonomy moving forward. Yet this is why Sempoyaffee and Escotchaby maneuvered their *huti* and *talwa* in the ways that they did in 1763. For instance, even before the Augusta conference convened in November, Escotchaby had visited the Spanish governor of Havana in the company of several other members from his *huti*. There he talked of rekindling a relationship between Coweta and the Lower *talwas* with the Spanish in Cuba, hoping to restore a semblance of the political system that Muscogee peoples had enjoyed in previous decades. As Spanish officials remarked after Escotchaby departed, "there are many more examples that could be used to justify the natural inclination and affection" of the Lower *talwas* to Spain, and Spanish agents debated ways to cultivate a future relationship with Coweta. Meanwhile Sempoyaffee made a point during the Augusta congress that trade, and the reduction of prices, was vital to the Muscogee-British alliance moving forward, especially if the Lower *talwas* were to cede land to the colonies. Naturally Sempoyaffee and Escotchaby envisioned Galphin playing a vital role in that respect.[47]

Despite such efforts, though, Muscogee *micos* such as Sempoyaffee and Escotchaby could not ignore the fact that their townspeople from the Lower and Upper *talwas* feared the treaty and land cession was the first step by which the English colonies would "divest them of territory they had claimed since the beginning" of time. In other words not all Muscogee peoples placed the same faith in appeasement as their *micos* did. The young men within the *talwas* believed that giving away territory represented the "greatest threat" to Muscogee independence. As Superintendent Stuart himself observed at the Augusta conference, it seemed "the Bulk of the lower Creek were displeased with their Chiefs for having ceded so much Land in the Provinces of Georgia and East Florida" and found many of those individuals to be "so tenacious of their Lands and so Jealous of Encroachments upon them" that Stuart cautioned his superiors not to demand any more land for "years to come." After 1763, then, Sempoyaffee and Escotchaby contended with not just the threat of British encroachments upon Muscogee territories, but also with the simmering resentments of Coweta's townspeople and namely the frustrations of the younger generations.[48]

Five

The Muscogee World
and Colonial Crisis, 1763–1775

In December 1765 Superintendent John Stuart addressed Muscogee *micos* with a heavy heart. A few months previous, "three white men named William Payne, George Payne, and James Hogg were hunting" when a "Party of Creek Indians met with them in the Woods and murdered them, and carried off their Horses, Guns, and other things." This was the second such violent incident in the last year, taking place in the wake of the Long Cane crisis when Muscogee hunters had killed fourteen people in South Carolina. When Stuart tried to demand satisfaction for the deaths, pleading with *micos* that the young men "do this without consulting you in the Contempt of your authority," talks quickly broke down. While Stuart had stated in 1764 that the "Seven Young Men [were] of no account" and should be punished, he either disregarded or did not know that one of the young men was Sempoyaffee's own son Limpike. This time, though, Stuart identified Limpike as the one who led those that killed the Paynes and Hogg.[1]

Despite Stuart's best efforts to seize Limpike in 1765, Sempoyaffee's son eluded the British for years. Following the violence, he and the young men sought refuge with the Cherokee, where "they were protected," undoubtedly assisted by Escotchaby. And for the next several years, British authorities continually renewed their demands for satisfaction, but in each case it always "threw the Indians into a ferment," which Stuart attributed to Limpike's being "Sempoyaffee's Son." When Stuart pressed several *micos* with trying to secure Limpike's capture in 1767, Sempoyaffee stopped meeting with British agents altogether. Meanwhile when Stuart sent talks to Sempoyaffee and Escotchaby to come to Augusta, they refused to comply. When Stuart eventually convinced Lower *micos,* including Sempoyaffee, to meet him a year later and again raised the issue of Limpike, Sempoyaffee stormed off and "declared he would die in place of his Son."[2]

Stuart had to wait almost another year before he saw Sempoyaffee again, only this time Sempoyaffee seemed resolved to settle the matter. He confessed, "I am now an old Man and give Publick Testimony that the English have always been our best Friends." After a brief pause, he addressed the matter of Limpike, saying that "since that Time my Son's Behaviour has covered me with Shame, and I never have appeared at any Publick Meeting, 'till now." Speaking plainly, he revealed that "I am grieving that my Blood should be capable of Hurting our Friends the English, and my grief is dearly Augmented by the reproaches of my own people." Sempoyaffee then pleaded with Stuart: Limpike "is my Son and I feel for him like a Father. You are advanced in Years and have Children; judge them of my feeling by your own." If Limpike could be forgiven, he vowed, "I will answer for his behavior in the future"; if Stuart could "intercede with the Great King for my Son's pardon . . . it will remove the Cloud which hangs over my Aged Head." Sempoyaffee concluded by placing the medal and commission that Stuart had given him years earlier, the symbols of Sempoyaffee's friendship to the colonies, on the table in front of them. Sempoyaffee concluded that "My Son's Behaviour has rendered me unworthy of them, take them back and bestow them on one more worthy."[3]

An astonished Stuart responded, "Friend Sempoyaffe, You have always been considered by me as a Good man . . . I am Sorry for the distress into which your Son's behavior has plunged you." While Stuart remained adamant that satisfaction was required, he did promise to ask King George III to consider pardoning Limpike and will "acquaint you with whatever I may receive relative to your Son." Stuart then picked up Sempoyaffee's effects from the table and returned them, stating, "I am Convinced that none of your Country men deserves it better." Following this exchange, Stuart reached out to the governors James Grant and James Wright about Sempoyaffee's request. Both Grant and Wright similarly thought it proper to contact "His Majesty" about a potential pardon. As Stuart confided, he thought the pardon was a good idea, since he believed that Sempoyaffee might prove "easier to Prevail on to become an Instrument in obtaining an Additional Cession of Land" from the Lower *talwas*. While we do not know if Limpike ever received the pardon, we do know his father signed the Treaty of Augusta (1773), one of the largest land cessions in the South in the eighteenth century, which may suggest that Limpike received amnesty.[4]

This is a remarkable event that underscores how little we still know about family and kinship among eighteenth-century Muscogee peoples and in matrilineal societies more generally. True, Limpike was Sempoyaffee's son, but being born in a matrilineal world, he became part of his mother's clan and lived among her people—in her *huti*—and no longer beloged to Sempoyaffee's clan and *huti*. Despite being Limpike's father by blood, Sempoyaffee would have played only a minimal role in Limpike's life, whereas Limpike's mother, maternal uncles, and other female-related kin were responsible for his care, education, and experiences as a young boy and man. And this is what makes Sempoyaffee's actions between 1765 and 1769 so incredible yet perplexing. To nearly derail his own *huti*'s ambitions and put his life on the line for Limpike, even when that son no longer shared any attachment to Sempoyaffee's *huti*, indicates how little we actually understand about family and kinship in the eighteenth-century Muscogee world. Further, another member of Sempoyaffee's *huti*, Escotchaby—who had no connections to Limpike according to matrilineal rules—similarly stuck his neck out when he undoubtedly intervened on Limpike's behalf with Cherokee peoples, who provided him with refuge after the attacks in 1765. One of the biggest takeaways from this affair, then, is that the family and kinship dynamics of the Muscogee world are far more malleable and uneven than scholars have yet to articulate and may even demonstrate that a Muscogee person's membership in a clan or *huti* extended to other people in ways that we do not yet fully understand or—because of the limitations of the colonial archives—may never understand. That is profoundly troubling.

With that said, this conflict between father and son is illustrative of the unprecedented challenges that Muscogee peoples faced in the aftermath of the Seven Years' War, with the continuing encroachments upon their lands, which in turn fueled violence between Muscogee peoples and the colonies. It is just as important, though, to recognize that Limpike's violent outbursts represented a profound disconnect between an older generation that tried to negotiate the colonial forces arrayed against them and the younger generations who believed negotiation was becoming less of a viable strategy for their people. This is not to suggest the tensions between *micos* and young men did not always exist within the Muscogee world; of course it did. But an unsettling pattern of British encroachments followed by violent conflict and then cessions of land emerged during the 1760s and 1770s and incensed the younger generations. As Lower and Upper *micos* repeatedly told British officials in this decade, their encroachments "will shortly bring on a war" and undermine their previous agreements, which also weakened the respect that younger generations had toward the authority of their *micos*, who in turn believed that it was no longer in their "power to stop the young people."[5]

Limpike's case also demonstrates that Sempoyaffee and Escotchaby's best-laid plans, which had effectively cemented their influence in Coweta by 1763 and by which they hoped to do even more to lead their *huti* and *talwa*, could all be undone by one's own family. Sempoyaffee had nearly stepped away from his role as *mico* because he did not want to sacrifice his son. Meanwhile Escotchaby had tempted fate by asking the Cherokee to intervene on Limpike's behalf. As Cherokee headmen such as Tiftoy afterward complained of Limpike and the other young men, they "are constantly in our Towns . . . bringing in Lying Talks which disturb and confuse our young men." Tiftoy also told Escotchaby specifically that if he did not recall those individuals to their *talwas*, Tiftoy would be forced to take action. A crisis was thus brewing in the South, as an increasingly aggressive empire—no longer held in check by other imperial powers—threatened Muscogee territories at the same time the generational tensions within the *talwas* escalated in unprecedented ways, all of which created a sense of disorder within the Muscogee world such that no amount of action seemed to restore balance. For Sempoyaffee and Escotchaby, their ability to lead their *huti* and *talwa* in a time of such crisis and imbalance was an unfathomable burden.[6]

1763–1773: A Decade of Crisis

The Seven Years' War and Treaty of Augusta ushered in unprecedented transformations to the Muscogee world that forced individuals such as Sempoyaffee and Escotchaby to make extraordinary decisions for the future of their *huti* and *talwa*. One of the ways in which they sought to navigate such change, and in hopes of restoring some semblance of the political system that had served the *talwas* so well in the past, was to rekindle a relationship with Spain. As early as 1763, even before the November congress, Escotchaby traveled to Havana with "his Youth, his Mother and other Caciques," where they met with Spanish agents in hopes of setting up some sort of relationship for the future. As British authorities feared, a renewed connection between Spain and the *talwas* might "furnish the Spaniards with an opportunity" to get back at Britain after their defeat in the Seven Years' War; at the same time, it would "render the management of the Creek nation (one of the most turbulent upon the continent) more difficult." Of all the individuals the English did not want to see conspiring with the Spanish, it was Escotchaby who was considered the "Best Affected to the Spaniards of any in the Nation" with whom he who carries on a "Clandestine correspondence."[7]

Whereas scholars have argued that Coweta's *micos* experienced a political decline among the Lower *talwas* during the 1760s and 1770s, eclipsed in particular by the *micos* of Chehaw,[8] Sempoyaffee and Escotchaby sought innovative strategies to bolster their authority within Coweta while at the same time projecting Coweta's continued importance among the other *talwas*, one of which was their negotiations with Spanish Havana. Whenever they ventured to Havana in person or sent a proxy such as Thlawhulgu or one of Escotchaby's "sons," everyone always returned "richly dressed" with goods and presents.[9] At other times they or their representatives met with the Spanish on the "Point of Florida" rather than in Cuba, where again Sempoyaffee, Escotchaby, or their proxies received a wealth of presents that ranged from gunpowder and "ammunition [to] laced Cloaths from the Spanish Governor." Naturally Sempoyaffee and Escotchaby redistributed such gifts to the members of their *huti* and *talwa,* which again accentuated their influence within Coweta. Escotchaby and the Spanish governors even talked about establishing a permanent trade in "horses, Deer Pelts, and other Goods" between Coweta and Havana. The potential for such a relationship clearly outweighed British threats to stop such activities, and all the Spanish asked in return was for Sempoyaffee and Escotchaby to convene a "Congress with the Chiefs of the Upper and Lower Nations, at the Mouth of Appalachicola River" whenever was convenient.[10]

To take further advantage of the situation, Escotchaby spread rumors that the Spanish intended to return to the mainland, news that not only put British authorities on edge but also made them easier to manipulate when it came to demanding presents and goods in exchange for the promises to stop visiting the Bay of Tampa or Havana. As Escotchaby coyly let it slip in one of the larger conferences between Superintendent Stuart and the Lower and Upper *micos,* he had granted the Spanish "Liberty in four or Five Moons" to meet them at the nearby Apalachicola River to decide where the Spanish could plant a new settlement "somewhere on the Sea Coast in the Bay of Appalache." From other *micos,* British agents learned that the Spanish governor wanted Escotchaby to "go to Havannah as he wanted much to see him there."[11] Imperial officials repeatedly tried to confront Escotchaby about his proceedings with the Spanish, when Stuart reminded him that "I need not tell you that the Spaniards are incapable of being such Friends to you as we are." In other cases British agents employed *micos* such as the Pumpkin King to keep an eye on Escotchaby, who went so far as to threaten Escotchaby that "I want some Scalps I shall be glad to hear that Spaniards are near my Towns. . . . I will go on a look for them." But none of these threats phased Escotchaby, who casually replied to Stuart and other imperial officials that "I Know nothing certain concerning the Spaniards otherwise I should not keep it a Secret from my Father." And in the end, fearing the return of a Spanish presence to the mainland, imperial administrators sent goods and presents to Coweta to try and prevent future meetings. Escotchaby, then, continued to play the English and Spanish off against one another during the 1760s and 1770s, and his *huti* and *talwa* reaped the material benefits of such efforts.[12]

One of Sempoyaffee and Escotchaby's other strategies was using their relationship with George Galphin to increase profits in the deerskin trade. For instance the trio perfected a scheme of establishing illegal out-stores (also called out-settlements) nearby Coweta, where Galphin's factors—half-Creek, half-European traders and storekeepers—intercepted Muscogee hunters and exchanged cheaper-priced goods for their deerskins. Galphin operated several of these out-stores with the consent and protection of Sempoyaffee and Escotchaby, including Pucknawhitla (also known as the Standing Peach Tree and the Coweta Lieutenant's Settlement), Chouaglas, Bigskin Creek, Clay-Catskee, and Buzzard's Roost. This is one of the many reasons that Galphin's factors, such as the White Boy, maintained the largest accounts at his Silver Bluff store, trafficking in thousands of pounds of deerskins week after week. Reciprocally Galphin imported an influx of goods totaling thousands of pounds sterling back into Coweta, much of which ended up in the hands of Sempoyaffee and Escotchaby. And when other *micos* threatened to shut down the illegal out-settlements, Sempoyaffee and Escotchaby mobilized to protect Galphin's stores. In one case Emistisiguo of Little Tallassee led a party of young men from the Upper *talwas* to "seize the Goods of all such persons" at Buzzard's Roost. When Emistisiguo arrived there, he and the young men seized much of the store's goods but left Galphin's trader—a nephew by the name of Edmund Barnard—alone. This suggests that Sempoyaffee and Escotchaby may have intervened or sent word to Emistisiguo not to molest Galphin's trader. Together Sempoyaffee, Escotchaby, and Galphin operated an "advantageous Trade" that benefitted their *huti* and *talwa* but angered British authorities and the other *micos,* who started to resent Coweta's fortunes.[13]

Whenever a rival out-store popped up in and around Coweta, Sempoyaffee and Escotchaby shrewdly put an immediate stop to such proceedings. For instance, British agents noted that despite permitting the illegal out-stores, Sempoyaffee and Escotchaby threatened to take away the goods of several traders who had erected rival out-settlements nearby and, if those traders failed to heed their words, would come and "pull the houses down" themselves. When a trader by the name of Carter continued to run his own out-store despite such warnings, Escotchaby made good on his threat. As Galphin later informed Superintendent Stuart, Escotchaby "took a good many Things" from Carter's store and sent them down to Galphin's Silver Bluff, although the "Powder Bullets and Paint were made away with," presumably by Escotchaby. As Escotchaby later told Galphin, he had raided Carter's out-settlement because "the fellow [was] making use of [Galphin's] Name" and, according to the "Governor and Beloved Man's Talk," he was within his rights to take "all the Goods they found people a Trading with in the Woods between Augusta

and the Nation." How convenient for Sempoyaffee, Escotchaby, and Galphin.[14]

Sempoyaffee, Escotchaby, and Galphin even entertained ideas of capital-
izing on the expansion of the deerskin trade to East Florida after 1763. In
summer 1768, Galphin and one of his merchant contacts, John Gordon, cor-
responded with the governor of East Florida, James Grant, about building a
store at St. Marks, a former Spanish garrison. As Gordon pitched the idea to
Grant, the store "would be of great utility if we should ever have any Dispute
with our numerous Creek neighbours" and would provide "protection to settlers against privateers and the Spanish banditti from Cuba." Grant reached
out to his superior, Frederick Haldimand, and advised Haldimand that instead of dismantling the St. Marks fort, Gordon would "establish a credible
Indian Store house there without loss of time." Grant and Gordon settled on
none other than Galphin to operate that store, who sent one of his trusted
confidants, Daniel McMurphy, to take charge. Grant proved so effusive about
the trade prospects in East Florida and working with Galphin that he also
granted Galphin the rights to build stores at the forts of Picolata and St.
John's, in effect gifting him with a majority share of the deerskin trade in East
Florida.[15]

The East Florida trade proved important to Sempoyaffee and Escotchaby
for several reasons. By adding to the veritable wealth of goods that poured
into Coweta during the 1760s and 1770s, the Florida deerskin trade accentuated Sempoyaffee and Escotchaby's influence in Coweta, as the members of
their *huti* and *talwa* continued to reap the benefits of their efforts. In addition having a presence in East Florida, where Coweta's hunters could trade,
allowed Sempoyaffee and Escotchaby to strengthen their connections to Havana covertly. As British authorities observed about the area surrounding the
St. Marks fort, there soon existed a "considerable settlement" of Muscogee
peoples who frequently "meet the Spaniards" around St. Marks.[16] This settlement, maybe even a *talofa* (satellite town) of Coweta, was led by Tunape,
who shared a peculiar and at times troubled relationship with Escotchaby
and Coweta's *micos*.[17] Nonetheless Sempoyaffee and Escotchaby invested a
lot into this Florida initiative, and it seemed to pay off in dividends for both
them and Galphin.[18]

Sempoyaffee, Escotchaby, and Galphin also collaborated when it came to
the new boundary lines that were negotiated between Muscogee and British
leaders during the 1760s and 1770s, which stemmed from misunderstandings
over where the 1763 line started and ended. Based upon his *huti*'s landed
responsibilities as well as in his capacity as the Cherokee king, Escotchaby
joined the English surveying parties in 1765 and 1768, which just so happened
to include Galphin. While colonial officials such as James Wright duplici-

tously wanted Galphin to "convince the Indians that the upper fork was understood at the Treaty to be the place from whence the said Line should begin"—contrary to what was agreed at Augusta—Galphin either refused to do so or Escotchaby immediately shut down such ideas. In 1768 Escotchaby and Galphin joined the surveying party led by Roderick McIntosh and Samuel Savery. Once again dishonesty was involved when the party's surveyors misidentified where the new boundary line was to be located. Whether intentional or not, the error threatened to create a violent dispute between the two sides and was only resolved when Galphin and Escotchaby stepped in to defuse tensions and renegotiate the terms of the line. It was later reported that one of the attending Muscogee men had gone so far as to point his gun at McIntosh and "pulled the trigger," but the gun misfired, and Escotchaby and Galphin quickly "calmed the hot heads."[19]

Despite the innovative strategies that Sempoyaffee and Escotchaby pursued on behalf of their *huti* and *talwa,* the commercial deerskin trade underwent paradigmatic shifts in the 1760s and 1770s that had profound repercussions for Muscogee peoples. In the aftermath of the Seven Years' War, imperial authorities led by Superintendent Stuart embarked on a series of reforms intended to curb the frequent abuses and exploitation of Muscogee hunters. However, Stuart's proposed Plan of 1764 failed, and what the empire instead created was a chaotic and unregulated mess as an influx of unlicensed traders flooded the markets with raw deerskins, peddled in illegal goods like rum, and defrauded Muscogee hunters out of their deerskins.[20] As Stuart had pleaded with his superiors in 1764, "I begg your Lordships leave to observe that some uniform Rates of decision between us & the Indians seem to be wanting," for when "an Indian is cheated or robbed by a Trader, the Latter seldom pays any regard to the decision . . . and the Indian remains without Redress."[21] Individual colonies also competed for the greater share of the deerskin trade, which only contributed to the flood of new, unlicensed traders who attempted to make a new living. As Emistisiguo of Little Tallassee aptly described the situation, "formerly the Trade was Carried on by a few People in their Principal Towns, but now great Numbers of Traders Come Amongst Them from All Parts and Trade about in the Woods and Hunting Grounds." As Emistisiguo gloomily concluded, "when there was but One Path it was Peaceable but not so Now, for there is Too Many Paths, and That these things and Confusion in the Trade have been the Cause and Foundation of all the Evils."[22]

The glut of unlicensed traders only grew worse throughout the decade and led to other debilitating problems in the deerskin trade. While the many traders offered greater quantities of goods at cheaper prices than licensed traders such as Galphin, their goods were of inferior quality, and their acquisition of deerskins was often duplicitous in nature. For example, many of these traders preferred raw deerskins instead of processed skins, which opened the door to "great Frauds" and the "Value of Skins greatly diminished." The unlicensed traders also operated the illegal out-stores that started to populate throughout Muscogee territories, where they intercepted Muscogee men returning from the hunt, plied the hunters with rum and other liquors, and exchanged "trifling goods" for deerskins or convinced the hunters that their skins were not as valuable as they believed. As Stuart described the situation, Muscogee peoples were deprived of the "means of cloathing themselves and Families, and of paying their just debts to the established Traders in the Towns to the great Detriment." Such rampant fraud and abuse cut into the profits of licensed traders such as Galphin, who in turn resorted to the same practices by "fitting out Traders in the Woods." Further, white hunters competed with Muscogee peoples for the *itchu,* encroached on Muscogee territories, and contributed to the "deer growing scarcer every year." Once again it was Stuart who reported to his superiors that the white hunters "do not confine themselves to our grounds at which the [Muscogee] are highly displeased." The state of the deerskin trade grew so perilous that Sempoyaffee and Escotchaby changed their tune when it came to their own out-settlements. As Sempoyaffee stated to British authorities at one particular congress, there existed too many "traders going about in the Woods and clandestinely trading with the Indians, and trafficking the Raw Skins to the Injury of the fair Trader," and if he met with any of them in the future, he would "look upon them as French or Spaniards, and not white Men, and treat them accordingly."[23]

The precarious and increasingly fraudulent nature of the deerskin trade translated into unfathomable levels of debt for Muscogee peoples. As the number of unlicensed traders spiraled out of control in this decade,[24] the more established traders such as Galphin started to accumulate their own debts and soon fell behind in paying their suppliers and merchants in the colonies and in London. Similarly the unlicensed traders were quite liberal with the amount of goods that they distributed to Muscogee hunters, goods that were to be paid back later when the hunters returned with their deerskins. More often than not, though, the amount and the prices of goods outstripped the value of the skins that Muscogee hunters brought to the traders, which gradually added up over the years. Often when the traders tried to collect the money that they believed was owed to them—notwithstanding the exploitive means at the heart of such transactions—the hunters responded with disbelief and in some cases disputed the matter violently. For instance, in March 1772 in the *talwa* of Tallassiehatchie, Muscogee townsmen attacked one of the traders by breaking open his door, taking his goods, and making him flee their community. As everyone's debts continued to grow, the traders sent petition after petition to imperial administrators in London demanding relief and warning that unless the empire took drastic measures, the traders faced "impending ruin" and a "burthen too intolerable."[25]

In addition to the deteriorating deerskin trade, the encroachments on Muscogee territories increased exponentially, despite the many promises at Augusta. As Lower and Upper *micos* reminded Superintendent Stuart and the colonial governors about their agreements in 1763, "it was the last land ever you would ask of us and if any red men should offer to give up any of our lands you would not harken to it." Thus the boundary line was "like a mountain, not to be passed," and furthermore, it was to be enforced by both sides, so that any encroaching settlers "should be sent off." While people on both sides did not expect the treaty would stop all the encroachments, most everyone believed that they had bought themselves some time before having to return to the issue. They were wrong. As Sempoyaffee put it best, the white people "settle[d] more numerous than before" and brought along the thousands of cattle and horses that infested their territories, which precipitated the "Buffalo, Deer, and Bear being drove off the Land and killed." As Sempoyaffee warned, the failure by imperial officials to abide by the agreements made at Augusta risked "a Disturbance betwixt Us which [you] do not want."[26]

It took less than two months after the Augusta treaty for encroachments on Muscogee territories to produce violence. In January 1764 seven young men—one of whom was Limpike—killed fourteen settlers at the Long Cane settlement in South Carolina. The resulting Long Cane crisis and Superintendent Stuart's efforts to get satisfaction dragged on for years. Meanwhile the violence continued to escalate, next with the killing of the Paynes and Hogg also at the hands of Limpike and other young men of Coweta, followed by several confrontations along the boundary line that was supposed to prevent such violence. In summer 1767 inhabitants from Augusta ventured into Muscogee territories, where they "burnt and plundered a small Indian Village consisting of about fifteen Families because they suspected that the Indians had stole some of their horses." The small settlement happened to be one of Coweta's *talofas* whose townspeople had no hand in taking the horses. Luckily for the Augustans, one of the townsmen—Howmatcha—did not retaliate but instead went to Galphin's Silver Bluff, where he sent a talk to Stuart and Escotchaby. As Howmatcha stated, even though his community's "houses are burnt & goods carried away," they did not want "any Disturbances" and hoped "the Governor will make [them] satisfied" for what was lost. Although Stuart reimbursed the Cowetas for the damages, he also took the opportunity to remind Escotchaby and the other *micos* to restrain the "the Young fellows to Leave off Stealing & Robbing the White People," for if any of them were killed, there would "be no Satisfaction required of the White People as what damage you do them [and] give them no Satisfaction for."[27]

But for every violent encounter that did not end in death, such as the one in summer 1767, there were several more such incidents where people on both sides lost their lives. Augusta's inhabitants razed Howmatcha's town in retaliation for an attack by several young men from the Lower *talwas* days earlier, who had killed two settlers on the Oconee River and then escaped into Cherokee territories. As Governor Wright remarked to his superiors in 1767, Muscogee peoples and the settlers seemed on the verge of war, and he believed it was "high time my Lord that this Matter was brought to a point, and those wretches should know that they shall not be suffered to murder His Majesty's Subjects when and where they please." The Oconee River proved to be the main source of contention between the two sides, given that it was supposed to represent the new boundary line between Muscogee territories and the colonies. But constant encroachments by the settlers, in close proximity to several Muscogee communities on the river, all but made violence inevitable. In 1770 eleven white men stumbled on a hunting camp along the Oconee after several horses were stolen from their homesteads. There they found two Muscogee men and proceeded to kill one of them and "whipped the other very Severely and left him tyed to a Tree and took away their Skins and every other Article they found there." Although imperial authorities attempted to prosecute the offenders, they did not lift a finger when it came to removing the settlers from the Oconee, despite the promises at Augusta in 1763. It should have come as no surprise, then, that several Muscogee men retaliated, this time claiming the life of John Carey, and more would have been killed if not for Galphin, who happened to be nearby at one of his cow pens and chased after the culprits. As Stuart described the growing encroachments on Muscogee lands, "it is a very general and interesting concern to all Indians, and however they may quarrel about other matters they will unite and make this a common cause."[28]

The violence hit particularly close to home for Escotchaby when it almost claimed the life of one of his sons in early 1770. As he described to Stuart, after "my young people made great complaints to me about the white people settling on the line and over it," he set out on horseback with his son to see "whether it was so or not, that there might be a stop put to it before any mischief happened." When Escotchaby and his son reached the Little River, they heard gunfire off in the woods and went to investigate. There they found a camp of white hunters who "killed a good many deer" and had large stocks of cattle with them, which was prohibited by the 1763 treaty. Escotchaby told the camp to "gather their cattle near the settlement for fear of my young people who were hunting and might kill some of them which would breed

mischief." But as Escotchaby and his son tried to leave, several of the hunters forcefully attempted to stop and restrain them. Although they ultimately
escaped, they lost two horses in the process. And when Escotchaby and his
son tried to locate those horses, they came upon yet another settlement where
the "white people kept store . . . and sold goods very cheap." Escotchaby sent
in his son to inquire about their missing horses and to purchase some gunpowder. But when his son approached the settlement, the residents disarmed
him and "tried to throw him down." When Escotchaby's son ran, the settlers
pursued him for two miles, all the while chucking wood and taking potshots
at him with their rifles, which "frightened him so much that he dropped his
bundle of skins." One of the gunshots nearly killed Escotchaby's son, as the
ball "went tho' his Blanket & shot pouch." As Escotchaby angrily concluded
his son's harrowing experience to Stuart, "It is very lucky my son is not killed."
What he did not have to say to Stuart is that if his son had been murdered,
there would have been hell to pay.[29]

This decade of trade abuse, encroachments, and violence also exacerbated
the tensions between the *micos* and the young men of each *talwa,* including
Coweta. According to eighteenth-century Muscogee worldviews, there existed a customary balance between a *talwa*'s civil leaders and the young men.
But the frequency and intensity of the violence that erupted in the 1760s
and 1770s started to produce a more "volatile and headstrong force in Creek
political life," led by the young men who increasingly resented their *micos,*
who seemed all too willing to appease British authorities, particularly when
it came to the demands for satisfaction and eventually land. As Escotchaby
described to Galphin in 1770, "the younge people is mad," and even though
"I talk to my People & does what lies in my power to keep them Quiet,"
there were still occasions when "they do mischief out of my sight." Many of
the young men not only stopped listening to their *micos* but also moved out
of the *talwas* to "form settlements near the Frontiers, where they withdraw
from Government of their ruling Chiefs and renders it impossible to keep
them in order or to prevent the thefts and violence so loudly complained of
by the white people." Even when Sempoyaffee, Escotchaby, and other *micos*
offered incentives to the young men to remain in the *talwa,* such as presents, increased trade prospects, or even the chance of earning war names by
attacking their rivals the Choctaw,[30] the younger generations focused their
attentions on the encroaching settlers, from whom "they Could get Every
thing they want."[31]

One of the primary motivations for the young men removing themselves
from the *talwa,* and from the oversight of their *micos,* was the desire to assert
their masculinity—and thereby attain rank within the *talwa*—at the same
time punishing the white settlers for their encroachments upon Muscogee

territories. As British agents aptly observed after the Seven Years' War, "many young men have arrived at the State of manhood Since they had war with any of their Neighbours, and have never had any opportunity of signalizing themselves by Warlike Exploits, by which they can only obtain War Names, and bear any rank in the Community." With limited opportunities to wage war after 1763, young men sought alternatives for doing so, and one strategy involved raiding the white settlements for horses, cattle, and other goods. At the same time, raiding doubled as a way for young men to strip themselves of their dependencies upon *micos,* who customarily distributed presents and goods to the *talwa* as a hallmark of their authority and influence. The young men could now do it all by themselves, which is why the *micos* and imperial authorities lamented the fact that they now "made it a practice to rob and plunder the Plantations."[32]

The young men who increasingly ignored the words of their *micos* or departed the *talwas* also used violence to send an explicit message to the settlements that bordered or crossed over the boundary line. The anger and frustrations that the young men felt were quite palpable, being on all sides "surrounded with English" who had "almost the whole possession" of the South. The recourse to violence, then, was "not done with a view to rob but only to assert our native rights" to the lands that increasingly changed hands to the settlers. As one *mico* summed up the mood of the young men, "If the governour cannot prevent the Virginia people from taking our lands, how does he think we can restrain our mad young men?" Group after group of these young men vented their frustrations upon the colonies. In May 1770 a party of young men from Coweta attacked Wrightsborough and stole several horses. Throughout the incident the two sides exchanged gunfire, and miraculously nobody died. Meanwhile young men from Okfuskee also traveled to the boundary line, where they attacked a second settlement and stole more horses, under the guise of hunting along the Oconee River. The town's residents chased after the Okfuskees and came upon a hunting camp where two men, who were unaffiliated with the theft, were staying. Thinking they had located the thieves, the settlers seized one of the men and "tyed and Whipped him" and then shot him at point-blank range. The victim proved to be a "beloved Man" who had "never done any harm to the white people." His death precipitated further retaliation from Muscogee peoples. As Galphin described the rapidly deteriorating situation along the boundary line, "If anything brings on a War," it would be the settlers, for "they and the Indians keep Robbing one another."[33]

Sempoyaffee, Escotchaby, and many other *micos* were astounded by how fast everything started to fall apart, despite the fact that—in Escotchaby's words—"he and the rest of the headmen Does Every thinge that lyes in their power to keep pease." While the *micos* continued to present the grievances of their young men to imperial authorities, they also articulated how they were increasingly unable to make the young men listen to them. Thus when Sempoyaffee promised to do "all in my power" to keep the path "straight and wash it Clean," he had little power to do so. And if the *micos* ever sought to exert their authority back over the young people, often at the behest of British authorities, it merely had the effect of inciting anger and resentment. In spring 1768, for instance, Escotchaby had to answer for the violence of his townsmen when he met with Governor James Grant. To secure satisfaction, Escotchaby somehow convinced the members of the killer's *huti* to take the killer's life, after which Escotchaby informed Grant that satisfaction was "taken." But Escotchaby cautioned Grant not to ask for anything more from him or his townspeople, "otherwise it will Breed a Civil Warr amongst themselves." What Escotchaby left unsaid was the fact that his efforts to secure satisfaction had likely cost him a lot personally in the eyes of his townspeople. He also did not revel in the efforts to police or punish his people, and he likely even agreed with them. But as a *mico,* it was his responsibility to both his *huti* and his *talwa* to try and ensure the balance between peace and conflict that was central to the Muscogee world. This did not mean, though, that Sempoyaffee and Escotchaby—or any *mico* for that matter—were happy about their roles, for Escotchaby himself remarked how he acted "more in behalf of the white people than of my own colour."[34]

As the patterns of encroachment and violence gripped the South, and Muscogee *micos* urgently sought to cultivate peace in a world increasingly beset by conflict, imperial agents tried to offer their own solutions. Because events had reached a tipping point by the early 1770s, even the commander in chief of British forces in North America, Thomas Gage, could not ignore that "the Indians in general grow daily more Jealous as the Settlers extend themselves more into their Country." One of the potential solutions proposed by British officials was to further adjust the boundary lines separating their two peoples, since "a great many Red & White people's not knowing the Line causes disturbance." The only problem with this idea was that British agents and Muscogee *micos* had already done that exact thing in 1765 and again in 1768. In 1765, at the Picolata congress that tweaked the boundary line, it had been Sempoyaffee and Escotchaby who had insisted to Stuart that they could "not give away any Land [to] the White People." When Stuart pressed the issue, both men "started at every Hint of Land that was thrown out." Yet the incessant requisitions for a new boundary line ultimately led to a cession of land near the St. Mary's River in East Florida. One might assume that Sempoyaffee and Escotchaby could not help but sympathize with the younger generations who increasingly resorted to violence to try and combat the loss of land. Escotchaby himself grew so disillusioned that he held a "private Conversation" with imperial authorities in December 1767, where he exasperatingly pleaded with Stuart "to have the Line settled" and to stop their demands for any more land.[35]

But the drama of the boundary line did not end there. Based upon conflicting reports of where the 1765 line started and ended, both sides were forced to convene again in 1768, led by an adamant Sempoyaffee and Escotchaby, who refused to part with more land. As Sempoyaffee and Escotchaby articulated to imperial agents, "the white People have gone & settled" over the line, and "if they catch one of them settling over the Bounds that they will kill all their Cattle, & if that will not do, they must take other means to prevent their settling over the Bounds." As the two sides tried to negotiate, Escotchaby proposed his own solution to the problem. He mentioned that when he had surveyed the previous line, he met with a small group of Quakers "who I like much they are good and peaceable." Therefore he desired that a "great Number of them may be encouraged to come and settle near the Line by which means the Virginians may be kept back from settling near us." To Escotchaby it seemed a reasonable request. However, Stuart immediately dismissed the idea. Escotchaby was so visibly frustrated afterward that when British agents invited him to join the *micos* going to Georgia months later, he refused. As one observer noted, "The [Young] Lieutenant does not Seem disposed to go to Augusta to Meet the Superintendent." Before parting company in 1768, Escotchaby also dropped a bombshell of a threat: "he Cannot Split his Body in two, for he Wanted to go to See the Spaniards & to Settle them on the Florida Point Where they are now a Visiting & that he would go & See them first." This threat scared imperial officials so much that they scrambled to try and "prevail on him to go to Mr. Galphin's to Meet Mr. Stuart." Once again, Escotchaby refused to do so.[36]

One of the underlying reasons that Escotchaby did not go to see Stuart at Galphin's was because his family's relationship with Galphin had recently taken a turn for the worse. What started as Galphin's dabbling in the same duplicitous practices as the other traders he competed with in the deerskin trade turned into what amounted to a betrayal of kinship by the early 1770s. For starters Galphin shepherded thousands of cattle through Muscogee territories for sale to the British garrisons in West Florida "to get a good Price for them as they have not as yet got many Stocks of Cattle in that Countrey." But several times he lost track of his livestock, which trampled through the *talwas* and corn fields and enraged *micos* and young men alike. Galphin also increasingly accepted raw skins over processed ones, and he also looked the other way when his traders took advantage of the hunters. For example, Francis Lewis—a "Hireling of Mr. Golphins"—made it a practice to sell liquor to the hunters at inflated prices in exchange for their deerskins and horses, and in the process he defrauded the hunters. This same Lewis was involved in a series of violent incidents due to his peddling alcohol as a substitute for payment, at one point angering several young men who threatened to shoot him and would have done so if not for several Muscogee women who put Lewis "into a Canoe and Carried him over the River." Both Lower and Upper *micos* also accused Galphin of refusing to send them ammunition and other goods that had been promised to them based on "what was agreed at the late Congress." Among the furious *micos* were Sempoyaffee and Escotchaby, who both alleged that Galphin had shorted the shipment to Coweta, as the "Baggs were too Small and not the Number agreed for." Galphin's increasingly disreputable reputation contributed to a widening distrust between him and Sempoyaffee and Escotchaby.[37]

Galphin's growing estrangement from Sempoyaffee, Escotchaby, and Coweta also revolved around the staggering debts that he accumulated in the deerskin trade during the 1760s and 1770s. As Coweta's primary supplier, he distributed a wealth of goods to Sempoyaffee and Escotchaby's *huti* and *talwa,* and as the competition with unlicensed traders reached new heights in the decade after the Seven Years' War, he started to owe more to his creditors in the colonies and Europe. In fact Galphin's debts hovered somewhere around ten thousand pounds by the early 1770s. It seems that he, to try and alleviate the burden of such debt, embraced the same duplicitous practices as his peers and, in the process, started to alienate Sempoyaffee and Escotchaby. The relationship between the three had soured so much by January 1774 that Sempoyaffee complained to British officials about Galphin's behavior and asked Stuart to intervene with him.[38] Unfortunately for Sempoyaffee and Escotchaby, they had gambled quite a bit on their connection to Galphin, and it now seemed their gamble was no longer paying off.[39]

Making matters worse between Sempoyaffee, Escotchaby, and Galphin was the fact that Galphin actively facilitated encroachments onto Muscogee lands during the late 1760s and early 1770s. In January 1765 Galphin with this friends Lachlan McGillivray and John Rae successfully petitioned the Georgia Assembly for fifty thousand acres along the Ogeechee River near the Creek Path in western Georgia, lands that had been recently ceded by the *talwas* in 1763. Between 1765 and 1771, Galphin attracted hundreds of families from Ireland who immigrated to that Ogeechee settlement, which was later called Queensborough. The Irish community proved so successful that Galphin petitioned for another fifty thousand acres, which was similarly populated by the "Protestant Families from the north of Ireland." While Galphin may have naively believed the immigrants would not encroach onto Muscogee territories, or at the very least he may have thought he could

control the community, he consistently failed to do so. In fact much of the violence that occurred between Muscogee and British peoples in the 1760s and
1770s occurred between Lower *talwas* such as Coweta and settlements such
as Queensborough. Whether it was the killing of John Carey by the Cowetas
in 1771 or the whipping death of a *mico* that same year, both sides increasingly saw each other as immediate threats to their ways of life. This is why
Queensborough residents declared in March 1772 that "they wou'd kill the
first Indian that come into their Settlement" and also petitioned the Georgia
Assembly to build forts around their community because of their "Continual
uneasiness" and fears "they will be cut off by the Indians."[40]

What might have been the nail in the coffin to Sempoyaffee and Escotchaby's relationship with Galphin was Galphin's demand for eighty-eight thousand acres of land for his Muscogee children. In spring 1772 he asked for
"23 miles" along the Ogeechee River and invoked Metawney's kinship ties to
Sempoyaffee and Escotchaby's *huti* to do so. Sempoyaffee, Escotchaby, and
Coweta's other *micos* responded angrily to Galphin's request but eventually
relented, although observers noted how Galphin's proposal met "with some
difficulty." The leading signatories for the cession were Sempoyaffee and Escotchaby, who also served as "Attorney" and signed the final deed that ceded
"full possession and seizure" of the lands to Galphin's children. It should be
noted that all of this occurred despite British restrictions against the ceding
of Indigenous lands to individuals. So why, then, did Sempoyaffee, Escotchaby, and Coweta's *micos* agree to Galphin's demand in the first place? Unfortunately, we do not know and can only speculate. My guess is that Sempoyaffee
and Escotchaby, with the members of their *huti*, hoped that Galphin—
despite all evidence to the contrary—could still be their solution to the empire's advance in the South. If that required sacrificing hunting grounds, to be
settled in theory by other members of their *huti* (in this case Galphin's children), then all the better instead of the Irish settlers from Queensborough.[41]

With all of the pressures mounting in Coweta—the encroachments on
Muscogee lands, Creek-on-settler violence, generational tensions, a deerskin
trade on the brink of collapse, and Galphin's duplicitous turn—Sempoyaffee
and Escotchaby faced an imminent crisis that threatened their *talwa*, their
huti, and their own positions as two of Coweta's leading *micos*. Despite everything they had done to try and steer their *huti* and *talwa* through the chaos
of the last decade, circumstances in 1773 seemed worse than they had in 1763.
While the problems that Sempoyaffee and Escotchaby endured since the
Seven Years' War were partly of their own making, the crisis had much more
to do with the colonizing forces that had been unleashed after 1763. And even
though every *mico* in all of the *talwas* responded in their own myriad ways
to the chaos, Sempoyaffee and Escotchaby acted in ways that were consistent

with the past, in the interests of their *huti* and *talwa,* and in their efforts to restore some semblance of balance to a Muscogee world that seemed increasingly disordered. Unfortunately things were about to get even more chaotic.

The Second Treaty of Augusta and the Coweta Conflict

In 1773 the Lower *talwas* ceded more than two million acres of land to the Georgia colony, an unprecedented cession among the Indigenous groups of the South. The origins of what became known as the Treaty of Augusta (1773) were rooted in Cherokee Country, where Cherokee headmen decided to cede millions of acres to the British Empire in 1771. The decision was based on the efforts of Cherokee leaders "to discharge our Debts, which Burthen we think it a great happiness to be eased of," and to placate imperial authorities' demands for satisfaction for the several violent incidents that had occurred in the past decade. The lands in question were not simply Cherokee lands, though, because Muscogee peoples "claimed part of the ceded land by right of conquest" in their conflicts with the Cherokee during the 1740s and 1750s. Even British agents observed the "greatest part of it was always deemed Creek property." Cherokee leaders at first dismissed Muscogee concerns, asserting that "the Land is ours, and not the Creeks, they know it well." But when several *micos* learned of Cherokee intentions, Escotchaby—as Cherokee king— immediately sent messengers to the Cherokee to "bring two of their head men" to Coweta at the time of the Busk, so that he "might Enquire of them whether they had given the Land . . . to the white people or not." Cherokee headmen quickly backpedaled after meeting with Escotchaby and informed British agents that "if there is any misunderstanding between Us and the Creeks about the Land, it shall be settled amongst ourselves." As Superintendent Stuart observed, the Lower *talwas* did not seem "so much against the cession of the lands as they are piqued with the Cherokees who they think ought to have consulted them on the affair."[42]

Meanwhile the governor of Georgia, James Wright, traveled to London to earn King George III's blessing for the cession at the same time the traders and merchants in the deerskin trade pressed Muscogee and Cherokee leaders to agree to it. As Wright framed the entire situation in his petition to the Crown, he envisioned the millions of acres could be quickly "sold and disposed of to such of his good subjects who might remove into this Province and purchase and settle thereon." Wright's temporary replacement as governor, James Habersham, managed the logistics of bringing Muscogee and Cherokee peoples to the treaty table, which Habersham considered of the "greatest Importance to this Colony." Reciprocally the traders and merchants coordinated in England to pressure Parliament and key figures in the imperial bureaucracy to consent to the cession, despite the restrictions under the Royal Proclamation of 1763. All these individuals were financially motivated as they sought to recoup the debts that now threatened, in their words, "impending ruin." In the end Governor Wright returned to Georgia with the British king's assent to the cession.[43]

While Cherokee headmen were on board with the new treaty, Muscogee peoples were not, at least not until Wright and other interested parties enlisted Galphin in their cause. For his part Galphin was one of the leading creditors who stood to reap a financial windfall from the treaty. It is hardly a coincidence that he led the traders and merchants who sent a memorial to the royal government in the summer 1771. Similarly Governors Wright and Habersham appealed to Galphin's financial stake in the proposed cession, which prompted Galphin to promise them "to get the Consent of the Lower Creeks" and "to ask for some more Land than what the Cherokees gave to pay the Debts due by the Creeks and the traders." Galphin was so invested in the scheme that he confided to Wright and Habersham that if the Lower *micos* refused to join the Cherokee in the treaty, he would "stop sending any Goods amongst them." From the beginning, then, Galphin was willing to coerce Muscogee peoples into signing the treaty.[44]

It seemed that Galphin had to convince Coweta's *micos* more than anyone else, since it was widely agreed that most of the territory in dispute "was under that town's jurisdiction." Although no record exists for how Galphin managed to convince Sempoyaffee, Escotchaby, and Coweta's other *micos* to consent to the treaty, or what he may have promised or threatened, we know he exploited his connection to Sempoyaffee and Escotchaby to make the treaty a reality. As Habersham wrote to Galphin by the summer of 1772, "you have my Thanks for the Trouble you have taken to get the Consent of the young Lieutenant and Symphihephy to join the Cherokees in the Cession of the Lands." This bombshell of a document tells us much, but also very little, like what were the two brothers thinking in ceding the lands despite being resistant to parting with any more territories in the past several years and at the same time being presented with evidence of what amounted to Galphin's betrayal of their trust? Further, Sempoyaffee and Escotchaby knew the English were lying when British authorities "agreed that said Lands should be all that should be ever desired." No one, least of all Sempoyaffee and Escotchaby, was oblivious to the fact that this had all happened before.[45]

While frustratingly limited by the lack of evidence, we do know that Sempoyaffee and Escotchaby did not agree to the treaty lightly. As Escotchaby addressed Stuart in September 1772, "We have considered your Talk to us and also considered the Many Complaints which our Traders have made about their Poverty and being unable to Pay the Merchants for the Goods which they supply us with." He then relented to the terms of the treaty and "agree[d] to give the great King some Land to pay our Traders with." However, Escotchaby refused to cede the lands "on this Side [of] Savannah River as far as the foot of the Mountain [which] is *Ours*. We drove the Cherokees up to the Mountain and they know the Land to be Ours; and asked leave to Plant Corn near Toogaloo old Town and promised that our people should have Something to Eat when they met them a Hunting." Escotchaby thus concluded his talk to Stuart.[46]

On the surface it seems that Escotchaby conciliated to yet another cession of land to the British Empire, for at one point he had confessed that "they were much tired with the Subject of Land and wanted to have done with it." But if we look at what exactly the Lower *micos* were willing to part with, and the demands that Escotchaby made of the British, appeasement appears more like shrewd maneuvering by Coweta's *micos,* who faced a no-win situation. Escotchaby and Coweta's other *micos* remained adamant that the only lands to be ceded were those seized from the Cherokee during the 1740s and 1750s. As Governor Wright frustratingly wrote, the Lower *micos* "could not be prevailed upon to cede the lands to the bank of the Oconee River which they said was their beloved hunting grounds." Therefore the Lower *talwas* only ceded lands that had been formerly Cherokee, sacrificing little to none of their own territories in the process. When Cherokee headmen agreed in secret to cede more territory along the Tugaloo River than what was originally asked for, Lower *micos* somehow uncovered the truth and, in council with British and Cherokee leaders in 1773, scolded the Cherokee for such behavior. As one *mico* chided Cherokee headmen in front of everyone, by what right did they "give away their lands"? The Lower *micos* then threatened to "dissolve the congress and return home, unless the Georgians consented to annul the secret treaty with the Cherokees." In addition Escotchaby requested that British agents provide gifts to "every town in the Lower Creeks" in response to such duplicity. He went so far as to demand "you will give us the Steelyard Trade the same as in the Cherokees," which was part of his efforts to placate the younger men of Coweta, for "this is what our Young Men desire." By the end of the negotiations, all the parties involved were fed up with one another, and the treaty proceedings ended not "intirely to the Satisfaction of the Parties." Given all the circumstances, though, Sempoyaffee, Escotchaby, and the Lower *micos* had circumvented the British and instead forced the Cherokee to make up the difference in lands with their own. When Governor Wright sent out surveying parties after the treaty, Escotchaby accompanied the surveyors to ensure the boundary lines remained as agreed on.[47] When disagreement arose, in the case of one surveyor who "determined upon the [wrong] point" of origin for the boundary line, Escotchaby and others challenged him and "said it was not right." The surveyor did not believe them and stated he "could not err." But the Muscogee answered they "knew better and that the little wicked instrument was a liar." The surveyor was eventually proven wrong, and the line fixed accordingly.[48]

Despite playing hardball with the Cherokee and British, Sempoyaffee and Escotchaby returned to Coweta disillusioned and aware that they had angered Coweta's young men. From the very beginning of the congress, young Muscogee men "were unwilling to submit to so large a demand" for land. When negotiations continued without their input, Coweta's young men in particular seemed on the verge of taking action "by force of arms" and were unable to "be brought to listen to reason and amicable terms." By the end of the treaty council, Sempoyaffee and Escotchaby could not ignore the fact that a "deep divide" had opened up between them and the young men of their *talwa,* who resented the continual loss of Muscogee territories, even if in this case it was former Cherokee lands. This is not to say that Sempoyaffee and Escotchaby were not frustrated and angry themselves or even sympathized with their townsmen. As British agents observed of Sempoyaffee's attitude after the treaty, he "behaved very ill" and acted in a "most dangerous" manner toward David Taitt, Superintendent Stuart's right-hand man. The brothers were also furious at Galphin and undoubtedly interpreted his actions in the negotiations as a betrayal. Sempoyaffee and Escotchaby likely talked to the other members of their *huti* about what had transpired and may have even debated whether to sever their connections to Galphin altogether. Fortunately, or unfortunately, Galphin took the decision out of their hands when he sent a letter to Coweta addressed to Escotchaby and Sempoyaffee, informing them "how far he had been their friend" and "telling them of his leaving off trade." After the letter was read aloud in the town square, it was observed that Escotchaby "behaved rather a little too rash," obviously enraged with Galphin one last time.[49]

While Sempoyaffee, Escotchaby, and Coweta's other *micos* contemplated what to do next, the young men of their *talwa* made the decision for them. After witnessing more than a decade of encroachments that culminated in the 1773 treaty—and followed by a flood of settlers from South Carolina, North Carolina, Georgia, and Pennsylvania who all flocked to the "Ceded Lands" in late 1773—a small group of men from Coweta set out on Christmas Day and killed members of the White family near the Ogeechee River. It is quite telling that the leader of the Coweta group was Howmatcha, the same individual whose *talofa* had been destroyed by settlers in 1767 and who had not resorted to violence in that case but instead communicated with Stuart and Escotchaby to ensure peace.[50] Six years later Howmatcha represented how disillusioned and frustrated the young men of Coweta had truly become. In fact his actions stemmed from his desire to get revenge, or satisfaction, for the murder of his brother by several settlers. He and the other young men "set out to the Place where his Brother was killed and followed the Tracts of the Horses to [the] White man's house on [the] Ogeechee," where they attacked the White family. Afterward Howmatcha and the young men returned to the Standing Peach Tree, one of Coweta's satellite towns, where they "told Mr. Galphin's Factor & others there that they had now spoiled the Path with the White People." It was hardly a coincidence that Howmatcha went to Galphin's factor the White Boy of Coweta: he stated that one of the reasons he went and killed the family on the Ogeechee River was because "no Lands must be given up but Blood for Blood," and he blamed Galphin for the settler invasion. Such accusations from Howmatcha and other young men from Coweta likely extended to Sempoyaffee and Escotchaby by proxy.[51]

Only a few weeks later, Coweta townsmen struck again. This time Coweta's young men attacked and killed six members of the Shirroll family as well as "set fire to the stockade . . . [and] one of the houses" before they were forced to retreat. In response to a second incident, the local militia mobilized in order to track down the Cowetas. But when the militiamen crossed the Ogeechee River, they were ambushed, and four militiamen were killed. One of those slain was Lt. Daniel Grant, whose "mangled body was found tied to a tree, his scalp and ears cut off, a gun-barrel thrust into his body supposed to have been red hot, twelve arrows sticking in his breast, a painted hatchet sticking in his head and a painted war-club laid upon his breast."[52] While Sempoyaffee, Escotchaby, and other Lower *micos* "disavowed having had any hand" in the violence, the young men of Coweta had delivered an explicit message to both their *micos* and imperial authorities: any more cessions of land or encroachments on Muscogee territories would not be tolerated. The message became unmistakably clear when it was discovered that the same Cowetas had set "several trees blazed" toward Pucknawhitla (Standing Peach Tree), "on one of which was an M with two strokes, and, at a little distance, a bundle of physic." Again it was hardly a coincidence that the Cowetas in this instance targeted Standing Peach Tree, known also as the Coweta (or Young) Lieutenant's Settlement.[53]

Panic and frenzy ensued in the colonies in 1774. Newspapers reported how the "Frontier Inhabitants of this Province with such Terrour . . . have deserted the Settlements, and abandoned their All," while imperial officials such as Governor William Bull believed the killings were an opening salvo in a "general War." News of the attacks spread throughout the British Empire as far as Belfast, where it was reported that the "Cowetas had taken up the hatchet against the English, killed all the traders in their nation, and above 30 of the country people." Governor Wright soon after mobilized other armed forces, asked for military support from South Carolina, resupplied and established new stockades, and requested a thousand redcoats from London, citing his fears of a "most Furious & desperate Warr." Wright also ordered an embargo upon the deerskin trade in hopes of forcing the *talwas* to begin negotiations.[54]

While Sempoyaffee and Escotchaby at first attempted to defuse the hostilities and restrain their townsmen from attacking the ceded land settlements, events conspired against them and eventually triggered their support for their young men. As Muscogee and British peoples clashed in the early months of 1774, several members of Sempoyaffee and Escotchaby's *huti* were killed during the fighting. But it was the loss of one of their beloved nephews, an individual for whom the entire *talwa* "grieved," that convinced Sempoyaffee and Escotchaby that enough was enough. Both men were reportedly saddened and angered "very much" and afterward "sent out people twice to take satisfaction, which they did." Sempoyaffee even joined one of these raids in the company of the Chavolkey Warrior, an attack that claimed several settlers' lives. The resulting violence, what I call the Coweta Conflict (1773–83),[55] effectively stopped the settlement of the ceded lands, and for all intents and purposes, Sempoyaffee and Escotchaby joined Coweta's young men in declaring war on the colonies.[56]

While Sempoyaffee joined the battle, Escotchaby solicited the support of the Spanish in Havana. Before the ink had even dried on the second Treaty of Augusta, Escotchaby traveled by "canoe to hunt for the Spaniards" to negotiate a stronger alliance. In addition to making his way to Cuba, Escotchaby sent representatives such as Estimslayche and members of his *huti* to request "Arms and Munitions" from the Spanish, which they stored in the *talwa*. At the outset of the Coweta Conflict, Escotchaby once again sent Estimslayche to Havana and asked for more weapons and supplies that they could use to expand the conflict into East Florida, with the aim of capturing the "Castle of San Marcos de Apalache" (fort at St. Marks). Escotchaby presumably had in mind wiping out the British fortification and Galphin's store, to be replaced by Spanish traders and soldiers. He asked the Spanish governor, the Marquis de la Torre, in 1774 for whatever he could spare to help them "conduct the crude war that they have declared against the" colonies. After he left Spanish agents remarked that there was a "Terrible Venom . . . coming from the said Indians toward the English," and they were persuaded that Escotchaby and the Cowetas "intend to make War." A year later Escotchaby again traveled to Cuba in the company of his wives and three children, who were showered with gifts, and he again asked the Spanish for their aid against the colonies. During their deliberations he blamed the colonies for the war and claimed Coweta had "killed 22 English" since the start of the conflict. He then requested that the Spanish governor send troops to the Bay of Tampa to support

Coweta. As British authorities anxiously noted, "the Young Lieutenant with two more Head Men were gone again to the Spaniards for Ammunition & other Necessaries to Carry on the War, as they promised that they would." When Escotchaby returned to Havana in the summer of 1775, he again asked the Spanish governor to assist his peoples' efforts to take the Bay of Tampa and pledged his "absolute obedience to His Majesty."[57]

In response to the Coweta Conflict, the *micos* of the Upper *talwas* attempted to resolve the violence on their own. Due to the embargo on the deerskin trade, all the *talwas* suffered, and as goods poured into Coweta from Havana, the same could not be said for the other *talwas*, especially the Upper *talwas*. Led by Emistisiguo of Little Tallassee, Upper *micos* were the first to reach out to British officials and promise to "take every method in their Power to Settle the Difference now Subsisting between their nation and Government amicably." However, they also warned Stuart that "they have not Influence enough to get the Murderers delivered up." Upper *micos* then sent messages and representatives to Coweta, and in one case Emistisiguo confronted Sempoyaffee in person, pleading with him on behalf of all the other *talwas* that the "Cowetas should not stop their trade." But the Upper *micos* did little to dissuade the Cowetas from their course of action. As the conflict continued, Emistisiguo hosted a second meeting with British agents where he again condemned Coweta and its people who had "shut up the path between us" and the colonies, and because of that Coweta "must stand for themselves." It was in that meeting that Emistisiguo asked whether British authorities and the traders would be willing to forge a new trade path to the Upper *talwas* from Pensacola and Mobile in West Florida. As Emistisiguo explained to Stuart, "The Cowetas who are the Front Part seems to want to bring us who are the back Part into poverty by their doing," so he instead proposed that there be "two paths, one to Pensacola and one to Mobile." The importance of Emistisiguo's proposal is that it would create a new trade path that would bypass Coweta altogether and undermine that *talwa*'s ability to turn the trade on and off by virtue of its strategic position along the Creek Path. This was an unprecedented threat for unprecedented times.[58]

Emistisiguo and the Upper *micos* were joined by the Cherokee, who similarly reached out to Coweta to try and broker a peace. In a talk sent to their "Brother" Escotchaby, the Wolf of Seneca, Chinisto of Sugar Town, the Bag of Toxaway, and a council of the Cherokee Beloved Women all asked Escotchaby and Coweta not to "bring any darkness over us, nor to Stop our Trading Path." Speaking as a Coweta king to a Cherokee king, the Bag of Toxaway shamed Escotchaby for his role in the violence and declared that even though "I have been your Beloved Man but as you are turned Rogues, I decline being so any Longer, in token whereof I send you this String of Beads." Escotchaby could not have taken the Bag of Toxaway's words lightly. Even the Pidgeon of Tugaloo, another Coweta king, remarked how the Cowetas "wanted to have a Ball Play or two with the Virginians, especially as it was them that begun the Affair, by killing first one of their people." But "for his own Part," the Pidgeon "wanted to live in Peace, for which Purpose he left the Cowetas." Sempoyaffee and Escotchaby could not ignore the fact that Coweta was on its own, as the Upper *talwas* and the Cherokee sought to prevent their attacks upon the colonies.[59]

It is likely within this context that Sempoyaffee, Escotchaby, and Coweta's other *micos* reached out to the Upper *talwa* of Okfuskee in 1774. After months of violence, Coweta's *micos* agreed to receive an envoy from Okfuskee. That emissary, the Mad Turkey, met with Escotchaby, who entrusted him with a message of reconciliation. The Mad Turkey then traveled to Silver Bluff and, in the presence of Superintendent Stuart and Galphin, related Escotchaby's "account for the reasons that he and the Cowetas had went to war," reasons that primarily revolved around the killing of several townsmen (as well as members of Sempoyaffee and Escotchaby's *huti*). But as Escotchaby confided, "now he was satisfied, and did not desire any war," and promised to stop all attacks on the settlers, who would be allowed to "come back to their settlements and plant as before." Yet the biggest takeaway for imperial authorities was the fact that Escotchaby "takes all the mischief that has been done hitherto upon himself, that it is not the act of a parcel of straggling mad young fellows, but a deliberate . . . revenge of one of the Head-Men." Colonial officials thereby rejected the terms of peace that Escotchaby proposed to them.[60]

The potential for reconciliation grew even more unlikely when the Mad Turkey was found dead several days later, murdered by one Thomas Fee. Despite the Mad Turkey's "friendly Errand," Fee and several other residents had invited him to drink with them, and when he agreed, Fee repeatedly struck the unsuspecting Mad Turkey with a bar of iron. Although Fee was eventually arrested,[61] it did not take long before four men came to the prison and forced the prison keeper at gunpoint to open Fee's cell. They then stole some horses and retreated to the western settlements. As one newspaper publisher suspected, the jailbreakers were "a set of men who . . . had some of their relations killed" during the Coweta Conflict and were "determined to kill any Indian they can come across friend or foe." The killing of the Mad Turkey was followed by several more murders, which claimed the life of the Elk, who was assassinated while passing through Cherokee territories, and the Buck, who was killed in East Florida. When imperial authorities attempted to apprehend the killers, they again could not be found. Like the young men of Coweta, the settlers continued to take matters into their own hands.[62]

The Cowetas thereby renewed their attacks upon the ceded lands, while Upper *micos* and imperial agents desperately sought to stem the violence. Ironically one of the individuals who tried to convince Sempoyaffee and Escotchaby to negotiate was Galphin. Maybe he believed that Escotchaby had somehow reached out to him when the Mad Turkey delivered his message at Silver Bluff. But whatever the case, Galphin sent a missive addressed to "My Friend" Escotchaby, in which he lamented, "I was very sorry when I heard the difference that was between your People & the white People upon the Ceded Lands." Galphin reminded Escotchaby that people had been killed on both sides and, to that effect, confided how "I am doing all that is in my Power to keep Peace here with your people & the White People & I hope you will do the same there." He then tried to entice Escotchaby with promises that "you never shall be poor as long as I live, let me know what you want & I will send it to you." Escotchaby, though, did not dignify Galphin's letter with a response, a message unto itself. Meanwhile the Upper *micos*—once again led by Emistisiguo—collaborated with several *micos* of the Lower *talwas* to try and carve out peace. At one point the Cusseta King and several other *micos* of Cusseta and Chehaw told imperial agents that they—rather than Coweta—would give satisfaction for the initial killings[63] and were somehow able to "put three of the Murderers to Death."[64]

Shortly thereafter a group of Upper and Lower micos signed a Treaty of Peace and Friendship with the colonies in late 1774, although Sempoyaffee, Escotchaby, and Coweta's other micos refused to go along. In fact Coweta sent only one representative to the treaty deliberations, a man by the name of Le Cuffee, who likely attended in order to report back to Coweta what had transpired between Muscogee and British leaders. Led by the Cusseta King for the Lower talwas and Emistisiguo for the Upper talwas, the two sides hammered out an agreement by which the deerskin trade was reopened in exchange for promises to execute several more of the men from Coweta who had first instigated the violence, to return all stolen horses and cattle, and to do away with all the "Settlements, Houses or Huts whatever shall be Built by an Indian" near the Ocmulgee River. But again the absence of Sempoyaffee, Escotchaby, and Coweta's other micos was quite telling of where they stood on the issue of peace. Everyone waited anxiously to see how Sempoyaffee, Escotchaby, and the Cowetas would react to news of the treaty. It should have come as no surprise to anyone that Sempoyaffee and Escotchaby did not lift a finger to comply with it. Thus the Coweta Conflict not only raged on into 1775 but also would be assimilated into the broader conflict that was the American Revolutionary War.[65]

Six

The Muscogee World in the Revolutionary Crisis, 1775–1783

In September 1776 the American commissioner for Indian affairs in the South, George Galphin, sent several letters to Coweta. While the contents of Galphin's letters are unknown, having been intercepted by British agents, we can gather that he had attempted to reach out to Sempoyaffee and Escotchaby. This was not the first nor the last time that Galphin tried to rekindle that relationship, but like every time before, the bad blood between the three remained. Completely unaware of Galphin's letter, Sempoyaffee and Escotchaby led a delegation of Lower *micos* to meet with British authorities in Florida, where they pledged their friendship to Superintendent Stuart and committed their *talwa* to a neutrality with Britain so long as the trade continued to flow. However, if we trust what Sempoyaffee told Thomas Brown a few days later, Coweta pledged to do even more: they had "thrown away the Virginians," and Sempoyaffee "intended himself to have apprehended" any of Galphin's agents that dared come around Coweta or any of the other Lower *talwas*.[1]

Meanwhile Escotchaby continued to strengthen the connection between Coweta and Havana. In both January and May 1776, he made the voyage to Cuba, where he met with Spanish officials, received gifts, and made plans for establishing a permanent trade between the Bay of Tampa and Havana. While Escotchaby hoped the Spanish might also "come backe" to the mainland, he likely knew he had only a slim chance of convincing the Spanish governor to do so, since he had been asking the Spanish to do just that for years. While the Spanish governor avoided answering Escotchaby directly, he nonetheless presented a wealth of gifts that Escotchaby later redistributed to the members of his *huti* and *talwa*. Both British and American officials observed such proceedings with trepidation, fearful that the Spanish might somehow influence Escotchaby to ally with one side over the other in the war.[2]

What Sempoyaffee's and Escotchaby's actions in 1776 demonstrate is the fact that the two brothers, and the people of Coweta more generally, continued to harbor an animosity toward the Americans—whom they generally associated with the settlers who encroached upon their lands—that ultimately precipitated their attacks upon the colonies-now-states. In short the Coweta Conflict was far from over and was ultimately absorbed into the larger Revolutionary War. Whereas the majority of the *talwas* were content with waiting patiently as a neutral party and even relished the opportunity to pit the Americans states against the British, Coweta's *micos* and its young men voluntarily aligned themselves against the revolutionaries. Therefore, contrary to existent scholarship that argues that Muscogee peoples—and most Indigenous groups in eastern North America—were "mostly uninvolved" or attempted to stay neutral in the early years of the Revolutionary War, Sempoyaffee, Escotchaby, and the Cowetas made a calculated decision at the outset of the war to continue their attacks against the Americans. Therefore, at the outset of the war, Sempoyaffee joined the young men of Coweta on the battlefield and Escotchaby pursued talks with the Spanish in Havana.[3]

Tragically Sempoyaffee and Escotchaby's story—and the story of their *huti*—comes to an unceremonious end by 1780. All traces of Sempoyaffee disappear from the historical record by mid to late 1779; there is no mention of his name by either the British, Spanish, or Americans when it comes to Coweta, the Coweta Conflict, Muscogee peoples more generally, or the peace with the many Indigenous groups of the South in 1783. As for Escotchaby, the records of the Portado del Archivo General de Indias briefly describe his death in Coweta in December 1779, after he presumably fell ill with some sort of sickness. Sempoyaffee and Escotchaby were not the only ones to vanish from the archives, for any references to the members of their *huti*—brothers or sisters, nephews or nieces, mothers or cousins—are similarly lost, as if they never existed in the first place. The only reason we ever learned anything about this Muscogee family was because of Sempoyaffee and Escotchaby, and once the brothers were gone, so too was the memory of their *huti*. In a sense the story of Sempoyaffee and Escotchaby's family ends abruptly with the Revolutionary War. Some scholars might call this a fitting conclusion, given that Sempoyaffee and Escotchaby presided over the many transformative changes that reshaped the Muscogee world during the eighteenth century, never to witness the dramatic dispossession and removal of Muscogee peoples by the United States in the early to mid-nineteenth century. However, I find the end to Sempoyaffee and Escotchaby's story to be profoundly troubling and a reminder of the violence that our archives and our national memory continues to perpetuate against the many generations of Indigenous Peoples who confronted unprecedented changes to their worlds, changes wrought primarily by Euro-American empires and colonialism. In a sense the creation of the United States in 1776 initiated the process of erasing Indigenous voices and histories such as those of Sempoyaffee, Escotchaby, and their *huti*.

The Coweta Conflict and the American Revolution

In summer 1775 John Stuart sent a message to be read aloud in all the Lower and Upper *talwas*. His message was intercepted by the revolutionaries, who replaced it with a talk by Galphin informing the *micos* and their townspeople that there now existed an "unhappy Dispute between the People of England and the white People of America." Galphin articulated how the conflict was just a "family quarrel" between the British Empire and its colonies, and he asked for Muscogee peoples to remain neutral. He also used the opportunity to suggest that Stuart and the British, unlike the revolutionaries, intended to involve the *talwas* in the war, even though Stuart promised otherwise in his letter. As Galphin concluded to the Lower and Upper *micos,* the Americans will "keep you supplied with goods and ammunition" and the conflict "will soon be over, & we desire you to have no concern in it."[4]

Sempoyaffee, Escotchaby, and Coweta's other *micos* did not react to Galphin's letter, yet when they received a letter from Stuart weeks later, they immediately replied. As the *micos* of Coweta and other Lower *talwas* responded to Stuart, "We have heard your talk and we like it and see it's the same as . . . Georgia sent us some time past." Sempoyaffee then spoke on behalf of the *talwas* when he confessed, "We heard there is some difference between the white People and we are all sorry to hear it," and he informed Stuart that the Americans had lately "sent us a handful of Powder and Lead." But after receiving Stuart's talk, which also asked the Lower *micos* to meet with him and indicated that they might expect gifts in return, Sempoyaffee emphasized how much he looked forward to seeing Stuart. While Sempoyaffee, in his capacity as speaker for the Lower *talwas,* pledged to not "join any one party" during the empire's dispute with the states, he did tell Stuart that he and the Cowetas "will have some more talk with you" when they met. What Sempoyaffee left unsaid was the fact that he and the people of Coweta entertained different ideas than the other *talwas* about what role they would play in the war.[5]

Sempoyaffee, Escotchaby, and the Cowetas thereby played a dangerous game in late 1775 that threatened to involve the *talwas* in the war. Unlike Coweta, the majority of Upper and Lower *talwas,* including Cusseta, Tallassee,

Okfuskee, and Yuchi, among others, wanted no part in the conflict. Therefore, when Galphin sent a spy into the Lower *talwas* to learn more about
Stuart's negotiations with Muscogee peoples, that individual learned that the
Cowetas continually threatened "to come out against the White People." But
as the spy told Galphin, the townspeople of Coweta were constantly held in
check by their sister town, Cusseta, who "made Answer and said they were
not the Master of the Land and if they did come out they would sent word to
their Friends, and immediately kill all the [British] or drive them all together
to Pensacola to starve." The reasons for disagreement between Coweta and
Cusseta were many but largely revolved around the hopes of Cusseta and
other *talwas* to keep the Creek Path open and—as Emistisiguo had attempted
during the Coweta Conflict—to open a new channel of trade to the British
in Florida. In short the majority of the Lower and Upper *micos* intended to
deal with the Revolution as they had with all the other conflicts that had
come before: by pitting the two sides against one another and without committing the *talwas* to one side or the other. While Sempoyaffee, Escotchaby,
and Coweta's *micos* envisioned a different role for their *talwa* in the conflict,
the *micos* of the other *talwas* consistently sought to counter the actions taken
by Coweta. This is why the *micos* of Cusseta, Tallassee, and Okfuskee instead
met with Galphin repeatedly during the war, like they did in November 1778,
where they reaffirmed the "white path from there to the Cussatas from thence
to the Tallassees and to the Okfuskees." When Coweta's young men joined
the fighting on the British side in 1776, Stukychee, "the great warrior of Cussita," and several young men from Cusseta and Yuchi joined in the defense of
Savannah against British forces and took several prisoners.[6]

To Sempoyaffee, Escotchaby, and the Cowetas, though, the revolutionaries
were the same people who continually encroached upon their lands in the
preceding decade, and thus the Coweta Conflict became a part of the Revolutionary War. As Galphin described the ongoing violence in October 1776,
it was the settlers—those "people upon the ceded land"—who killed several
Muscogee peoples from the Lower *talwas* and threatened to "kill them wher-
ever they meet them." Doctor Wills, an elected member of the new Georgia
Assembly, secretly intended to seize "all the ammunition and to have fell
upon the Indians and killed them, and declared war with them." Moreover no
one could mistake the intent of the many settlers from Georgia who sought to
capitalize on the chaos of the war to join "2 Surveyors & Several people over
the Indian Line, running out Land." But when the people of Coweta attacked
the surveying parties and other encroaching settlers, these same "Ceded Land
people" petitioned the revolutionary leadership, such as Gen. Charles Lee,
to "exterminate and rout those savages out of their nation" and volunteered
themselves "at the hazard of their lives and fortunes, to unite together for so

desirable a purpose." Even officers in the Continental Army, such as Samuel
Elbert, genuinely believed that the "Fire & Sword are the only arguments that
can avail with [the Muscogee]—and though harsh in the execution, are eventually the most humane measures that can be adopted." It is no wonder, then,
that when Sempoyaffee met with Superintendent Stuart in September 1776,
he vehemently declared that he had "thrown away the Virginians & purpose
to hold you fast" instead.[7]

Therefore, as early as fall 1776, several parties of young men from Coweta
attempted to punish the Georgia settlers who sought to exploit the war to
seize Muscogee lands. The Cowetas first attacked the settlements along the
Altamaha and Broad Rivers, and when several young men were killed during
those raids, the Cowetas sought "revenge for the [men] they had lost" in those
skirmishes. Particular to Sempoyaffee and Escotchaby, one of the young men
who was killed in the early months of the war was yet another nephew. When
Galphin learned of that fact, he sent a trader to try and "quiet the minds of
Simpiaphy and the other relations of the person killed until we shall have
Taken every Step in our power to bring the Murderer to Justice." But Galphin's promises meant next to nothing to Sempoyaffee and Escotchaby. The
loss of another member of the *huti,* in addition to Galphin's tacit threats that
retaliation would produce a "general war" and the loss of trade, only strength-
ened their resolve to stop the settler invasion. Galphin and the revolutionaries
could not mistake their intent after 1776 when they received "black beads"
from Coweta, which signified that the Creek Path from Charleston and Augusta to the *talwas* had too much "Blood Spilt" upon it for peace to exist.[8]

Sempoyaffee thereafter incited the young men of Coweta to attack the
ceded lands. In May 1777 it was reported that "one hundred and thirty of the
Cowetas" attacked one of the forts upon the Ogeechee River, which ended
in several deaths on both sides, including a member of the Tiger clan. It is
important to note in this case that the Cowetas targeted the most visible
symbol of the encroachments upon Muscogee lands: a fort. As Daniel Ingram has demonstrated in his work, Indigenous groups viewed European
fortifications in their territories as both a literal and symbolic presence of
empire, and in times of conflict those constructs became targets of attack.
In the wake of such violence, Sempoyaffee demanded assistance from Upper
micos such as the Mad Dog of Tuckabatchee, demanding he "get the Warriors
of Tuckabatchee, Savannah, Coosada, & OakChoys Towns to send out men"
against Georgia. When Sempoyaffee learned that several Upper and Lower
talwas were instead sending representatives to attend a congress with Galphin
in summer 1777, he grew so "irritated" that he led "five partys . . . against
the Settlements of Georgia," and those attacks claimed the lives of dozens on
both sides. This was followed by "a considerable number of Cowetas Indians"

who harassed western Georgia in August 1777 and ambushed a militia unit, which left "20 men dead upon the spot." Even when famine struck the *talwas* in summer 1777, this did not deter Sempoyaffee and the young men of Coweta as they continued to assault the ceded lands. As British agents marveled, the Cowetas were their only "steady friends" among the *talwas* and "not a single man . . . from the Cowetaw Town" wavered from their war against the revolutionaries.[9]

The fall and winter of 1777 proved no different, as Sempoyaffee urged the young men of Coweta to continue punishing the ceded lands with a vengeance.[10] It seems for the most part that with the coming of the winter, the Cowetas switched from targeting the forts and settlements to the "armed scouting parties of the rebels," although British agents naively believed the Cowetas did so out of a sincere desire to avoid "doing any injury to the unarmed inhabitants." This seems unlikely, based on the fact the settlers/revolutionaries had not shown such temperament and judiciousness when attacking Muscogee peoples since 1763. In one instance Sempoyaffee boasted to British officials that more than "220 men" from Coweta attacked the "upper part of Georgia." If not an exaggeration, this meant a majority of Coweta's warrior population joined this one assault. Sempoyaffee also revealed that this mass attack was in response to the several *micos* from Cusseta, Chehaw, Tallassee, and Okfuskee who visited Galphin. When Sempoyaffee met with Stuart later, he went so far as to ask the British to build a fort around Coweta to fortify his *talwa*, likely motivated after "hearing of the marching of the rebels towards them." Although the threat never materialized, Sempoyaffee thought it prudent to ask Stuart to send boats up the Coosa River with weapons, provisions, and other supplies so that Coweta was "enabled to defend ourselves in case of an Attack." By the end of 1777, the Coweta Conflict had become a full-fledged war.[11]

Sempoyaffee and Escotchaby continually sought to convince the other *talwas* to abandon their neutrality and join their war. In May 1777 Sempoyaffee spread news throughout the *talwas* that he was "well pleased to hear of the promises made by the Choctaws" to side with the British. Afterward he solicited the support of Okfuskee and Tallassee, although to no avail. But this did not discourage Sempoyaffee, for he sent the "war hoop" among the Upper *talwas* several times in 1777 to try and galvanize the young men of those *talwas* to join Coweta. Interestingly enough, it was Alexander McGillivray of Little Tallassee—the future leader who would attempt to unify the *talwas* after the Revolutionary War—who conversed with Sempoyaffee about bringing the young men against Georgia and the ceded lands. In one instance McGillivray trekked back and forth from Coweta to the Upper *talwas* bearing a "message from Sempoyaffee" and, upon his arrival, spread word throughout the *talwas* about Coweta's plans for the fall and winter of 1777. Sempoyaffee also reached out to Emistisiguo, who had emerged as an influential voice in recent years among the Upper *talwas,* and to enlist his support. Although Emistisiguo declined to act with Coweta in the early years of the conflict, he later led his *talwa's* young men against the revolutionaries. Sempoyaffee and Escotchaby also never stopped trying to convince the *micos* of Cusseta, Okfuskee, and Tallassee to change their course.[12]

However, Cusseta, Tallassee, and Okfuskee's *micos* actively resisted Sempoyaffee and Escotchaby's efforts to set their communities against the Americans. As the Cowetas ramped up their attacks upon the ceded lands in summer 1777, the Handsome Fellow led a delegation of *micos* from Cusseta, Tallassee, and Okfuskee to Charleston, where they met with Galphin and received a great "quantity of Goods, Arms, and Ammunition." At this congress the governor of South Carolina, John Rutledge, assured the *micos* that all they desired from the *talwas* was to remain neutral throughout the conflict. Handsome Fellow then handed Rutledge an eagle tail and rattle trap that he wanted Rutledge to send to the Continental Congress in Philadelphia, being symbols of peace and friendship. Handsome Fellow also produced several commissions that he had received from Superintendent Stuart prior to the war and "threw" them down on the table, a visible rejection of British efforts to enlist the neutral *talwas.* After the proceedings, though, Handsome Fellow and his party were nearly killed by the same revolutionaries they had just affirmed their friendship with. Before the delegation left Charleston, they were intercepted by a Captain Dooley of the Continental Army, who "forcibly" seized the *micos* and "carried them into Georgia at Augusta where they are kept Close prisoners." Galphin tried to stop Dooley, claiming it would "put us at the Eve of a War," but Dooley had lost a brother to the Cowetas and now sought to take his vengeance. Before Dooley could do just that, though, he was arrested, and Handsome Fellow and the *micos* were freed. More important, though, what should have been an experience that would have turned the *micos* of Cusseta, Okfuskee, and Tallassee against the Americans was instead blamed on "Stuart & his Emissaries." Somehow Galphin framed Dooley as one of Stuart's agents, which thereby changed the entire narrative, and after that harrowing experience, Handsome Fellow—believing that Stuart and the British were responsible—vowed "vengeance" against the British.[13]

When Handsome Fellow and the other *micos* arrived back in their *talwas,* they met with their townsmen and plotted to expel British agents from their territories. Therefore in September 1777 the young men of Okfuskee, Tallassee, Cusseta, and Yuchi together "drove all Stuarts Commissaries & Disaffected traders out of there nattion & plundered them all," seizing an untold wealth of goods, weapons, and supplies that were all redistributed among sympathetic *talwas*. As one of those agents, William McIntosh, remarked after the fact, "a fellow called Long Crop from the Cussitaws with some others yesterday came over here with a View to take my Scalp, but he mist his aim." Although McIntosh genuinely believed his life was in danger, it was more likely that Long Crop and the Cussetas intended to scare him off more than anything else. After the British commissaries fled, the women of Cusseta "went over to their houses and pulled them down," sending an unmistakable message to both the British and the Cowetas. As Galphin gloated to Henry Laurens after receiving word of the British exodus from the *talwas*, "we have got all Stuarts [men] Drove out of the nation."[14]

What Galphin did not mention, though, was that several of the British agents who fled the *talwas* had found sanctuary at Coweta. In the case of McIntosh, after being shot at by Long Crop, he was whisked away by several young men who took him to Coweta and there "guarded his house for several days and nights" before escorting him back down to Pensacola.[15] Sempoyaffee even tried to retrieve McIntosh's effects, storming over to Cusseta and demanding they "deliver them up the Commissaries' Goods." Sempoyaffee and the young men of Coweta were so "irritated" with Cusseta, Okfuskee, and Tallassee that several groups attacked a Georgia "Scouting Party" and plundered several supply trains along the Creek Path. In recognition of Coweta's staunch support, Stuart and the governor of West Florida, Patrick Tonyn, gave them "Galphin's property" that had been confiscated at various points during the war and promised to "reward them generously if they brought him or those employed by him prisoners to me or to Pensacola." Despite the efforts of the revolutionaries and friendly *talwas* to keep Muscogee peoples out of the war, it was instead Sempoyaffee and the Cowetas who effectively "spoilt Galphin's path" and "made it as crooked as Ever." As one *mico* of Cusseta blamed Coweta's *micos* for the violence: "If you had taken my Talk to be Peaceable this Would not have happened."[16]

Sempoyaffee continued to instigate the young men of Coweta to attack the ceded lands in 1778, which ultimately convinced a number of other Lower and Upper *talwas* to abandon their neutrality and join against the revolutionaries. In the early months, a party from Coweta harassed the westernmost settlements of Georgia and in one of their raids decimated a "party of the rebel rangers." But the violence once again took a darker turn for Sempoyaffee and Escotchaby's *huti*, when another one of their nephews was killed in battle. All over again, an enraged Sempoyaffee joined the young men of Coweta who attacked the ceded lands, and it was estimated they "killed 20 or 30 Inhabitants." The violence of 1778 proved so intense that it convinced the revolutionary leadership that all the *talwas*, even the friendly ones, "have broke with Us," despite Galphin's warnings that "it is only a Part of the Nation" and that the "greater Part are still our Friends." Nonetheless Coweta's relentless attacks against the Americans started to have an effect on the other *talwas* by mid to late 1778. As Alexander McGillivray wrote to Stuart, several other Lower and Upper *talwas* such as Chehaw now agreed with Coweta and seemed determined to "carry their point [to] the whole Nation." Together Coweta and other *talwas* started to "spread terror" in Georgia and South Carolina, which the revolutionaries feared "from all appearances there is the greatest probability of a rupture with those Indians."[17]

Between early 1778 and late 1779, Sempoyaffee and the Cowetas were thus joined by several other *talwas* that raided the ceded lands. In November 1778 Sempoyaffee himself led a party of young men from Coweta to the Oconee River, where they attacked several settlements in Georgia and "intend[ed] to watch the Enemies motion till spring." Coweta townsmen also joined in the defense of the British stronghold of St. Augustine, when it was feared Spanish forces were launching an attack from Havana. And by the end of 1778, Coweta emerged as a staging base for joint British-Muscogee assaults upon the ceded lands, a role that continued well into the next year when British strategists set into motion their Southern Strategy. As British generals deployed more forces to the southern colonies to turn the tide of the war—with the support of the loyalists, Indigenous groups, and the enslaved population —the Cowetas were one of the first allies to offer their support to the British army. And when Galphin tried to pressure Cusseta's, Okfuskee's, and Tallassee's *micos* to try and deter Coweta from its continued course, Will's Friend confessed they had no idea why the Cowetas were still "killing the Virginia People." Yet everyone knew why: the incessant encroachments upon Muscogee territories for more than a decade.[18]

Whereas Sempoyaffee spearheaded Coweta's war effort, Escotchaby colluded with their neighbors the Cherokee. At the outset of the conflict, Muscogee *micos* and Cherokee headmen talked on and off about what role they might play in the war together, while most everyone else hoped to remain aloof from the war. However, certain individuals in both worlds, Sempoyaffee and Escotchaby among the Muscogee and Dragging Canoe of the Cherokee, were fed up with the treaties and encroachments and believed now was the time to strike at the colonies. Therefore Cherokee headmen visited Coweta in June 1775 and declared to their Cherokee king that their business was to renew the "ancient" friendship between them, although they also talked about matters of war. And unlike the Muscogee *talwas,* a number of Cherokee towns went to war against the colonies in 1776. All the while Escotchaby talked with Cherokee headmen about supporting their efforts militarily, which Galphin observed with great anxiety, for when "the Cherokees broke out with us I knew they would send to the Creeks to join them." Galphin's fears were fully realized at the Battle of Fincastle in summer 1776,[19] where several Muscogee men—presumably from Coweta since no other *talwa* joined the war at that point—fought with the Cherokee against the Americans. In addition Escotchaby facilitated the "fifty horse-loads of ammunition" that Coweta and a few other *talwas* "sent off to the Cherokees." At first Dragging Canoe and the Cherokee seized the upper hand against South Carolina and Georgia in early to mid-1776. But after that the revolutionaries responded with several punitive expeditions[20] that effectively laid waste to Cherokee communities.[21]

The sheer violence that the revolutionaries employed against the Cherokee ultimately convinced Escotchaby and Coweta to stop supporting the Cherokee. As Stuart believed, the Cherokees' "distressed situation" is "constantly before the eyes of the other Indian nations" and dampened everyone's spirits to support them. Amid the violence Escotchaby offered Cherokee peoples what he could, especially a place of safety in Coweta and other Lower *talwas,* to which a "great many of them" accepted his offer and relocated to Muscogee territories. The Cherokees who removed in and after 1776 quickly acclimated to their new surroundings and planted what British agents observed as "fine Fields of Corn" in Coweta. And while Cherokee leaders such as Dragging Canoe disparaged Muscogee peoples "with not having assisted them in their distress," the refugees who relocated to Coweta shared "vivid accounts of the invasions" that had convinced Escotchaby that his *talwa*'s course of action had been the right one. It should come as no surprise that later in the war, many of these Cherokee refugees joined Sempoyaffee and Coweta's young men in their "expedition[s] to Georgia."[22]

Meanwhile Escotchaby negotiated with the Spanish throughout the war, despite the fact that Spain financially assisted the revolutionaries beginning in 1776 and entered the war against Britain in 1779.[23] As early as 1775, Escotchaby and a dozen other townspeople from Coweta went to Havana by canoe, where they talked about continuing trade between Cuba and the Tampa Bay. As Claudio Saunt notes, the Spanish approached these negotiations seriously, with a desire for Coweta foodstuffs and an outlet for the molasses they produced on the island, which "spoke to the immediate needs of Cuba's population." In doing so Escotchaby labored intently not only to provide a source of economic support for Coweta during the war, but he also may have thought even longer term than that: a trade for the foreseeable future that no matter who won the war, Coweta could still depend on its connection to Havana. Therefore Escotchaby and the Spanish governor engaged in talks about establishing a trade in "horses, Deer Pelts, and other Goods which abound in their Lands" in 1775 and 1776. Escotchaby also offered the Spanish to "protect and defend the Spanish Boats that engage in the fishing off that Coast" during the war, which may have seemed quite attractive to the Spanish because British ships continually patrolled the waters between Pensacola and St. Augustine. Escotchaby followed through on such promises when he sent delegations to Havana in February 1776[24] and again in early 1777, followed by a small party led by Tibulayche, who, at Escotchaby's behest, once again renewed the Coweta-Havana relationship. For the remainder of the war, Escotchaby sustained a lifeline of trade to Havana for his *huti* and *talwa,* and at one point he invited the Spanish back to East Florida near the "Apalachee old fields." He presumably intended the Spanish presence to check British and American interests in and around Muscogee territories, complete with the customary gifts.[25]

Despite Sempoyaffee and Escotchaby's efforts during the Revolutionary War, more than a decade of violence between their *talwa* and the colonies started to wear on the young men of Coweta. As early as October 1777, British agents noted that Coweta's "young people" started to "fault the Old for sending them to War" so often and earning them the "censure" of the other *talwas.* Some of these young men also denounced Escotchaby's request to the Spanish "that they would be sent a Priest to baptize them, teach the Doctrine, confess them and attend (to them) when they die." While such demands were uncharacteristic of Escotchaby and likely part of his efforts to strengthen the Spanish connection, such a prospect no doubt alarmed people in Coweta. Meanwhile a few of the young men, such as "Jeagay a head warrior of the Cowetas" and Fine Bones, "one of the head warriors of the Cowetas," decided they had had enough of the violence and joined the *micos* of Okfuskee, Cusseta, and Tallassee in talking with the Americans. At one such talk, Fine Bones confided to Galphin that "I take your talk and will kill no more white people," although he reiterated that the entire reason the Coweta Conflict exploded in 1773 was because "the Virginia People first began by killing our people." Such changes in the opinions and actions of some of Coweta's young men is a testament to the fact many had reached the limits of their willingness to wage war, whereas Sempoyaffee and Escotchaby continued to push for it. Such disagreements between some of Coweta's young men and Sempoyaffee and Escotchaby gradually reached a tipping point in September 1779.[26]

It was Estimape who ultimately challenged Escotchaby and Coweta's other *micos.* Estimape is quite the paradox, having never existed in either the British or Spanish archives up until September 1779, and was likely one of the nameless "young men" that Europeans observed time and again alongside more prominent individuals and *micos.* In any event Estimape made an independent voyage to Havana in summer 1779 and brought back word to Coweta that the Spanish intended to return to the mainland, which was "celebrated" in the town square. Unbeknownst to Escotchaby, though, the Spanish governor had made an additional agreement with Estimape, "who had never failed to deliver to them [Spanish] what he was offered." The Spanish governor worked out a deal with Estimape in which "all of the lands of West Florida" would be put under the protection of the Spanish Crown, and when the war ended, it would be Estimape—or in the event of his death, his "sons or brothers" (i.e., Estimape's *huti*)—who would assume custody of those lands. Thus in summer 1779 Estimape and the Spanish agreed to supplant Escotchaby and Coweta's other *micos* as the primary voice of leadership for the *talwa*.[27]

But Escotchaby soon suspected that Estimape was up to something. As Spanish agents anxiously noted in December 1779, Escotchaby and the "Caciques [*micos*] of the Town of Cabeta" were concerned about Estimape, who seemed "angered" by certain actions Coweta's *micos* had taken in late 1779. Escotchaby and Coweta's *micos* were wise to be wary of Estimape, but they underestimated Estimape's ability to cultivate the support of Coweta's young people. As Escotchaby learned firsthand in fall 1779, Estimape confronted him in the town square in front of all the townspeople, where Estimape threatened to "dispose of" Escotchaby and the other *micos*. Escotchaby soon recognized that they faced an unprecedented threat from the young people of their *talwa*. Meanwhile Estimape returned to Havana, where he informed Spanish authorities about what had transpired, and they made plans accordingly. While Estimape gathered "arms and Munitions," Escotchaby waited anxiously for the young man's return. But when Escotchaby received word that Estimape was about to arrive back in Florida in December 1779, he set out for "that same spot to receive Estimape" with the rest of Coweta's *micos*. The stage was set for a dramatic confrontation.[28]

Estimape failed to appear, though, instead delayed in Havana by the Spanish governor, which prompted Escotchaby to return to Coweta, and it was there without any fanfare that Escotchaby "just Died."[29] And with that the story of Sempoyaffee and Escotchaby comes to an anticlimactic end. Along with Escotchaby's death, Sempoyaffee all but disappears from the archival record by mid to late 1779,[30] and with their passing their *huti*'s story also ends abruptly.[31] Despite the richness of their story and what it can tell us about the depths of the Muscogee world in the eighteenth century, the Revolutionary War ultimately concludes their story. In the wake of their deaths, the *micos* who supported the revolutionaries signed the Treaty of Augusta (1783), which seemingly settled "all differences between the said parties" and proclaimed that all enmities from the previous twenty years "shall cease and be forgotten." Nothing could have been further from the truth, of course. While Sempoyaffee and Escotchaby did not live long enough to see the end of the Coweta Conflict, although presumably members of their *huti* did, they would have recognized the insidious nature of that treaty and the provision that stipulated "a new line shall be drawn without delay . . . to begin on [the] Savannah River, where the present line strikes it," and extend as far east into the Muscogee territories as possible. The lands ceded by the *micos* in 1783 just so happened to include the lands between the Ogeechee and Oconee Rivers, the very territories that Sempoyaffee and Escotchaby had gone to war to protect from the colonies a decade previous.[32]

Conclusion

After Sempoyaffee's and Escotchaby's passing by 1780, the Muscogee world continued to experience profound change. The creation of the United States heralded a new era and forever changed the dynamics between Muscogee and Euro-American peoples. From its inception the United States was a settler republic, hell-bent on dispossessing the Indigenous Peoples of North America and resettling their territories with Euro-American farmers. Although Kathleen DuVal has revealed how fragile the American imperial project was in the 1780s and 1790s, exploited by a host of individuals including the Muscogee leaders Alexander McGillivray and the Tallassee King, such fragility did not offset the rabid violence that was ushered in by the settler republic. In ways reminiscent of the violence between the *talwas* and the colonies during the 1760s and 1770s, the decades after the Revolutionary War were defined by frequent conflict, often between the state of Georgia and Muscogee peoples. As Secretary of War Henry Knox described to George Washington in July 1789, the protracted violence in the South threatened a "serious war" with the *talwas,* who "have been making inroads into Georgia, and . . . the outrages committed by them have excited an alarm" and may "require the interference of the United States." The primary source of conflict was no different than in previous decades: treaties and encroachments. Or as Alexander McGillivray best described the situation, the "Georgians have brought the war on themselves, by manifesting . . . persecuting spirits towards us. Our situation does by no means admit of our giving away our lands."[1]

By the turn of the nineteenth century, Sempoyaffee and Escotchaby would have no longer recognized elements of the Muscogee world. For instance kinship no longer acted in the ways it had in the eighteenth century.

The emergence of several new leaders within Muscogee society, those born of Muscogee mothers and European fathers such as McGillivray, as well as the introduction of the federal government's Plan for Civilization, started to invert kinship ties from matrilineal to patrilineal. While Muscogee peoples resisted such change, the very idea of kinship was now under assault by the turn of the nineteenth century. Similarly the Muscogee world had tipped overwhelmingly toward the side of violence and disorder in the recent decades, a product of Muscogee peoples' incessant conflicts with the state of Georgia. With that said, though, Muscogee peoples responded in creative ways, just as Sempoyaffee and Escotchaby had throughout the eighteenth century. In the case of McGillivray, he—like other individuals before him—articulated a nascent sense of Muscogee nationhood, to unify the *talwas* against the threat of the United States. As Thomas Brown reported in 1783, McGillivray was "elected by the chiefs of the Creeks, the King and Head Warrior of all the Nation." While other *micos* such as the Tallassee King and Nea Mico of Cusseta asserted a more *talwa*-centered political model as in the past, McGillivray embodied the transformative changes that continued to reshape the Muscogee world by the early nineteenth century.[2]

In particular McGillivray articulated a long-germinating idea of confederacy and union that Muscogee leaders had toyed with for nearly a century, and he continued to exploit the many rivalries that existed in the United States, and with the neighboring Spanish, to make a vision of Muscogee nationhood real. Although McGillivray's emphasis on the "defence of their rights as men" was rather new, his determination to protect "the limits of our country" and the fact that "we are now, as we always have been, an independent and free people," was not. McGillivray gave voice to a form of "nation-based resistance" and "independent nationhood" similar to what Americans had fought for during the revolution. In effect McGillivray aligned such revolutionary ideals with the struggles of Muscogee peoples to retain their territories and ways of life. McGillivray also played the various actors in the South against one another to help make his vision of Muscogee nationhood real, particularly his negotiations with the federal government to offset the "unhappy differences which have for some time subsisted between the inhabitants . . . of South Carolina and Georgia." It was also McGillivray who complained to George Washington of the encroachments on their territories by American settlers. Like Escotchaby, he also entertained Spanish agents who pledged to assist Muscogee peoples in "defending their rights to their lands." And for a time McGillivray's intrigues paid off, such as the Treaty of Peace and Friendship with the United States that provided a temporary reprieve from violence. McGillivray and Muscogee peoples thereby closed the eighteenth century with a "greater coalescence" as a nation while also "preserving the privileges of *talwa* autonomy," a mixture of past and present.[3]

The precedents and traditions that McGillivray drew upon were ultimately rooted in the eighteenth-century Muscogee world that Sempoyaffee and Escotchaby helped to shape, a world defined by one's family and kinship. And it is through the story of these two brothers we learn more about the fundamental building blocks of the eighteenth-century Muscogee world in ways that scholars have not yet fully articulated as much as town and community identities, regional affiliations, or national aspirations. We can also utilize the consensus of scholarship related to Muscogee history and culture to contextualize the early lives of these two men and the other members of their *huti* and how critical those family relationships were to Sempoyaffee and Escotchaby throughout their lives. Particularly as the two brothers ascended the ranks of leadership within Coweta—as *tustenogy*, Cherokee king, and *micos*—Sempoyaffee and Escotchaby always acted in the interests of their immediate and extended relatives. At the same time, they balanced the welfare of their *huti* with the good of their *talwa*, which at times aligned in near-perfect ways and in other instances not at all, which incited conflict with Coweta's other *micos*, the other *talwas*, Indigenous groups such as the Cherokee, and of course Europeans. Nonetheless Sempoyaffee and Escotchaby acted in ways that they believed was best for their *huti* and *talwa*, especially when it came to their interactions with European empires. As Superintendent Stuart described in 1764, there existed "so many Headmen" in every *talwa* such as Coweta, but each "Headmen's" family and clan were always working behind the scenes and orchestrating events beyond the sight of Europeans. Sempoyaffee and Escotchaby thereby embodied the calculating, shrewd, and deft negotiations that their *huti* made within the eighteenth-century Muscogee world.[4]

Thus Sempoyaffee and Escotchaby help us to explore how a family confronted the profound transformations that reshaped the Muscogee world during the eighteenth century. As *micos*, the *tustenogy*, and Cherokee king, the two brothers provided avenues for their family and clan members to negotiate the changing world around them, as well as more generally for the people of their *talwa*. At times Sempoyaffee and Escotchaby managed to navigate and redirect the transformative and invasive forces of European colonialism. But at other times they did not. Sempoyaffee and Escotchaby's story is not theirs alone, for they are merely one of the multitude of families in the Muscogee world—and in Indigenous North America more generally—who similarly grappled with the profound changes to their worlds in the eighteenth century. Each of these families, as illustrated by Sempoyaffee and Escotchaby,

wielded a power to shape their worlds anew at the same time the forces beyond them—of empire and colonialism—conspired against their efforts.

With that said, there are severe limitations to our understandings of the
broader narrative of this Muscogee family, for we do not have their entire
story. This inability to reproduce the full story of one Muscogee family's experiences in eighteenth-century America is a product of the archival violence
that has been done to this family and every other Indigenous family for centuries. So much has been lost, and even though scholars have become more
creative and sophisticated in getting around the restrictions of the colonial
archives, there is sometimes only so much that one can do. It is frustrating,
maddening, and altogether painful to be unable to relate this family's narrative in its entirety. Instead all we have are the fragments, and even then the
fragments do not add up.

Finally, Sempoyaffee and Escotchaby's experiences reflect the intimate
entanglement of the Muscogee and imperial worlds in eighteenth-century
America. From the deerskin trade to the intermarriage of Indigenous and European peoples, to the looming threat of encroachment and the negotiations
to bring about peace, the many contours of the Muscogee world blended
with that of the Spanish, French, and English, so much so that one could
not exist or thrive without the other. The interdependence of Muscogee and
European worlds thereby forced both sides to integrate one another into
their worlds, at the same time they confronted the various challenges that
came with such entanglement. After 1763, though, the intersections of Muscogee and European worlds became increasingly characterized by antagonism
and violence, as seen in the deteriorating relationship between Sempoyaffee, Escotchaby, and Galphin. In Galphin's case, his betrayal of Sempoyaffee,
Escotchaby, and their *huti* represented a perverse and intimate form of colonialism that emerged out of this entanglement of Indigenous and imperial
worlds in eighteenth-century America.

This is ultimately my goodbye to Sempoyaffee, Escotchaby, and their *huti*,
a journey that started in a graduate research seminar a lifetime ago. It took me
more than a decade to write their story. In hindsight my dissertation should
have been about these two brothers and the members of their *huti* . . . but it
wasn't. This book is partly my efforts at making some kind of peace—a troubled peace at that—with the decisions I made more than a decade ago.

I hope that the story of Sempoyaffee, Escotchaby, and their *huti* is acces-
sible, a family biography of the early American and Indigenous pasts. Stories
personalize the past in ways that nothing else can, especially when it comes
to the worlds and peoples who seem so far removed from our present. Only
they are not. The story of Sempoyaffee, Escotchaby, and the members of their

huti can tell us a lot about where we have come from, where we are today, and where we are going, in the same ways they drew upon their Creation Stories and the stories of their ancestors to explain the world that they lived in and how they negotiated the forces of colonialism throughout their lives. It all comes back to family and the stories told by one's family.

ABBREVIATIONS

Ballindalloch   James Grant of Ballindalloch Papers, 1740–1819. David Library of the American Revolution.

BD-SC   Board of Trade and Secretaries of State: America and West Indies Original Correspondence, Board of Trade & Secretaries of State: South Carolina, 1733–1775. CO 5/363–387. British National Archives.

CIT   Creek Indian Letters, Talks and Treaties, 1705–1837. Hargrett Rare Book and Manuscript Library.

CRG   *The Colonial Records of the State of Georgia.* Edited by Allen D. Candler et al. 39 vols.

DAR   *Documents of the American Revolution, 1770–1783.* Edited by K. G. Davies. 21 vols.

DRIA 1   *Documents Relating to Indian Affairs, May 21, 1750–August 7, 1754.* Colonial Records of South Carolina, Series 2. Edited by William L. McDowell Jr.

DRIA 2   *Documents Relating to Indian Affairs, 1754–1765.* Colonial Records of South Carolina, Series 2. Edited by William L. McDowell Jr.

EAID   *Early American Indian Documents, 1607–1789.* 27 vols. General editor, Alden T. Vaughan. Washington, DC: University Publications of America, 1979–2004.

EFL   America and West Indies, Original Correspondence, Board of Trade and Secretary of State: East Florida, 1763–1777. CO 5/540–73. British National Archives.

FHO   The Indian Frontier in British East Florida: Letters to Governor James Grant from Soldiers and Indian Traders at Fort St. Marks of Apalache, 1763–1784. Edited by James Hill. Florida History Online.

Gage   Thomas Gage Papers, 1754–1807, American Series. William L. Clements Library.

General de Indias   Transcriptions of Records from Portada del Archivo General de Indias, Texas Tech University Center in Seville, Spain, Edward E. Ayer Manuscript Collection, MS #1236, Newberry Library, Chicago.

GGL 1779   George Galphin Letters, 1777–1779. South Carolina Historical Society.

GGL 1780   George Galphin Letters, 1778–1780. Newberry Library.

GGZ   Georgia Gazette, 1763–1776. University of North Texas.

HL   *The Papers of Henry Laurens, 1746–1792.* Edited by Philip M. Hamer and
              David R. Chesnutt. 16 vols. Columbia, SC, 1968–2003.

Indian Affairs   America and West Indies, Original Correspondence. Secretary of
              State: Indian Affairs, 1763–1784. CO 5/65–CO5/82. British National Archives.

Payne   John Howard Payne Papers, 1794–1842. 14 vols. Edward E. Ayer Manuscript
              Collection, Newberry Library

Penn Gazette   *Pennsylvania Gazette,* 1728–1800. South Caroliniana Library.

Plantations General   Records of the Colonial Office: Original Correspondence, Plan-
              tations General, 1689–1952. CO 323. British National Archives.

SCCJ   South Carolina Journals of His Majesty's Council, 1721–1774. ST0704-
              ST0712. South Carolina Department of Archives and History.

SCG   *South Carolina Gazette,* 1732–1775. South Caroliniana Library.

WHL   William Henry Lyttleton Papers, 1756–1760, William L. Clements Library.

NOTES

Introduction

1. Edmond Atkin to Henry Ellis, 25 January 1760, Henry Ellis Papers.
2. Ibid.
3. Ibid.
4. Ibid.
5. SCG, 6 October 1759 ("Frenchified"); Henry Ellis to William Henry Lyttleton, 5 February 1760, WHL, box 11: June–August 1759 ("worst person"); Council in Savannah with Henry Ellis, 10 October 1759, in Candler, *Colonial Records of the State of Georgia*, 7:160–67 ("lying Talks"); Lyttleton to Captain Paul Demere, 20 March 1759, Letterbooks of William Henry Lyttleton ("Fort"); SCG, 22 March 1760 ("neuter"); Atkin to Ellis, 25 January 1760 ("Commission"); Atkin to Lyttleton, 17 June 1759, WHL, box 11 (Ufylegey).
6. Atkin to Lyttleton, 13 February 1760, WHL, box 14 ("ill"); Atkin to Ellis, 25 January 1760; Atkin to Lyttleton, 2 October 1759, WHL, box 12: September–October 1759 ("Madness"); Ellis to Lyttleton, 16 October 1759, WHL, box 12 ("conduct," "discontent"); Ellis to Lyttleton, 27 August 1759, WHL, box 11 ("Journey"); Corkran, *Creek Frontier*, 200–201; Juricek, *Colonial Georgia and the Creeks*, 236–40.
7. For the colonial archives, see Stoler, *Along the Archival Grain*; Mt. Pleasant, Wigginton, and Wisecup, "Materials and Methods in Native American and Indigenous Studies"; Fuentes, *Dispossessed Lives*; Hartman, *Lose Your Mother*; Kimmerer, *Braiding Sweetgrass*; Mihesuah, *Natives and Academics*; Mihesuah, *So You Want to Write About American Indians?*; Trouillot, *Silencing the Past*; Farge, *Allure of the Archives*.
8. Atkin to Ellis, 25 January 1760; Corkran, *Creek Frontier*, 200–201.
9. Piker, *Four Deaths of Acorn Whistler*, 79.
10. Saunt, "Native South," 54.
11. Miles, *Ties That Bind*; A. P. Hudson, *Real Native Genius*; Anderson, *Betrayal of Faith*; Little, *Many Captivities of Esther Wheelwright*; Cleves, *Charity and Sylvia*; Pulsipher, *Swindler Sachem*; Oberg, *Professional Indian*; Oberg, *Uncas*; Piker, *Four Deaths of Acorn Whistler*; Hahn, *Life and Times of Mary Musgrove*; Crane, *Killed Strangely*; Shannon, *Indian Captive, Indian King*; Perdue, *Cherokee Women*; Rountree, *Pocahontas, Powhatan, and Opechancanough*; Dunbar, *Never Caught*, xi.

12. Pearsall et al., "Centering Families in Atlantic History"; Morgan, *Laboring Women;* Palmer, *Intimate Bonds;* Rothman, *Notorious in the Neighborhood;* Scott and Hebrard, *Freedom Papers;* Gordon-Reed, *Hemingses of Monticello.*

13. Trivellato, *Familiarity of Strangers;* Hancock, *Citizens of the World;* Beiler, *Immigrant and Entrepreneur;* O'Neill, *Opened Letter;* Matson, *Merchants and Empire.*

14. Romney, *New Netherland Connections;* Stoler, "Tense and Tender Ties"; Stoler, *Haunted by Empire;* Rothschild, *Inner Life of Empires;* Ghosh, *Sex and the Family in Colonial India;* Perry, *Colonial Relations;* Pearsall, *Atlantic Families.*

15. Hyde, *Empires, Nations, and Families;* Demos, *Unredeemed Captive;* Lewis, *Pursuit of Happiness;* Hurtado, *Intimate Frontiers;* Catton, *Rainy Lake House;* Graybill, *Red and the White;* Isaac, *Landon Carter's Uneasy Kingdom.*

16. Stremlau, *Sustaining the Cherokee Family;* Child, *Boarding School Seasons;* Peterson, *Indians in the Family;* Brooks, *Our Beloved Kin;* Inman, *Brothers and Friends;* Adams, *Who Belongs?;* Saunt, *Black, White, and Indian;* Doerfler, *Those Who Belong;* Bohaker, "'Nindoodemag'"; McDonnell, *Masters of Empire;* Frank, *Creeks and Southerners;* Sleeper-Smith, *Indian Women and French Men;* Denial, *Making Marriage;* Demos, *Unredeemed Captive.*

17. Piker, *Four Deaths of Acorn Whistler,* 102, 136–37.

18. Fullagar, *Warrior, the Voyager, and the Artist,* 9.

19. Blackhawk, *Violence over the Land,* 1, 5, 9.

20. DuVal, *Independence Lost,* xiv, xix.

Chapter One

1. Chekilli Speech. Also printed in *CRG,* 20:381–87.

2. Grantham, *Creation Myths and Legends of the Creek Indians,* 57 ("hegemonic"). Eighteenth-century Muscogee peoples were made up of a diverse set of ethnic and language groups that included the Alabama, Hitchiti, Tallapoosa, Abeka, Hitchiti, and Yuchi, among others.

3. Hahn, "Cussita Migration Legend," 57–59.

4. Chekilli Speech.

5. Ibid.

6. The four brothers not only assumed leadership of the *talwa* in one another's absence but also served as one another's proxies to imperial authorities, as Sempoyaffee did when "desired by the Young Lieutenant [Escotchaby] to tell the Superintendent that he was still his friend & Brother" despite staying home because "his Wife was Sick." At a Meeting of the Head Men of the Upper Creek Nation, 14 July 1 763, *CRG,* 10:70–71; Proceedings of the Picolata Congress, 21 January 1766, Gage, vol. 47.

7. John Stuart to James Grant, 15 March 1769, in Hill, *Spanish Correspondence concerning the Uchiz Indians* ("Land Affairs"). As Thomas Nairne observed in 1708, Muscogee peoples "reckon all their fameiles from the mothers side and have not the least regard who is their father . . . the greatest Judgment in the world [is] reckoning kindred from the woman's side." Nairne, *Nairne's Muskhogean Journals,* 61–62.

8. C. Hudson, *Southeastern Indians*, 184 (family and kinship); Green, *Politics of Indian Removal*, 14–15 (kinship); Journal of the Proceedings of a Congress at Augusta, 12–14 November 1768, GAGE, vol. 137 ("old man"); Edmond Atkin to Henry Ellis, 25 January 1760, Henry Ellis Papers ("eldest," "Second Man of Coweta"); Atkin to William Henry Lyttleton, 17 June 1759, WHL, box 11 ("ruling"); John Stuart to James Grant, 15 March 1769, in Hill, *Spanish Correspondence concerning the Uchiz Indians* ("privilege"); Juan Josef Eligio de la Puente, 26 December 1777, *FHO* (Spanish East Florida).

9. C. Hudson, *Southeastern Indians*, 192–93 ("social entity"). As Charles Hudson describes the clan, it "was a category of people who believed themselves to be blood relatives, but who could not actually trace their relationships to each other through known ancestral links" and nonetheless treated one another as family based upon their clan relationships. C. Hudson, *Southeastern Indians*, 185–86, 190–92. For more details about Muscogee peoples and matrilineal kinship, see Hewitt and Swanton, "Notes on the Creek Indians"; Braund, "Guardians of Tradition and Handmaidens to Change"; Bell, "Separate People"; Speck, "Creek Indians of Taskigi Town."

10. Historians and anthropologists have pieced together the following clans of the Muscogee world (some of which may or may not have existed in the eighteenth century and some of which may have been merely subsets of other clans): Bear, Wind, Panther, Tiger, Deer, Turkey, Eagle (or Bird, Hawk), Fox, Raccoon, Beaver, Fish, Alligator, Snake, Buzzard, Skunk, Rabbit, Mud-Potato, Wolf, Toad, and Otter. Speck, "Creek Indians of Taskigi Town," 115; Nairne, *Nairne's Muskhogean Journals*, 60; Hewitt and Swanton, "Notes on the Creek Indians," 128–29.

11. The extenuating evidence comes from several reports that Sempoyaffee and Escotchaby were Togulki's "uncles." In one instance Sempoyaffee identified himself as Togulki's uncle and as "deputed to speak for him and all the rest present who are the head Men." Togulki was of the Tiger clan, and as uncles in a matrilineal society, where uncles took a very active role in teaching children, it may be likely that Sempoyaffee and Escotchaby were a part of the Tiger family as well. Provincial Congress with the Headmen of Coweta and Cusseta, 10 October 1759, *EAID*, 11:300–304; Corkran, *Creek Frontier*, 172–73, 200, 282–83; Haynes, *Patrolling the Border*, 30.

12. In the aftermath of the Long Cane crisis in January 1764, it was reported that one of Sempoyaffee's sons had been involved and that all the culprits were "of such note and influence in the nation (chiefly of the Bear family, one of the greatest in it)." *SCG*, 28 January 1764.

13. Piker, *Four Deaths of Acorn Whistler*, 101–2; James Wright to the Earl of Hillsborough, 8 December 1770, *CRG*, vol. 37, pt. 2, 489–90 (Tiger clan, "principal"); William McIntosh to John Stuart, 29 May 1777, EFL, CO 5/557, 607–9 ("numerably"); *SCG*, 28 January 1764 ("Bear").

14. It should be noted that despite punishing the act of adultery, Muscogee peoples "did not restrict women's sexual affairs" in general, because Muscogee women possessed the right "to make use of her body" however she wished. Frank, *Creeks and Southerners*, 37; C. Hudson, *Southeastern Indians*, 232.

15. C. Hudson, *Southeastern Indians*, 192–93, 195 (taboos); Speck, "Creek Indians

of Taskigi Town," 115 (taboos); Green, *Politics of Indian Removal,* 4 (identity, clan, justice); Wright, *Creeks and Seminoles,* 18–20 (clan); Griffith, *McIntosh and Weatherford,* 10–11 (clan); Benjamin Hawkins, "A Sketch of the Creek Country in the Years 1798 and 1799," in Foster, *Collected Works of Benjamin Hawkins,* 73 ("maternal"), 74 (adultery, "crop," "satisfaction"); Letter by Juan Josef Eligio de la Puente, 26 December 1777, General de Indias ("Youth"); Alexander Cameron to John Stuart, 1 March 1774, Board of Trade and Secretaries of State: America and West Indies, Original Correspondence—Indian Affairs, Surveys, Etc. CO 5/75, folder 79, (satisfaction).

16. This is also referred to as matrilocal residency. Ethridge, *Creek Country,* 74.

17. Ibid. (*huti,* matrilineage, "land"); C. Hudson, *Southeastern Indians,* 190 ("lineages"), 192–93 ("membership"), 213 ("block"), 292 (gardens), 313 (lands); Hewitt and Swanton, "Notes on the Creek Indians," 128 (*huti*); Braund, "Guardians of Tradition and Handmaidens to Change," 240–41 (*huti*); Green, *Politics of Indian Removal,* 5–6 (matrilocal residence, clan); Griffith, *McIntosh and Weatherford,* 11 (matrilocal residence); Slaughter, *William Bartram,* 563–66 (buildings).

18. It is important to recognize that Creation Stories are stories—oral traditions—handed down across generations, in contrast to myths and legends, as these stories have been characterized for centuries. These are stories with real meaning and purpose in the Muscogee world, which defy the mythical or fantastical elements that are implied when people call them legends or myths. Smithers, *Native Southerners,* 19, 24; Woodward, *Woodward's Reminiscences of the Creek,* 16–17.

19. The Cusseta Migration Story was one of many different versions of the same Creation Story. As US agent Benjamin Hawkins clarified in the 1790s: "There is some diversity in the accounts given by the Muskhogees of their origin," such as the delegation of *micos* who traveled to Washington, DC, in 1826 and related how "the nation had issued out of a cave near the Alabama river" rather than emerging out of the ground to the west as told by Chigelli in 1735. In addition Louis Leclerc Milfort asserted that the Muscogee peoples' ancestors "set their course toward the north" out of Mexico and "went up as far as the headwaters of the Red River" and eastward until they settled along the Chattahoochee, Oconee, and Ogeechee Rivers. Meanwhile Thomas Woodward recounted in the late 1780s how "the Muscogees, from their own account, made but a short stay on the Mississippi . . . [and] emigrated to Alabama and Georgia," and he was "inclined to credit the Indian tradition." William Bartram similarly recounted in 1773 that "if we are to give credit to the account the Creeks give of themselves . . . [they] established themselves after their emigration from the west, beyond the Mississippi, their original native country. . . . On this long journey they suffered great and innumerable difficulties." There is also Benjamin Hawkins's account from the 1790s that "all tradition[s] among the Creeks points to the country west of the Mississippi, as the original habitant of those tribes . . . on the authority of Tusseloiah Micco" and that they "spread out from thence to Oc-mul-gee, O-co-nee, Savannah [Rivers], and down on the seacoast, towards Charleston." Meanwhile Caleb Swan stated in 1791 that it was during the migration west that Muscogee peoples gradually coalesced and "gained attachment" to each other. There is also the Tuckabatchee account of the Cusseta Migration Story, in which "two Coweta men came from the

northwest. . . . This produced more people who came flocking around," after which they came to the Tuckabatchee, who appointed the Cowetas as "the leaders" and "drifted eastward until they came to the sea." Or as Legus Perryman described to John Swanton more than a century later, the "Coweta say that they came out from under the earth and . . . traveled eastward slowly, stopping a long time where the hunting was good . . . until they came at last to a river . . . [and] traveled on again eastward" until "they found . . . the Ocean." Perryman, though, identified the emergence point of the Cowetas—"Il'afoni, 'the backbone'"—as the Rocky Mountains. All of this is a testament to the great diversity of Creation Stories and how their meanings changed over time but still reflected the core foundational beliefs for Muscogee peoples. Milfort, *Memoirs*, 103, 113–14, 162–65, 181–82; Woodward, *Woodward's Reminiscences of the Creek*, 16–17, 25; Slaughter, *William Bartram*, 67; Hawkins, "Sketch of the Creek Country in the Years 1798 and 1799," 13–14, 19, 81–83; Caleb Swan Journal Extracts, 2 May 1791, B284.d.vol.32, American Philosophical Society, Philadelphia; Grantham, *Creation Myths and Legends of the Creek Indians*, 130–31, 162–64.

20. Smithers, *Native Southerners*, 15–16 ("meaning"); Grantham, *Creation Myths and Legends of the Creek Indians*, 5–6, 84 ("accounting," sacred time); John Stuart to William Tryon, 28 May 1766, *Colonial and State Records of North Carolina*, 7: 213–15 ("importance"); Nairne, *Nairne's Muskhogean Journals*, 36 ("Mississippi"); Pope, *Tour through the Southern and Western Territories*, 52–54 ("ten thousand"); Green, *Politics of Indian Removal*, 5 (maternal uncles).

21. Muscogee peoples generally thought that the "Upper World, the world beyond the sky, was the realm of powerful spiritual beings and departed souls. It was permeated with powers of perfection, order, permanence, clarity, and periodicity. The Lower World, the world below the earth and the waters, was also perceived as the habitat of many powerful spiritual beings. It was the realm of powers exactly contrary to those of the Upper World: reversals, madness, creativity, fertility, and chaos. These two worlds, permeated with different and opposing forces, should not, however, be thought of in the European sense of good and evil, but only as different and opposing." Grantham, *Creation Myths and Legends of the Creek Indians*, 21; Leitch, *Creeks and Seminoles*, 24–25.

22. As John Pope observed of Muscogee peoples after the American Revolution, "No People under Heaven are more attached to, or swerve less from, the Customs of their Ancestors than the Creeks." Pope, *Tour through the Southern and Western Territories*, 62.

23. In several variations of Muscogee Creation Stories, tobacco is considered "the greatest medicine there is," with many functions, including symbolizing the peace between peoples (hence smoking tobacco to produce white smoke) and serving as an offering at the water's edge in hopes of safe crossing (the crossing of water being similar to the crossing into the Lower World). Grantham, *Creation Myths and Legends of the Creek Indians*, 239–40.

24. Philemon Kemp to James Wright, 9 June 1771, *DAR*, 3:118–21 (Above); Pope, *Tour through the Southern and Western Territories*, 52–55 ("Taker"); *SCG*, 9 June 1773 (Giver of Breath); Tallassee King to the Georgia Governor and Council, 20 September

1784, CIT ("Master of the Breath"); Talk from the Mortar and Handsome Fellow, 8 May 1763, *CRG,* 9:70–77 ("All"); Letter 16, Bossu, *Travels in the Interior of North America,* 141–51 (Life); "Congress with the Lower Creeks at Augusta: Proceedings Following the Treaty," 14 November 1768, *EAID,* 12:75–78 ("Land"); Proceedings of the Assembled Estates of the Lower Creek Nation, 11 August 1739, CIT ("Ancestors," "Custom"); Upper Creeks to Henry Ellis, 25 April 1760, *EAID,* 11:316–17 ("Bones"); Grantham, *Creation Myths and Legends of the Creek Indians,* 12 (Worlds), 54 (dreams, visions), 239–40; Hawkins, "Sketch of the Creek Country in the Years 1798 and 1799," 80; Swanton, *Creek Religion and Medicine,* 484 (fire, Grandfather); 490 (snakes), 495–96 (birds), 515 (dreams, visions), 523–24 (dances), 549 (totems), 636–38 (medicines); Talk from the Upper Creeks to the Lower Creeks, 23 March 1774, Indian Affairs, CO 5/75, folder 71 ("Bodies"); John Stuart, Map of the Southern Indian District in America, 1764, Plantations General, CO 323/17, folder 240 ("Beast").

25. Grantham, *Creation Myths and Legends of the Creek Indians,* 21 (Worlds, precarious, "opposing"); 1 July 1735, in Reese, *Our First Visit in America,* 205 ("above," "dark").

26. While historians have long articulated that Muscogee peoples distinguished themselves from one another on account of their settlement patterns—the Upper *talwas* were located along the Tallapoosa, Coosa, and Alabama Rivers, and the Lower *talwas* were located along the Chattahoochee, Flint, and Ocmulgee Rivers—and political interests, it is important to note how the Upper and Lower *talwas* likely represented another manifestation of the moiety system and the cosmic balance that were so important to eighteenth-century Muscogee worldviews. Braund, *Deerskins and Duffels,* 6–7.

27. It should be noted that J. Leitch Wright Jr. believes that the importance of the moiety system declined considerably over the course of the eighteenth century. Wright, *Creeks and Seminoles,* 16–18.

28. The Upper Creeks to John Stuart, 20 April 1767, *EAID,* 12:335 ("different nation," "intermeddle"); George Galphin to the S.C. Council of Safety, 15 October 1775, in *HL,* 10:467–69 (Coweta/Cusseta, red/white towns); Braund, *Deerskins and Duffels,* 7 ("councils"); Caleb Swan Journal Extracts, 2 May 1791, 33–34 (*micos*/war leaders); Ethridge, *Creek Country,* 94 (moieties, red/white); Piker, *Four Deaths of Acorn Whistler,* 146–47 (moieties, red/white); Lankford, "Red and White," 75–77 (moieties, red/white); Smith, *Coosa,* 60 (moieties); Juricek, *Colonial Georgia and the Creeks,* 3 (moieties); Hewitt and Swanton, "Notes on the Creek Indians," 124–25 (civil/military balance), 128 (Hathagalgi, Tcilokogalga, "Whites," "red"); Green, *Politics of Indian Removal,* 7, 11–12 (moiety system, Hathagalgi, Tcilokogalga, Upper/Lower); Leitch, *Creeks and Seminoles,* 3, 17 (Upper/Lower, moiety system).

29. In all their variations, Muscogee Creation Stories involve a Corn Woman or Corn Mother, who not only gave life to her people by birthing children but also cultivated corn from the earth to feed her family and community. In many of these stories, Corn Mother or Corn Woman produced corn from her body, in some cases by washing her feet or shedding sores. According to one story, Corn Woman stumbled upon orphan children, whom she took under her care, and "she rubbed herself as one rubs

roasting ears and made bread of what came off." She then informed the children, "I am your mother. You can eat bread made out of [my] white corn." The next day, Corn Woman was nowhere to be found, but when the children went to the corncrib "and opened the door . . . it was full of corn." In other variations Corn Woman likewise sacrificed her body to feed her people. Grantham, *Creation Myths and Legends of the Creek Indians*, 235–53.

30. Piker, *Okfuskee*, 163–65 (generative, destructive powers); Stern, *Lives in Objects*, 25–26 ("fertility"); Bell, "Separate People," 333–34 (menstruation, pregnancy), 335 (*hompita haya, sofki*); Talk from George Galphin to the Tallassee King, 7 November 1779, GGL 1780 ("Mother"); *SCG*, 31 January 1774 ("Mother Towns"); Hahn, *Invention of the Creek Nation*, 12–13 (foundation/mother towns); Treaty Proceedings at the Ogeechee Congress, 17 June 1777, GGL 1779 ("Breast"); C. Hudson, *Southeastern Indians*, 268 (female custody); Perdue, *Cherokee Women*, 29 (menstruation, pregnancy); Braund, *Deerskins and Duffels*, 14–15 (menstruation, pregnancy); Speck, "Creek Indians of Taskigi Town," 116 (segregation, pregnancy); Griffith, *McIntosh and Weatherford*, 14–15 (female labors, separation).

31. Hahn, *Life and Times of Mary Musgrove*, 9 (genders, labors); C. Hudson, *Southeastern Indians*, 259 (genders, labors); Braund, "Guardians of Tradition and Handmaidens to Change," 242–43 (complementary gender roles, preservation); Frank, *Creeks and Southerners*, 27 (genders); Piker, *Okfuskee*, 190 (genders); LeMaster, *Brothers Born of One Mother*, 71 (genders); Bell, "Separate People," 332 (generative power), 333–34 (genders, separation),

32. This phenomenon is similar to what James Taylor Carson calls the "vernacular of paths" and roads. Carson, *Making an Atlantic World*, 78–79.

33. Letter 16, Bossu, *Travels in the Interior of North America*, 141–51 ("earth," blood, "land"); Jacobs, *Appalachian Indian Frontier*, 62 ("peace"); 11 February 1760, WHL, box 14 (peace with all); Upper Creek Headmen to John Stuart, 1 May 1771, *EAID*, 12:97 ("white"); Philemon Kemp to James Wright, 9 June 1771, *DAR*, 3:118–21 ("road"); Tallassee King to the Georgia Governor and Council, 20 September 1784, *CIT*, 159–60 (emblems); Proceedings of the First Picolata Congress, 15–18 November 1765, *EAID*, 12:454–62 ("giving," "mind"); Upper Creek "Great Talk" to John Stuart, 4 February 1774, *EAID*, 12:136–37 (white); Talk from the Upper Creeks to the Lower Creeks ("Earth").

34. Piker also notes "there were many variations on the basic formulae for the Creek Busk, a ceremony that could last for eight days" or as little as three. Each Busk differed in variation from *talwa* to *talwa*, given that the Busk in Coweta was likely practiced slightly differently than in Tallassee or Chehaw. Piker, *Okfuskee*, 162; Swanton, *Creek Religion and Medicine*, 568–89, 604–5.

35. Swanton, "Green Corn Dance," 178 (Busk, forgiveness); Piker, *Okfuskee*, 112–15 (town square), 117–18 (Busk); Green, *Politics of Indian Removal*, 15–16 (Busk, *poskita*); Thomas Brown to the Earl of Cornwallis, 16 July 1780, Charles Cornwallis Papers (ripening); C. Hudson, *Southeastern Indians*, 366–67 (cosmic balance, Middle World), 374–75 ("turning point"); Grantham, *Creation Myths and Legends of the Creek Indians*, 81–82 (cosmic balance, Middle World); Milfort, *Memoirs*, 135 (quarrels); Stern,

Lives in Objects, 30 (Middle World); Pope, *Tour through the Southern and Western Territories*, 55 (town square); Braund, *Deerskins and Duffels*, 15 (town square); Hawkins, "Sketch of the Creek Country in the Years 1798 and 1799," 80 ("Boosketau"); Wright, *Creeks and Seminoles*, 27 (Mississippian origins); John Stuart to Lord George Germain, 10 August 1778, in Boehm, *Records of the British Public Records Office*, reel 8, vol. 79 ("Feast"); Griffith, *McIntosh and Weatherford*, 19–22 (Busk).

36. To "make new fire," the ceremony leader "took the fire, and kindled it on the hearth in the [town] square." The leader of the Busk then took seven kernels from the "First Fruits," the first seven ears of the new corn, "marked them, and threw them into the fire, together with a small piece of meat, praying this being done the women and children might partake of the new fruits." Letter from John Howard Payne (1835), qtd. in Corkran, *Creek Frontier*, 36–39.

37. After purifying themselves, two men and two women were appointed singers to lead the male and female dancers in the turkey dance (*pine obungau*), tadpole dance (*toccoyulegau*), long dance (*obungau chapco*), mad dance (*obungau haujo*), and gun dance (*itsh obungau*), all in celebration of the First Fruits. In accordance with the separation of genders in the Muscogee world, "the women danced in a place by themselves, the men danced in the square ground" until night. Hawkins, "Sketch of the Creek Country in the Years 1798 and 1799," 75–80.

38. *Daily Register*, 9 July 1751, in Urlsperger, *Detailed Reports on the Salzburger Emigrants*, 15:88–89 (gender separations); Stern, *Lives in Objects*, 30 (men/women); C. Hudson, *Southeastern Indians*, 366–68, 371–74 (Busk), 375 (gender separations); Speck, "Creek Indians of Taskigi Town," 142 (Busk); letter from John Howard Payne (Busk); Grantham, *Creation Myths and Legends of the Creek Indians*, 67–69, 74–82 (Busk); Swanton, *Creek Religion and Medicine*, 548–57, 568–71 (Busk); Hewitt and Swanton, "Notes on the Creek Indians," 151 (Busk).

39. Bossu, letter 16 (seasons, labors, work); Piker, *Okfuskee*, 81 (season, child's labors); Braund, *Deerskins and Duffels*, 14 (child's labors); Braund, "Guardians of Tradition and Handmaidens to Change," 242–43 (child's labors); Ethridge, *Creek Country*, 60–1, 141 (child's labors); 9 July 1751, Urlsperger, *Detailed Reports on the Salzburger Emigrants*, 17:88–89 (child's labors); *Letters of Benjamin Hawkins*, 3 December 1796, 22 (guides, messengers); 24 January 1797, 64 (livestock); Hawkins, "Sketch of the Creek Country in the Years 1798 and 1799," 53 (fishing); Foster, *Archaeology of the Lower Muscogee Creek Indians*, 139 ("intercropping"), 190 (mixed economy); Green, *Politics of Indian Removal*, 3–4 (labors); Griffith, *McIntosh and Weatherford*, 13 (child's labors, fishing).

40. The ball game took place not only "between the Men of the Town" but also at times between specific matrilineages and *talwas*, which often created rivalries such as the one between Yuchi and Chehaw. In addition ball games usually involved some form of wager, "consisting of Broaches, Bracelets, Gorgets, Medals, Paints, Arms and Ammunition . . . [or] whole Family Stock of Food and Raiment." Ball games also served the purpose of resolving conflict between families within the *talwa* as well as between *talwas* themselves, such as the "sister towns" Coweta and Cusseta, which "are always at odds, especially in the ball games." Taitt, "David Taitt's Journal of a

Journey," 517 (8 March 1772), 546 (24 March 1772); Pope, *Tour through the Southern and Western Territories,* 49–51; Speck, "Creek Indians of Taskigi Town," 143.

41. Swanton, *Early History of the Creek Indians and Their Neighbors,* 540 (age restrictions); Swanton, *Creek Religion and Medicine,* 523 (dancing, singing, knowledge), 534–35 (social dances); Slaughter, *William Bartram,* 402 (instruments, "time"), 404 (ball game), 546–48 (chunkey yard); Braund, *Deerskins and Duffels,* 17 ("stone disk," "hurled"); Wright, *Creeks and Seminoles,* 38 (dances); Green, *Politics of Indian Removal,* 10–11 (ball game); Griffith, *McIntosh and Weatherford,* 29–34 (ball game, chunkey, training).

42. Although deer was the most popular animal because of the deerskin trade, men also hunted bear, beaver, buffalo, and other small fur-bearing animals. James Wright to the Earl of Dartmouth, 10 August 1773, *DAR,* 6:202; At a Meeting of the Head Men of the Upper Creek Nation, 14 July 1763, *CRG,* 9:70–77; Green, *Politics of Indian Removal,* 3–4.

43. Talk of Upper and Lower Creeks to Henry Ellis, 25 April 1760, *EAID,* 11:316–17 ("Pains," "Cloathing"); Coweta Origin Migration Story, in Grantham, *Creation Myths and Legends of the Creek Indians,* 130–31 ("earth," "good"); Swanton, *Creek Religion and Medicine,* 516–17 (success).

44. The processing of deerskins was a laborious task that involved scraping the fat and meat from the skins, stretching them on frames to dry in the sun, and then soaking them in a solution of water and deer brains. This was followed by scraping off all the hair, stretching and drying again, then smoking the skins over a firepit, after which they were decorated with dyes and pigments before being smoked one last time. Braund, *Deerskins and Duffels,* 68.

45. Nathaniel Sheidley, "Hunting and the Politics of Masculinity in Cherokee Treaty-Making," 170–71 (hunting and masculinity); James Wright to the Earl of Dartmouth, 10 August 1773, *DAR,* 6:202 ("beloved"); Braund, *Deerskins and Duffels,* 62–68 (hunting season, hunting grounds, family hunting, family labors, winter camps); Piker, *Okfuskee,* 78–79 (hunting labors, gendered labors), 81 (hunting season); Wright, *Creeks and Seminoles,* 63–64 (hunting season, Ogeechee-Oconee, women and men hunting parties); Busso, letter 16 (hunting season); Ethridge, *Creek Country,* 135–36 (hunting grounds); David Taitt to John Stuart, 22 November 1772, *DAR,* 5:224–25 (Tensaw); C. Hudson, *Southeastern Indians,* 18–19 (hunting grounds); Stern, *Lives in Objects,* 23 (those at home).

46. Muscogee territories consisted of a network of inter-*talwa* paths such as the Cusseta Path, Coweta Path, Yuchi Path, and Chehaw Path. Each *talwa* also had its own individual pathways that connected it to the other *talwas* or branched off the Creek Path. Ethridge, *Creek Country,* 122–25.

47. Carson, *Making an Atlantic World,* 81 ("world of paths"); James Wright to Emistisiguo and Creek Indians, 5 September 1768, *CRG,* 9:571–82 (hunting paths); Ethridge, *Creek Country,* 32 ("waterways"), 122–25 (paths, Chickasaw/Cherokee Path); Foster, *Archaeology of the Lower Muscogee Creek Indians,* 33 (paths); Caleb Swan Journal Extracts, 2 May 1791, 11–13 (water systems).

48. Ethridge, *Creek Country,* 103–4 ("dependent"); Stuart, Report and Map of the

Southern Indian District, 1764, Plantations General, CO 323/17, folder 240 ("Exploits"); John Stuart to the Lords Commissioners of Trade and Plantations, n.d., Plantations General, CO 323/17, folder 170 ("War Names"); John Stuart to William Howe, 23 August 1777, British Headquarters Papers of the British Army, 649 ("Quantity," "content"); Green, *Politics of Indian Removal,* 7–8 (military rank, rank/titles); Wright, *Creeks and Seminoles,* 39–40 (warfare); Griffith, *McIntosh and Weatherford,* 23–29 (war titles, warfare).

49. Lankford, "Red and White," 64–65 (generational tensions, balance); Conference between James Wright and the Upper Creeks, 14 April 1774, *DAR,* 8:90–95 ("bloody," "unruly," "peaceful"); Busso, letter 16 (red/white); John Stuart to the Lords Commissioners of Trade and Plantations, ("Plunging"); Treaty Proceedings at the Ogeechee Congress, 17 June 1777, GGL 1779 ("restrained"); The Mortar of Okchai to John Stuart, 20 May 1769, *EAID,* 12:89 ("Heart").

50. Gatschet, *Migration Legend of the Creek Indians,* 159 (puberty); C. Hudson, *Southeastern Indians,* 244 (sex); Hawkins, "Sketch of the Creek Country in the Years 1798 and 1799," 79 (hothouse); Swanton, *Creek Religion and Medicine,* 584 ("war-physic"); Stuart, Report and Map of the Southern Indian District, ("war dance," "Reputation"); Will's Friend and Half-Breed of Okfuskee to George Galphin, 9 June 1778, GGL 1779 (eagle dance); Myer, "Indian Trails of the Southeast," 749–50 (war paths); 12 August 1725, Fitch, "Journal of Captain Tobias Fitch," 12 August 1725, 191 ("Strong"); McLoughlin, "Cherokee Anomie," 456 (warfare); Speck, "Creek Indians of Taskigi Town," 118 (warfare); 29 April 1752, in Salley, *Journal of the Commons House of Assembly,* 261 (attacks); Roderick McIntosh to John Stuart, 16 November 1767, *EAID,* 12:340–41 (prisoners); Legardere to Governor Johnstone, 27 March 1766, *EAID,* 12:292–93 (trophies); Stuart, Report and Map of the Southern Indian District (tokens).

51. Taitt, "David Taitt's Journal of a Journey through the Creek Country," 22 May 1772, 558 (return from war, trophies); Hawkins, "Sketch of the Creek Country in the Years 1798 and 1799," 70 (war name), 78–79 (Busk, ceremony, grits, physic, emetics, sweating, visions, water); Piker, *Four Deaths of Acorn Whistler,* 184 ("remains"); Stuart, Report and Map of the Southern Indian District, ("Respect"); Bell, "Separate People," 336–37 (Busk); James Grant to John Stuart, 1 February 1769, *FHO* and Ballindalloch (one eye); Green, *Politics of Indian Removal,* 8 (manhood initiation, name); Griffith, *McIntosh and Weatherford,* 24–25 (initiation).

52. Protocols included sitting in arranged fashion in the warrior's cabin, drinking *cassina* and smoking tobacco to cleanse body and mind, sweating and bathing to purify, listening to and observing the hierarchy of authority in council with *micos,* and a host of other responsibilities. Speck, "Creek Indians of Taskigi Town," 116 (new responsibilities); Bell, "Separate People," 336–37 (new responsibilities); Hawkins, "Sketch of the Creek Country in the Years 1798 and 1799," 71 (warrior's cabin); Milfort, *Memoirs,* 91–92 (*cassina,* town square councils).

53. Speck, "Creek Indians of Taskigi Town," 116 (new responsibilities); Bell, "Separate People," 336–37 (new responsibilities); Hawkins, "Sketch of the Creek Country in the Years 1798 and 1799," 76–77 (Busk, men's dances); Swanton, *Creek Religion and*

Medicine, 538–39 (town square councils, ceremonies); Pope, *Tour through the Southern and Western Territories*, 55–56 (abstinence).

Chapter Two

1. George Galphin to Vice President Parker, 4 November 1750, *EAID*, 9:213–14 ("writing"); James Glen to the Lords Commissioners for Trade and Plantations, 2 October 1750, James Glen Papers ("Emperor"); George Galphin to Commissioner Pinckney, 3 November 1750, *DRIA 1*, 4–5 ("Officers").

2. Last Will and Testament of George Galphin (Metawney); Galphin to Parker, 4 November 1750 ("Convercation," "mistchef," "willing").

3. Galphin to Parker, 4 November 1750 ("head war king"); Stephen Forrester to James Grant, spring 1768, Ballindalloch ("warriors").

4. As Piker describes, one's "family connections . . . play[ed] a profound role in Creek politics," given that "family . . . meant clan, the social center of Creek life, just as town was the political center." Thus family not only was "a critical component of eighteenth-century Creek local life" but also was crucial for "structuring political relations within a community" or *talwa*. Piker, *Four Deaths of Acorn Whistler*, 101–2, 136–37.

5. Speck, "Creek Indians of Taskigi Town," III (*talwa*); Braund, *Deerskins and Duffels*, 15 (*talwa*); Hahn, *Invention of the Creek Nation*, 18–19, 123–24 (*talwa*, "independent"); Ethridge, *Creek Country*, 93 (*talwa*); Piker, *Okfuskee*, 7 (*talwa*); Foster, *Archaeology of the Lower Muscogee Creek Indians*, 22 (*talwa*); Piker, *Four Deaths of Acorn Whistler*, 135 (*talwa*); Carter, "Observations of John Stuart and Governor James Grant," 828 ("Republicks"), 829–30 ("contending").

6. Journal of a Conference between the American Commissioners and Creeks at Augusta, 16–19 March 1776, *EAID*, 12:183–90 ("leading Towns"); Hahn, *Invention of the Creek Nation*, 12–13 ("foundation"); Swanton, *Early History of the Creek Indians and Their Neighbors*, 225 ("Tall Coweta"); Grantham, *Creation Myths and Legends of the Creek Indians*, 164–65 (Tuckabatchee-Coweta Alliance).

7. Hahn, *Invention of the Creek Nation*, 3–4 ("Coweta Resolution"), 7–8 ("autonomy," "enterprise"); The Mortar of Okchai to John Stuart, 13 August 1764, *EAID*, 12:14 ("Great Old Path"); Conference between James Wright and the Upper Creeks, 14 April 1774, *DAR*, 8:90–95 ("opened," "shut up," "stop"); Juricek, *Colonial Georgia and the Creeks*, 7 (Creek Path importance to Coweta); William Bull to the Lords Commissioners of Trade, 25 May 1738, James Glen Papers ("inlett"); The Wolf and the Upper Creeks to John Stuart, 1764, *CRG*, 9:148–49 ("law"); Milfort, *Memoirs*, 93–94 ("principal," "assemblies"); Meeting at Fort Augusta, 11 February 1760, WHL, box 14 ("nothing"); Upper Creeks to John Stuart, 20 April 1767, *EAID*, 12:335 ("different nation"); Green, *Politics of Indian Removal*, 20–22 (Brims).

8. The diverse and cosmopolitan nature of Muscogee *talwas* has been well documented. As one Shawnee Indian put it best to English authorities in 1774: "Altho' I am a Shawnese, but am only a visit from the Creek Country which is my Home." Private Intelligence from a Shawanese Indian from Alexander McKee, 1774, Indian Affairs,

CO 5/75, folder 147. See also Salley, "Creek Indian Tribes in 1725"; Slaughter, *William Bartram*, 316–18, 371–73; Emond Atkin to Henry Ellis, 25 January 1760, Henry Ellis Papers; David Taitt to John Stuart, 17 March 1772, in Taitt, "David Taitt's Journal of a Journey through Creek Country"; Milfort, *Memoirs*, 114–15, 185–88; Hawkins, "Sketch of the Creek Country in the Years 1798 and 1799," 14; South Carolina Council Proceedings, 24 January 1726/27, Board of Trade and Secretaries of State: America and West Indies, Original Correspondence—South Carolina, CO 5/387, folder 245; Stuart, Report and Map of the Southern Indian District, 1764, Plantations General, folder 240.

9. Slaughter, *William Bartram*, 563 ("streets"); James Wright to Emistisiguo and Gun Merchant, 25 June 1771, *CRG*, 9:370–71 ("Englishmen"); Daily Register, 19 November 1735, in Ulsperger, *Detailed Reports on the Salzburger Emigrants*, 2:207–08 ("Englishmen"); 2 May 1791, Caleb Swan Journal Extracts, 1790–1791 ("Numbers"); Francis Le Jau, Letter Books of the Society for the Propagation of the Gospel in Foreign Parts, 9 February 1711 ("language"), 1 February 1710 ("parts"); William E. Myer, "Indian Trails of the Southeast," 750, 823, 828, 847 (paths); Ethridge, *Creek Country*, 1 ("purely," "lives"); Green, *Politics of Indian Removal*, 14 (cosmopolitan *talwas*); Wright, *Creeks and Seminoles*, 3–12 (cosmopolitan *talwas*).

10. Even though red and white *talwas*—the moiety system—were essential to the ceremonial, political, and social functions of the eighteenth-century Muscogee world, the designations of red and white towns changed with time depending on a host of factors, including a particular town's war record or certain wagers taken during annual ball games. This is why Cusseta *micos*, despite being of a white *talwa*, identified Cusseta as a "war town" rather than a white *talwa* at certain times. "Proceedings of the First Picolata Congress," 15–17 November 1765, *EAID*, 12:454–62.

11. While maintaining the moiety system was the ideal, it was not always the reality. For instance, Okfuskee breached its own responsibilities as a white *talwa* by killing several of its resident traders in 1760, and because such "mischief was done by the white Town, and not by the War Towns . . . there [is] a great black Cloud spread over our Land." Gun Merchant and Okfuskee Captain to James Wright and Georgia Council, 7 November 1760, *CRG*, 8:417–22.

12. Slaughter, *William Bartram*, 316–18 ("bloody," captives murdered, "sacred," "deputies"); Gatschet, *Migration Legend of the Creek Indians*, 111 (civil-peace leadership), 121 (*kiyapa*); Alexander McGillivray to James Seagrove, 9 October 1792, in US Congress, *American State Papers, Vol. I*, 322 ("War town"); Lankford, "Red and White," 55–56 (red/white, young/elder, "diplomacy"); Hewitt and Swanton, "Notes on the Creek Indians," 124–25 (*kipayalgi*, "affairs"); Conference between James Wright and the Upper Creeks, 14 April 1774, *DAR*, 8:90–95 ("shut up"); Piker, *Four Deaths of Acorn Whistler*, 158 (sister towns); Upper Creek "Great Talk" to John Stuart, 4 February 1774, *EAID*, 12:136–37 ("blood").

13. Based on the timing of the individuals who identified themselves as Coweta's *tustenogy* and/or relinquished that title, we can estimate that Sempoyaffee assumed the mantle in 1746 or 1747. Prior to Sempoyaffee, Coweta's *tustenogy* was Chigelli, who stepped away from that role at the "last Busk" in December 1746/47. Malatchi to

Alexander Heron, 7 December 1747, *EAID*, 11:26; Galphin to Parker, 4 November 1750.

14. Slaughter, *William Bartram*, 316–18 ("bloody"); Gatschet, *Migration Legend of the Creek Indians*, 159 ("Great Warrior," "raids," "one," *micos*); Council Minutes, 9 September 1749, *Board of Trade and Secretaries of State: America and West Indies, Original Correspondence, South Carolina*, CO 5/459, folder 130–37 ("War Dance," "feat"); Stuart, "Map of the Southern Indian District in America," 1764, Plantations General ("Influence," "Bearer"); *SCG*, 12–19 July 1760 ("fond").

15. Hewitt and Swanton "Notes on the Creek Indians," 136 (outlet, stop); Talk from the Lower Creek Headmen to Governor James Glen, 25 July 1750, SCCJ (scouts); Affidavit of Joseph Dawes, 4 August 1772, *DAR*, 5:162 ("for war"); Patrick Carr to George Galphin, 4 November 1778, GGL 1779; Gatschet, *Migration Legend of the Creek Indians*, 168 (war leader–*mico* deliberations, "interpose"); Alexander Wylly to Captain Croft, 10 May 1740, BD-SC CO 5/368, folder 13 ("War Cabin," "Whoop"); A Treaty between South Carolina and Creek Nation, 25 June 1753, BD-SC, CO 5/374, folder 157 (outlet); Green, *Politics of Indian Removal*, 7–9 (political authority); Wright, *Creeks and Seminoles*, 17–18 (political authority).

16. Alexander Wylly to William Bull, 10 May 1740, BD-SC, folder 179 ("corn"); Chicken, "Journal of Colonel George Chicken," 2 August 1725, 115–17 (Head Warrior, "Warr"); Interpreter's Report on James Oglethorpe's Talk with the Chehaw War Captains, 7 April 1743, *EAID*, 12:108–9 ("Powder"); Emistisiguo's Talk to John Stuart, 19 April 1772, Indian Affairs, CO 5/73, folder 272–73; Speck, "Creek Indians of Taskigi Town," 114 (religious specialist); Green, *Politics of Indian Removal*, 8 (*hills haya*); GGZ, 25 May 1774 ("physic," "M"); Grantham, *Creation Myths and Legends of the Creek Indians*, 51, 53 ("bundle," "objects," "proper"); *Belfast News Letter*, 6 June 1760 ("marks"); *SCG*, 14 February 1774 ("Club").

17. To reinforce the "red" nature of such actions, the canoes that Muscogee men traveled in during their expeditions were called "red canoes . . . of war." Alexander Wylly to William Bull, 10 May 1740, BD-SC, folder 179.

18. John Stuart to the Earl of Hillsborough, 12 June 1772, *DAR*, 5:114–17 ("conquest"); 10 May 1740, BD-SC, folder 179 (painted, travel); Caleb Swan Journal Extracts, 2 May 1791 ("War Path"); Stuart to the Earl of Dartmouth, 13 February 1774, *DAR*, 8:48–49 ("ambush"); Provincial Council Talk with a Lower Creek War Party, 14 April 1760, *EAID*, 11:313–16 ("Scalps," "Songs"); George Galphin to Commissioner Pinckney, 3 November 1750, *DRIA 1*, 4–5 (captives, "400"); James Glen to the Lords Commissioners for Trade and Plantations, July 1750, Dalhousie Muniments Papers, 87–88 ("burn't"); Cherokee Vertical Files, 27 August 1776 ("Property"), 1 October 1776 ("line"); Fitch, "Journal of Captain Tobias Fitch," 8 November 1725, 201 (song); Roderick McIntosh to John Stuart, 16 November 1767, *EAID*, 12:340–41 ("Physicking," "mourning").

19. As John Swanton described the office of the *tustenogy*: "He was the Sheriff or Chief of Police within the town as well as the Head Warrior outside of it." Hewitt and Swanton, "Notes on the Creek Indians," 136.

20. Conference between Governor James Wright and Upper Creek Leaders, 14

April 1774, *DAR*, 8:90–95 ("mischief"); Talk from Escotchaby to John Stuart, 26 April 1770, *DAR*, 86–87 ("stop"); A Treaty between the Government of South Carolina and the Creek Nation, 25 June 1753, BD-SC, CO 5/374, folder 157 ("Home," "ill will"); *Penn Gazette*, 30 August 1753 (investigation); Fitch, "Journal of Captain Tobias Fitch," 12 August 1725, 191 ("Strong"); Stuart, Report and Map of the Southern Indian District (stain).

21. When the young men took matters into their own hands and indiscriminately killed Europeans, the *tustenogy* by necessity joined the other *micos* in pledging "friendship and fidelity" despite potentially cultivating the "hostilities" of their young people. *GGZ*, 30 August 1764.

22. Hewitt and Swanton, "Notes on the Creek Indians," 139 (town councils); Post-Talk Conference with Upper Creeks, n.d. 1771, *CRG* 38 I-A: 254–61 (Chickasaw); Cherokee Vertical Files, 1 October 1776 (Chote); Henry Laurens to John Rutledge, 1 December 1777, in *HL*, 12:117 ("Rattle Trap"); Charles Stuart to John Stuart, 17 June 1770, *DAR*, 2:108–10 ("prejudice," "hunt"); *Penn Gazette*, 30 August 1753; A Treaty between the Government of South Carolina and the Creek Nation, 25 June 1753, BD-SC, CO 5/374, folder 157 ("Room").

23. Hewitt and Swanton, "Notes on the Creek Indians," 151 ("immemorial," "health," "Land"); Affidavit of Joseph Dawes, 4 August 1772, *DAR*, 5:162 ("guns"); Stuart, "Map of the Southern Indian District in America" ("white people").

24. Fitch, "Journal of Captain Tobias Fitch," 20 July 1725, 178; Piker, *Okfuskee*, 176–77 (generational tensions); Lankford, "Red and White," 64–65, 75–77 (generational tensions, manhood); 2 May 1791, Caleb Swan Journal Extracts ("rage"); Charles Stuart to John Stuart, *DAR*, 103–04 (reputation); John Stuart to the Lords Commissioners of Trade and Plantations, n.d., Plantations General, CO 323/17, folder 170 ("Plunge").

25. George Galphin to James Glen, 24 August 1753, SCCJ, Roll ST 0709 (Sempoyaffee, "long," "Norward"); *Belfast News Letter*, 6 June 1760 ("marks"); Treaty between South Carolina and Creek Nation, 25 June 1753, BD-SC, CO 5/374, folder 157 ("restrained"); *SCG*, 12–19 July 1760 ("madmen").

26. Affidavit of Joseph Dawes, 4 August 1772, *DAR*, 5:162 (white people); Charles Stuart to John Stuart, 17 June 1770, *DAR*, 2:108–10 (white people, "hunt"); James Glen to the Board of Trade, 14 April 1756, BD-SC, CO 5/375, folder 97 ("ill blood"); Treaty Proceedings at the Ogeechee Congress, 17 June 1777, GGL 1779 ("Nation").

27. As Claudio Saunt observes, "Creek towns and clans were joined by their common commitment to the white path that existed in constant tension with the red," and despite dabbling in the red path at times, it was the duty of the *talwa*'s leaders, particularly the *micos* and *tustenogy*, to maintain peace among their peoples and with other groups. Saunt, *New Order of Things*, 22.

28. Conference between James Wright and the Upper Creeks ("ancestors"); Cherokee Chiefs to John Stuart, 22 September 1766, Plantations General, CO 323/24, folder 98; *SCG*, 12–19 July 1760 ("unanimously"); James Glen to Malatchi, the Wolf King, the Red Coat King, the Otassee King, and other Creek Headmen, May 1753, James Glen Papers ("kindle"); *Penn Gazette*, 30 August 1753 ("complied," "washed").

29. Sempoyaffee's ascendancy as *tustenogy* came in the wake of the decades-long political upheavals resulting from the Yamasee War, a war that nearly wiped out South Carolina, that brought an end to the Indian slave trade in the South, accelerated the "Africanization" of slavery, and created lasting enmity between the Muscogee, Cherokee, and Haudenosaunee peoples. For more information regarding the Yamasee War, see Ramsey, *Yamasee War;* Gallay, *Indian Slave Trade;* Oatis, *Colonial Complex;* Dubcovsky, *Informed Power;* Ethridge, *Mapping the Mississippian Shatter Zone;* and Shefveland, *Anglo-Native Virginia.*

30. As Hahn has demonstrated in his work on the Coweta Resolution of 1718, the politics of neutrality was pioneered by Brims of Coweta during the early eighteenth century and provided a precedent in the *talwa's* future dealings with Europeans. Hahn, *Invention of the Creek Nation,* 116–19.

31. The relationship between Muscogee peoples and the new Georgia colony has been well documented by Julie Ann Sweet, John T. Juricek, and David H. Corkran. Sweet, *Negotiating for Georgia;* Juricek, *Colonial Georgia and the Creeks;* Corkran, *Creek Frontier.*

32. Fort Toulouse was established after the Treaty of Utrecht in 1717, a "magazine for Trade" that was "converted into a strong and regular Fort." The Representation of Charles Pinckney regarding the Creek Indians, 2 December 1756, BD-SC, CO 5/375, folders 148–50. For further information about Fort Toulouse, see Thomas, *Fort Toulouse.*

33. Colonel Johnson to Board of Trade, 12 January 1719/20, *Board of Trade and Secretaries of State: America and West Indies, Original Correspondence, Proprieties,* CO 5/1265, folder 381 ("Midway"); Talk from the Young Tallassee King to George Galphin, 15 December 1778, GGL 1780 ("Mothers"); Diron d'Artaguette to Count de Maurepas, 17 October 1729, in Rowland and Dunbar, *Mississippi Provincial Archives,* vol. 4, series 690, 28 ("devoted"); 10 May 1740, BD-SC, CO 5/388, folder 179; James Oglethorpe to Harman Verelst, 15 June 1739, *EAID,* 11:92; Sweet, *Negotiating for Georgia,* 149 (war); Juricek, *Colonial Georgia and the Creeks,* 114 (war); Corkran, *Creek Frontier,* 103 (war); A Talk deliver'd to the Indians of the Upper & Lower Creeks Nations, 28 May 1751, BD-SC, CO 5/373, folder 99 ("Ancestors").

34. Thomas Brown to the Earl of Cornwallis, 28 June 1780, Charles Cornwallis Papers ("seat"); Upper Creek Headmen to John Stuart, 1 May 1771, *EAID,* 12:97 (Charleston); The Mortar and Upper Creek Headmen to Stuart, 22 July 1764, *EAID,* 12:217–19 (Augusta); Braund, *Deerskins and Duffels,* 30 (English-Creek relationship), 127 ("economy"); Hahn, *Life and Times of Mary Musgrove,* 30 (economy); John Bartram's Account of the First Picolata Congress, 15–20 November 1765, *EAID,* 12:462–63 ("Exchange"); Hall, *Zamumo's Gifts,* 9.

35. Carter, "Observations of John Stuart and Governor James Grant," 829–30 ("contending"); Edmond Atkin to Henry Ellis, 25 January 1760, Henry Ellis Papers ("vile").

36. As John Swanton described the process of selecting a *mico,* the elders of the *talwa* in conjunction with the other *micos* "considered the matter for a long time. They studied the character and qualifications of the best men that the particular group of clans had. . . . The names of a dozen men might be mentioned at first, and

the number then narrowed down to one." Hewitt and Swanton, "Notes on the Creek Indians," 133–34.

37. C. Hudson, *Southeastern Indians*, 223–24 ("devoted"); Ethridge, *Creek Country*, 103 ("blood"); Piker, *Okfuskee*, 17 ("consensual," "support"); Hahn, *Invention of the Creek Nation*, 231; Hewitt and Swanton, "Notes on the Creek Indians," 133–34.

38. After the death of Brims, Malatchi came under the tutorship of Chigelli, a former *tustenogy* turned *mico*, who "had the Power . . . in his Hands by the old Men, till Malatchi came to the Age of Maturity." Upon reaching manhood, Malatchi started to divest himself of Chigelli's oversight and, in May 1740, threatened "if Chigellie opposed him, [he would] cut off his Head." William Stephen's Report on Malatchi's Talk with James Oglethorpe, 2–3 May 1740, *EAID*, 11:102.

39. For a definitive biography of Mary Bosomworth, see Hahn, *Life and Times of Mary Musgrove*.

40. Piker, *Four Deaths of Acorn Whistler*, 14 ("powerful"), 101–2, 138 (Malatchi-Bosomworth); Juricek, *Colonial Georgia and the Creeks*, 47 (Malatchi), 84–86 (1736); James Glen to Malatchi, the Wolf King, the Red Coat King, the Otassee King, and other Creek Headmen, May 1753, James Glen Papers ("no other"); Hahn, *Invention of the Creek Nation*, 193, 196–97, 202 (Malatchi); Glen to the Lords Commissioners for Trade and Plantations, 2 October 1750, James Glen Papers ("Emperor," "Interest"); South Carolina Council Minutes, 4 September 1749, CO 5/459, folders 130–37 ("Childhood"); A Treaty between South Carolina and Creek Nation, 25 June 1753, BD-SC, CO 5/374, folder 157 ("sister"); Hahn, *Life and Times of Mary Musgrove*, 14 (Malatchi-Bosomworth).

41. The Gun Merchant of Okchai, Captain Aleck of Cusseta, the Red Coat King of Okfuskee, and the Dog King of Okfuskee all opposed Malatchi's and Bosomworth's intrigues. In one memorable instance, the Gun Merchant—when meeting with English officials in December 1755—remarked that the Upper *micos* "were not consulted in regard to such Treaties yet they agreed to the Grant of lands . . . because they looked upon the Coweta Town as the head and most ancient." But when Malatchi supported Bosomworth's claims and tried to void the treaties made with the Georgia colony, the Gun Merchant observed that if Malatchi "pretend[ed] to countermand or invalidate any Grants of Lands made by them to their Friends [he] would be Acting like Children." William Little's Talks with Creek Headmen at Augusta, 15–18 December 1755, *EAID*, 11:239–41; Piker, *Four Deaths of Acorn Whistler*, 147, 187; Juricek, *Colonial Georgia and the Creeks*, 161.

42. Declaration of Lower Creek Headmen Recognizing Malatchi as their Natural Prince, 14 December 1747, *EAID*, 11:155–56 ("Prince," "War King"); George Galphin to Vice President Parker, 4 November 1750, *EAID*, 11:213–14 ("Mary," "willing," "pleased"); Hahn, *Life and Times of Mary Musgrove*, 178 (limits); Piker, *Four Deaths of Acorn Whistler*, 81–82 ("coercive").

43. It is well established in the historiography that European men—particularly traders in the fur and deerskin trades—frequently coupled with women of the Indigenous communities that they were embedded within. As Kathryn Braund argues, "It was a common and necessary precaution for traders to secure protection from the

village chief, usually by marriage to a close female relative," a "visible testimony of a trade alliance" between the *talwas* and Europeans. Braund, *Deerskins and Duffels,* 78, 83–86, Hahn, *Life and Times of Mary Musgrove,* 13–14; LeMaster, *Brothers Born of One Mother,* 134, 157; Frank, *Creeks and Southerners,* 4, 9–11, 16; Piker, *Okfuskee,* 140–41. Some other eminent works about intercultural sexual relationships are Sleeper-Smith, *Indian Women and French Men;* Van Kirk, *Many Tender Ties;* Perdue, *Cherokee Women;* Kidwell, "Indian Women as Cultural Mediators"; K. Brown, "Anglo-Indian Gender Frontier"; and J. S. H. Brown, *Strangers in Blood.*

44. As Thomas Nairne recounted in 1708, Muscogee peoples "call their Uncles and aunts, father and mothers, their Cuzons both of the first and second remove, Brothers and Sisters." Nairne, *Nairne's Muskhogean Journals,* 62.

45. This is what happened in 1768 when Upper *micos* led by Emistisiguo of Little Tallassee sought to shut down several out-stores, one of which was Galphin's store at Buzzard's Roost. In this case Sempoyaffee and Escotchaby warned off Emistisiguo. But for those traders who did not enjoy such kinship ties, such as John Spencer, the results were disastrous. All of Spencer's goods were taken "by force," and his assailants threatened "to level his house with the Ground." 10 May 1740, BD-SC, CO 5/388, folder 179 (Buzzard's Roost, Spencer, "force," "level").

46. Dumont, *Colonial Georgia Genealogical Data,* 40–41 ("Sister"); Bonds, Bills of Sale, and Deeds of Gift, 27 October 1809, book D, Le Conte Genealogical Collection ("connexion"); Tallassee King's Talk to the Georgia Governor and Council, 22 September 1784, CIT ("Indian"); George Galphin to the Young Lieutenant [Escotchaby] of Coweta, 23 March 1774, in Boehm, *Records of the British Public Records Office,* reel 7, vol. 75 ("My Friend," "Brother"); Braund, *Deerskins and Duffels,* 87 (lifelong friendship).

47. Although Galphin learned the Muscogee language, he never fully grasped it. As he admitted to the governor of South Carolina in May 1754: "According to your desire I interpreted your Letter to Malatchi as well as lay in my Power there was but one man in the lower Towns that could Interpret better than my self." George Galphin to Governor James Glen, 29 May 1754, SCCJ, roll ST0709.

48. George Galphin to unknown [John Stuart?], 19 February 1771, Indian Affairs, CO 5/72 ("Satisfied"); "Account for Half-Breed Abraham" 23 June 1772, Silver Bluff Trading Post Account Book; "Account for the White Boy," 23 June 1772, Silver Bluff Trading Post Account Book; Talk from the Lower Creek Headmen to Governor James Glen, 25 July 1750, SCCJ, ST0707 ("sent about," Galphin as interpreter); Governor Thomas Boone's Response to Escotchaby of Coweta, 12 May 1762, *EAID,* 14:185—87; Talk from Escotchaby to John Stuart, 26 April 1770, *DAR,* 2:86–87 ("war," "line").

49. As Hahn argues, Malatchi and Bosomworth devised a "creative set of documents intended to solidify Mary's claims . . . presumed to elevate Mary to a position of leadership in the Creek Nation" and thereby supplant the treaty between the *talwas* and Georgia, using an "Indian-to-Indian transaction" between Malatchi and Bosomworth. Hahn, *Life and Times of Mary Musgrove,* 163.

50. Talk of Chickilli Tuskeestonduah, Chief of the Warriors in the Creek Nation, to Major William Horton, 4 December 1746, *CRG,* vol. 36.

51. Malatchi consistently defended Bosomworth's claims to the islands and by

extension Muscogee sovereignty, As late as 1753, he asserted that "Mrs. Bosomworth my Sister was in Possession of the Land in Georgia, that other People now claim, long before there was any Settlement at all of English in that Country; the Land was her own Right and nobody had any Claim there to but herself. But finding that the People of Georgia made Encroachments upon *our* Lands, we sent to Mrs. Bosomworth and advised her to go to the Great King and relate the whole Affair to Him, and to make Our Complaint." In this instance Malatchi acted through Bosomworth when she represented her case in London, in an attempt to put himself on equal level with King George II and thereby achieve recognition of Muscogee independence and sovereignty from the English Crown. A Treaty between South Carolina and Creek Nation, 25 June 1753, BD-SC CO 5/374, folder 157.

52. Malatchi's Speech to Heron, 7 December 1747, *EAID*, 11:148–52; Declaration of Lower Creek Headmen Recognizing Malatchi as Their Natural Prince, 14 December 1747, *EAID*, 11:155–56; Hahn, *Life and Times of Mary Musgrove*, 172–73.

53. Talk from the Lower Creek Headmen to Governor James Glen ("Powerful"); Governor James Glen to the President and Assistants of Georgia, October 1750, *CRG*, vol. 30 (Fort Toulouse, "Arms"); George Galphin to Commissioner Pinckney, 3 November 1750, *DRIA 1*, 4–5 (deed); George Galphin to Vice President Park and Assistants, 4 November 1750, *EAID* 11:213-14 ("Colours"); At a Meeting of the President and Assistants in Council, 25 September 1750, *CRG*, 6:331 ("Malatche").

54. George Galphin to Vice President Park and Assistants, 4 November 1750, *EAID*, 11:213–14 ("Convercation," "pleased"); Extract of a Journal from the Creek Nation, 11 April 1747, *CRG*, 27:11–12 ("Linguist," "Gun").

55. Talk from the Lower Creek Headmen to Governor James Glen ("Words"); Galphin to Pinckney, 3 November 1750 ("Colours"); Glen to the Lords Commissioners for Trade and Plantations, 2 October 1750, James Glen Papers ("Admittance"); At a Meeting of the President and Assistants in Council, 4 October 1750, *CRG*, 6:341–42 (Clark, "Store"); Juricek, *Colonial Georgia and the Creeks*, 135–36 (Galphin-Malatchi confrontation).

56. George Galphin to Vice President Parker, 4 November 1750, *EAID*, 11:213–14; Juricek, *Colonial Georgia and the Creeks*, 179–80; Hahn, *Life and Times of Mary Musgrove*, 187–88.

57. Galphin to Parker, 4 November 1750 ("Disanoll"); Juricek, *Colonial Georgia and the Creeks*, 184–85 ("deceit," "duped," "Dark"); Graham's Deed from the Upper Creeks, 28 May 1751, *EAID*, 11:219–21; Upper Creek Repudiation of Graham Deed, 23 September 1752, *EAID*, 11:224–26.

58. Talk Deliver'd to the Indians of the Upper and Lower Creeks Nations, 28 May 1751, BD-SC, CO 5/373, folder 99 ("profest"); James Glen to the Board of Trade, 14 April 1756, BD-SC, CO 5/375, folder 97 (encroachments, "Whoop"); George Galphin to Glen, 12 May 1754, *DRIA 1*, 499 (letters, "approve"); Malatchi to Glen, 12 May 1754, *DRIA 1*, 499–500 ("sent up," "Day"); Galphin to Glen, 1 August 1753, SCCJ, ST0709 ("Quietness"); Galphin to Parker, 4 November 1750 (Sempoyaffee-Malatchi); Galphin to Glen, 24 August 1753, SCCJ, Roll ST0709 ("gangs"); Hahn, *Invention of the Creek Nation*, 225 (Malatchi's death).

59. Lower Creeks to Governor John Reynolds, 13 October 1756, *EAID*, 11:245–46 (Sempoyaffee as speaker, "Friendship," "incroach"); John Stuart to the Earl of Hillsborough, 28 December 1768, *EAID*, 12:347–48 ("weight"); Proceedings of the First Picolata Congress, 15–18 November 1765, *EAID*, 12:454–62 (Coweta *mico*).

60. John Stuart to the Earl of Dartmouth, 25 October 1775, *DAR*, 11:167 ("extensive"); Letter from Governor Henry Ellis, 2 August 1758, SCCJ, STo711 ("License"); Slaughter, *William Bartram*, 259–61 ("connexions"); Stephens, *State of the Province of Georgia* (Yuchi); George Galphin to unknown [John Stuart?], 19 February 1771 (Silver Bluff stay); Galphin to Stuart, 2 June 1768, Gage, vol. 78 (Silver Bluff stay).

The documents never allude to the identity of Sempoyaffee's spouse, although we know they had at least two children, Limpike and another son known only as "Warrior." John Stuart to the Earl of Hillsborough, 28 December 1768, *EAID*, 12:347–48; Stuart to James Grant, 2 July 1767, Ballindalloch, microfilm 687, reel 17; Grant to Stuart, 5 February 1769, Ballindalloch, microfilm 687, reel 2.

Chapter Three

1. Coweta's *micos* remembered the Tugaloo Incident as the origins of their "old Grudge" against the Cherokees, which started when the Cherokee joined "the Carolina Army in the [Yamasee] War in 1715." When a Muscogee delegation visited Tugaloo to make peace, the Cherokee attacked the delegation, and "11 [were] killed and 1 given to ye white men to be shot that night." As Brims of Coweta remembered the violence in Tugaloo, "we have Nothing of Making a peace with The Cherokeys. For them men that was killed by the Cherokeys of Mine When the White people were there is not over with Me as yet, nor never shall be While there is a Cowwataid Living." Cherokee leaders also recognized that the actions taken in Tugaloo "brought upon themselves and their families a continued war," even though the Cherokee continued to blame Muscogee peoples for the continuing violence. Jacobs, *Appalachian Indian Frontier*, 62 ("Grudge"); Chicken, "Journal of Colonel George Chicken," 27 December 1715, 345 ("killed"); 5 December 1715, 336 ("peace"); Fitch, "Journal of Captain Tobias Fitch," 12 August 1725, 182 ("Cowwataid"); Hatley, *Dividing Paths*, 26 ("continued"); Talk from the Lower Creek Headmen to Governor James Glen, 25 July 1750, SCCJ; Charles Hicks to John Ross, 4 May 1826, Payne, vol. 7, folder 1.

2. George Galphin to James Glen, 24 August 1753, SCCJ, roll STo709 ("Peace"); Diron d'Artaguette to Count de Maurepas, 24 October 1737, in Rowland and Sanders, *Mississippi Provincial Archives*, 2:146–47 (Tugaloo); Saluy's Talk to Governor Thomas Boone, January 1764, Plantations General, CO 323/17, folder 172 ("Grudge").

3. Henry Ellis to William Henry Lyttleton, 5 February 1760, WHL, box 14 (Escotchaby as Cherokee king).

4. Lower Creeks to John Stuart, 19 September 1772, *EAID*, 12:113–14 (Coweta king); Charles Hicks to John Ross, 4 May 1826, Payne, vol. 7, folder 1 (Okchai kings, "actors"); Hicks to Ross, 1 March 1826, Payne, vol. 7, folder 1 ("ancient," "revolutionary," "intercourse"); Launey to Colonel W. Lindsay, 18 June 1838, Payne, vol. 5,

folder 19 ("brotherly"); *Penn Gazette,* 30 August 1753, ("look upon"); Charles Hicks Letter, n.d., Payne, vol. 2 ("Chief"); Charles Hicks Letter, n.d., Payne, vol. 6, pt. 2 ("brother"); Hicks to Ross, 1 February 1826, Payne, vol. 6, pt. 2 ("connected").

5. This is not to say that scholars have missed out on this intra-Indigenous world altogether. As early as 1971, Robert F. Berkhofer Jr. implored historians of American history to pay more attention to "intra- and inter-tribal political organization." Patricia Galloway did so when she famously pieced together the life of a Choctaw intermediary—the Alibamon Mingo—who facilitated peaceful relations, trade, and fictive kinship with Europeans and Native neighbors. Meanwhile Joshua Piker's insights into the Fanni Mico, who similarly fostered relationships with European and Muscogee peoples, provide a parallel to that of the Alibamon Mingo. As Galloway and Piker demonstrate, the Indigenous Peoples of the South "believed that a corporate group could adopt an individual who would serve as a mediator between his natal polity and his adopted one," as these individuals "united social worlds [and] represented a creative melding of the familial and the political." Other historians such as Clara Sue Kidwell, Juliana Barr, Ned Blackhawk, James Brooks, Michael McDonnell, Kathleen DuVal, and Michael Witgen, among others, have similarly grappled with intra-Native exchange in their work. However, it is worth noting that these scholars use individuals such as the Alibamon Mingo and Fanni Mico primarily to excavate Native-European interactions more than intra-Indigenous ones. Berkhofer, "Political Context of a New Indian History," 380; Galloway, "Four Ages of Alibamon Mico"; Piker, *Okfuskee,* 22 ("corporate group").

6. Journal of the Superintendent's Proceedings of the Congress at Augusta, 12–14 November 1768, Gage, vol. 137 ("women"); White Outerbridge to William Henry Lyttleton, 2 July 1759, WHL, box 11 ("Incampt"); At a Meeting of the Cherokee Indians, 8 June 1771, *Board of Trade and Secretaries of State: America and West Indies, Original Correspondence: Georgia,* CO 5/661, folders 211–12 ("mixed"); Talk from the Cherokees to Alexander Cameron, 8 August 1775, Henry Laurens Papers, box 7, folder 13 ("Brothers"); Raymond Demere to William Henry Lyttleton, 15 May 1759, Letterbooks of William Henry Lyttleton (Coosawhatchie); Raymond Demere to William Henry Lyttleton, 26 March 1759, Letterbooks of William Henry Lyttleton (Night-assay old); *SCG,* 14 February 1774 (Pucknawhitla); Account of an Indian Woman Called the Buffalo Skin, 1 August 1759, Letterbooks of William Henry Lyttleton ("houses," "Affairs"); Journal of an Expedition in 1776 against the Cherokee, 1 October 1776 ("rendezvous," Chote); Boulware, *Deconstructing the Cherokee Nation,* 22 (Creek-Cherokee interactions).

7. Charles Hicks to John Ross, 4 May 1826, Payne, vol. 7, folder 1 (messengers); Raymond Demere to William Henry Lyttleton, 11 July 1757, Letterbooks of William Henry Lyttleton ("meeting"); James Wright to Earl of Dartmouth, 17 June 1773, *DAR,* 6:156–58 ("confederacy"); Demere to Lyttleton, 20 July 1757, Letterbooks of William Henry Lyttleton ("informed"); Talk from the Headmen and Warriors of the Upper Creeks, 1 May 1771, Indian Affairs, CO 5/72, folders 346–47 ("Cattle"); Conference of Alexander Cameron with Lower/Middle Cherokees, 25 February 1775, *EAID,* 14:350–51 ("Beads").

8. As Hatley demonstrates, "Cherokees and Creeks seem to have shared . . . lands as hunting grounds, a subtle cooperation which tended to maintain a reserve of deer for hard times. Border towns such as Estatoe and Tugaloo, nominally Cherokee, had long preserved kinship with the Creeks as a kind of insurance against aggression." Hatley, *Dividing Paths*, 82.

9. Coulter, *Journal of William Stephens*, 10 December 1742, 149 ("Company"); White Outerbridge to William Henry Lyttleton, 12 February 1760, WHL, box 14 ("Winter"); Report of Colonels Christian and Lewis ("Highwassey"); Hatley, *Dividing Paths*, 22 (Cherokee travel in Creek territories for trade); South Carolina Council Minutes, 20 June 1760, *Board of Trade and Secretaries of State: America and West Indies, Sessional Papers, Council Assembly*, CO 5/474, Folder 74 (joint trade paths); *SCG*, 22 March 1760 ("Goods"); Alexander Cameron to John Stuart, 4 July 1774, Indian Affairs, CO 5/75, folder 186 ("Towns"); South Carolina Council Minutes, 4 September 1749, CO 5/459, folders 130–37 (Cherokee Busk).

10. As Boulware further notes: "The Cherokee towns of Settico, Chilhowee, and Toskegee, for instance, are believed to be Iroquoian corruptions of Muskogean words. The result, according to Charles Hudson, is that 'the linguistic frontier in eastern Tennessee shifted in favor of the Cherokees in early historical times, after the period of initial Spanish exploration.'" Boulware, *Deconstructing the Cherokee Nation*, 39.

11. The relationship between Muscogee and Cherokee peoples might best be thought of as one of intermittent peace broken up continuously by violence. For instance, even after Muscogee and Cherokee leaders restored a semblance of peace after the Tugaloo Incident in 1715, the Muscogee continued "in warr against the Cherokeyes" while the Cherokee also traded attacks with the *talwas*, all periodically between 1715 and 1740. Even more telling is the response of *micos* from Cusseta after learning that "it was a firm Peace" between their people and the Cherokee, who revealed "they thought so too but that the Cherokees about six Days before had killed 2 Women and had carried four alive . . . [and were now] going out to War against the Cherokees." Fitch, "Journal of Captain Tobias Fitch," 12 August 1725, 190; Benoit to Perier, 29 March 1732, in Rowland and Sanders, *Mississippi Provincial Archives*, 120–21; James Oglethorpe to Board of Trade, January 1737, James Edward Oglethorpe Papers; Perdue, *Cherokee Women*, 95; George Galphin to Commissioner Pinckney, 3 November 1750 (18 October 1749), *DRIA 1*, 4–5.

12. One of the other grievances that *micos* gave for the incessant conflict with the Cherokee was that the Cherokee allowed the Nottowagoes (Northward Indians) to pass through their territories to attack the *talwas*. As European and Muscogee leaders both noted: "The Nottowagoes" are "suffer[ed] to live among [the Cherokee] will always be killing us which will break the War out a fresh again." Or as Malatchi described, "whilst the Cherokees encourage these Northern Indians to come through their Towns to make War upon us, such a Peace cannot take Effect." South Carolina Commons Journal, 20 June 1748, *Journal of the Commons House of Assembly of South Carolina: 19 January 1748–29 June 1748*, 335–36 ("Nottowagoes," "Countenance"); Talk from the Lower Creek Headmen to Governor James Glen, 25 July 1750, SCCJ ("Suffer"); *Penn Gazette*, 30 August 1753 ("War").

13. Woodward, *Woodward's Reminiscences of the Creek*, 133 ("continual," Chote); Boulware, *Deconstructing the Cherokee Nation*, 39 ("ancestors"); 27 August 1776, Cherokee Vertical Files ("Property"); King, *Memoirs of Lt. Henry Timberlake*, xv; At a Meeting of the Cherokee Indians, 8 June 1771, CO 5/661, folders 211–12 ("it well"); Charles R. Hicks to John Ross, 4 May 1826, Payne, vol. 7, folder 1 ("skins," "frequent"); Lower Creek Headmen to Governor James Glen, 25 July 1750, SCCJ ("Grounds," "People"); Fitch, "Journal of Captain Tobias Fitch," 12 August 1725, 191 ("Strong").

14. As Tyler Boulware argues, the Muscogee-Cherokee Wars of the 1740s and 1750s were "the longest and most destructive conflict . . . during the eighteenth century" in the South, a product of the "Lower Creeks [who] shifted from sporadic raids to full-scale attacks against the Lower Cherokee[s]." Boulware, *Deconstructing the Cherokee Nation*, 57–58.

15. The executions in Tallauhassee lived on in the memories of Muscogee peoples. When Benjamin Hawkins visited that community in January 1798, he "was shown in an old field some stakes to which the Cherokees had been tied in the last war they had with the Creeks about 40 years past when taken prisoners. Three of the stakes remain. Here the captives were tied and here they received their doom, which with the exception of young lads and a few women was the torture till death." "Letters of Benjamin Hawkins," 23 January 1797, 63.

16. Charles Hicks to John Ross, 4 May 1826, Payne, vol. 7, folder 1 ("invasion"); Governor James Glen to Board of Trade, 16 December 1752, BD-SC, CO 5/374, folder 69; Patrick Brown to Glen, 25 April 1752, *DRIA 1*, 246–47 ("distressed"); George Galphin to Glen, 20 April 1753, *DRIA 1*, 257–58; Boulware, *Deconstructing the Cherokee Nation*, 59 (violence); Oliphant, *Peace and War on the Anglo-Cherokee Frontier*, 19 (Estatoe, Echoi); Tasattee of Hiwassee to Glen, 28 November 1752, *DRIA 1*, 363 ("destroy"); Deposition of John Elliot, 25 May 1752, *DRIA 1*, 249 ("Fear"); Glen to the Committee on Indian Affairs, 9 May 1751, *DRIA 1*, 54–55 (captivity); Glen to the Lord Commissioners, 15 July 1750, Records in the British Public Record Office Relating to South Carolina, vol. 24, 1750–51 ("killed").

17. A Speech by Malatchi Opiya Mico to the Lt. Col. Alexander Heron, 7 December 1747, *CRG*, 27:315–25; 29 April 1752, *Journal of the Commons House of Assembly of South Carolina: 14 November 1751 to 7 October 1752*, 261 ("Blood-shed," "Cruelties"); *EAID*, 13:213 (April 1750); Governor James Glen to Board of Trade, 25 June 1753, BD-SC, CO 5/374, folder 150 ("Terror," "Leader"); Piker, *Okfuskee*, 86 (conquest, grounds).

18. Cherokee fears were well founded, given the assassination of five Cherokee men in Charlestown by the Creeks the previous year. As Governor Glen described the killings, "a large Body of the Lower Creeks . . . followed them and came up with them as they were sat down, not expecting any harm, when the Creeks fell upon and killed 3 of them . . . an Act not only perfidious to the Cherokees, but very outrageous and injurious to us and which happend at our very Door." Talk of the Acorn Whistler to Governor James Glen, 1752, *DRIA 1*, 229–30. Joshua Piker has detailed this specific event, known as the "Acorn Whistler Crisis," in his *Four Deaths of Acorn Whistler*.

19. *Penn Gazette,* 30 August 1753.

20. The Coweta-Okfuskee rivalry has been well documented; see Piker, *Okfuskee,* 146–47. Up to that point, it had been Okfuskee who mediated with the Cherokee, such as in 1749 when "three Creek Embassadors [from Okfuskee] with five Cherokee Embassadors from the Cherokee Nation" arrived in Charlestown, "which overjoyed the Creeks to see their People return safe from the Cherokees. They treated the Cherokee Embassadors friendly." 25 May 1749, *Journal of the Commons House of Assembly of South Carolina: 28 March 1749 to 19 March 1750,* 193.

21. Okfuskee enjoyed connections with the Cherokee communities of Hiwassee and Estatoe. Piker, *Four Deaths of Acorn Whistler,* 150, 155.

22. Ibid., 151, 154 (Okfuskee-Estatoe), 175–176 ("fought"); Piker, *Okfuskee,* 49–50 (Okfuskee-Cherokees); *Penn Gazette,* 30 August 1753 ("complied," "Man"); Talk of the Over Hill Cherokees, 14 May 1751, *DRIA 1,* 64 ("Friends").

23. List of the Number of Men from the Upper and Lower Creek Nations now at Charles Town, 4 June 1753, *DRIA 1,* 410; George Galphin to Governor James Glen, 1 August 1753, *DRIA 1,* 378 ("going out," "before long"); Piker, *Four Deaths of Acorn Whistler,* 186–87 (Okfuskee-Malatchi); Proceedings of the Council Concerning Indian Affairs, May–August 1753, *DRIA 1,* 407–8 ("Home," "displeased," "Children," "Power"); James Germany to Lachlan McGillivray, 15 July 1753, *DRIA 1,* 378–79; Red Coat King of Okfuskee, 26 July 1753, *DRIA 1,* 379–80.

24. I base this assumption on the fact that Escotchaby was appointed by Cherokee leaders as the first Cherokee king of Coweta, the *talwa* that was recognized as "the principal [one] in re-establishing peace" between Muscogee and Cherokee peoples in the early 1750s. Thus Escotchaby likely served as one of two "messengers of peace" that were originally sent from Coweta to negotiate an end to the war with the Cherokee. Charles Hicks to John Ross, 4 May 1826, Payne, vol. 7, folder 1.

25. Hicks to Ross, 4 May 1826; Piker, *Four Deaths of Acorn Whistler,* 175–76 (Cherokee kings, Coweta kings). The Pidgeon of Tugaloo appears several other times in the documentary record, particularly in Alexander Cameron to John Stuart, 3 June 1774, *EAID,* 14:356–58.

26. Braund, *Deerskins and Duffels,* 133; South Carolina Council Minutes, 2 October 1754, CO 5/471 ("Destroying," "Woods," "Complain"); Andrew McLean to John Stuart, 21 June 1771, Indian Affairs, CO 5/72, folder 332 (emblems); Hahn, *Invention of the Creek Nation,* 225–28 (Malatchi's death); James Glen to Board of Trade, 14 April 1756, *Board of Trade and Secretaries of State: America and West Indies, Original Correspondence, North Carolina, Sessional Papers,* CO 5/357, folder 97 (Malatchi's death).

27. Alexander Cameron to John Stuart, 19 March 1771, Indian Affairs, CO 5/72, folder 219 (tobacco, "honor"); Stuart, "Map of the Southern Indian District in America," ("conservator"); Cameron to Stuart, 3 June 1774, *EAID,* 14:356–58; Payne, vol. 6, pt. 2, 17–19 ("brother"); Payne, vol. II, 260 ("Chief"); Payne, vol. 6, pt. 2, 31–35 ("connected"); Journal of the Proceedings of a Congress at Augusta, 12–14 November 1768, Gage, vol. 137.

28. The practice of appointing Cherokee kings and Coweta kings is similar to previous precedents like the Fanni Mico, the individual who mediated between

Muscogee and Chickasaw peoples during times of conflict. As European observers noted about the Cherokee, "In every Town in the Cherokee Nation, are Beloved men appointed by the Creeks, Chickasaws, Catawbas, & other Nations with whom they are at Peace" in order to remain at peace. Stuart, "Map of the Southern Indian District in America," 1764, Plantations General; Hatley, *Dividing Paths,* 82. For further information about the Fanni Mico, see Piker, *Okfuskee,* 25–26, 45–46.

29. It is also my speculation that when the Cherokee delegation traveled to Okfuskee in late 1753 or early 1754 and met with the Upper *micos* to formalize the peace and install a Cherokee King among the Upper *talwas,* that individual was the Mortar of Okchai. My speculation stems from the fact that Escotchaby and the Mortar were both identified as "attached" to the Cherokee during the Seven Years' War and were constantly sending talks to and visiting Cherokee communities during the 1750s and 1760s.

30. As Cherokee headmen revealed in 1826, "there is some account related by traditioners of the inter-change of names of towns having been swapt between the two nations." Charles Hicks to John Ross, 4 May 1826.

31. Launey to Col. W. Lindsay, 18 June 1838, Payne, vol. 5, folder 19 ("brotherly"); Nairne, *Nairne's Muskhogean Journals,* 40 ("protector"); Governor James Glen to the Committee on Indian Affairs, 9 May 1751, *DRIA 1,* 54–55 ("agreed"); Talk of the Cherokees with the Mortar and Creeks, 8 November 1773, Indian Affairs, CO 5/75, folder 19 (Mortar, Chote king, Coosa king, Okchai-Chote); Andrew Pickens to unknown, 15 October 1787, Andrew Pickens Papers (Little Turkey); Alexander Cameron to John Stuart, 9 February 1774, Indian Affairs, CO 5/75, folder 77 (Young Turkey); 14 October 1760, *Belfast News-Letter,* Belfast (Ireland) Newspaper Collection ("Channel"); Alexander Cameron to John Stuart, 3 June 1774, *EAID,* 14:356–58 (Coweta-Tugaloo); Raymond Demere to William Henry Lyttleton, 11 July 1757, Letterbooks of William Henry Lyttleton (Okchai-Chote); Piker, *Four Deaths of Acorn Whistler,* 24–25 (Okfuskee-Hiwassee); South Carolina Council Minutes, 4 September 1749, CO 5/459, folders 130–37 (Tallassee); Charles R. Hicks to John Ross, 1 March 1826, Payne, vol. 7, folder 1 (Coweta-Tugaloo-Keowee); Boulware, *Deconstructing the Cherokee Nation,* 156 (Coweta-Tugaloo); Talk from the Lower and Middle Cherokees and Their Beloved Women to the Cowetas, 21 February 1774, *EAID,* 14:348–49 (Coweta-Toxaway); *SCG,* 29 March 1760 (Coweta-Estatoe); Saluy's Talk to Governor Thomas Boone, January 1764, Plantations General, CO 323/17, folder 172 ("Grudge").

32. Escotchaby and his Cherokee "wife" had three sons, the oldest of which accompanied him to all his major conferences with British and Spanish authorities in the 1760s and 1770s, emerged as a renowned hunter in his own right, and was entrusted by his father as his intermediary with Cherokees and Europeans whenever he was absent. Similarly Escotchaby's second son joined his father at the major councils during the 1760s and 1770s, such as the one at Picolata, although this second son was only identified as "Child" while the eldest "a Young Man." As for the third son, the only evidence for his presence is his being one of "de tres hijos . . . el Indio Escuchape de Nacion Uchiz casique" in Havana when meeting with Spanish authorities in May

1775. Congress Proceedings at Picolata, 21 January 1766, Gage, vol. 47 (Escotchaby's wife, eldest son at Picolata-English); George Roupell to John Stuart, 10 December 1767, Gage, vol. 73 (eldest son, "presents," second son at Picolata, "Child," "Young Man"); Stuart to James Grant, 4 August 1769, Ballindalloch, reel 17 (eldest son in Havana, eldest son negotiating for Escotchaby); Escotchaby to Stuart, 26 April 1770, *DAR*, 2:86–87 (eldest son deerskin hunter); Declaration of Rafael de la Luz, 2 May 1775, General de Indias ("tres hijos").

33. Journal of the Proceedings of a Congress at Augusta, 12–14 November 1768, Gage, vol. 137 ("brother," "know you"); Alexander Cameron to John Stuart, 2 August 1774, Indian Affairs, CO 5/75, folder 174 ("Interpreter, "Speaks"); Raymond Demere to William Henry Lyttleton, 12 May 1759, Letterbooks of William Henry Lyttleton ("stay'd").

34. Payne, vol. 2, 269 ("Bench"), 260 ("Rights"); Charles Hicks to John Ross, 4 May 1826, Payne, vol. 7, folder 1 ("Councils," "Rights"); Raymond Demere to William Henry Lyttleton, 9 July 1757, Letterbooks of William Henry Lyttleton ("Summons"); White Outerbridge to Lyttleton, 12 February 1760, WHL, box 14 ("Pidgeon").

35. A Treaty between South Carolina and Creek Nation, 25 June 1753, BD-SC, CO 5/374, folder 157 ("Years"); Nairne, *Nairne's Muskhogean Journals,* 40 ("safety"); Alexander Cameron to John Stuart, 4 July 1774, Indian Affairs, CO 5/75, folder 186 (Little Turkey); Talk from the Lower and Middle Cherokees and Their Beloved Women to the Cowetas (Tiftoy, Bag, "darkness").

36. While this example was specific to the Upper *talwas* in this case, it was the Red Coat King of Okfuskee—one of the Cherokee kings—who hosted and traveled with Cherokee delegations. We also know that several of these same visits between Muscogee and Cherokee peoples were made to and from the Lower *talwas* and likely Coweta, where they would have met Escotchaby. Journal of the Council of South Carolina, 3 September 1754, *Board of Trade and Secretaries of State: America and West Indies, Original Correspondence, South Carolina, Sessional Papers,* CO 5/471.

37. Journal of the Council of South Carolina, 3 September 1754, CO 5/471; South Carolina Council Minutes, 4 September 1749, CO 5/459, folders 130–37.

38. Daniel Pepper to William Henry Lyttleton, 27 June 1757, Letterbooks of William Henry Lyttleton ("Safety"); Lt. Governor William Bull to General Jeffrey Amherst, 24 January 1761, *Board of Trade and Secretaries of State: America and West Indies, Original Correspondence, Military and Naval Dispatches,* CO 5/61, folder 181 ("remove"); William Bull to Board of Trade, 29 January 1761, BD-SC, CO 5/377, folder 50 ("Army"); John Stuart to William Howe, 11 June 1777, *Carleton Papers,* reel 6 ("Fields"); Launey to Col. W. Lindsay, 18 June 1838, Payne, vol. 5, folder 19 ("protection").

39. White Outerbridge to William Henry Lyttleton, 12 February 1760, WHL, box 14 ("gangs"); Journal of the Proceedings of a Congress at Augusta, 12–14 November 1768, Gage, vol. 137 (Tiftoy-Escotchaby); Henry Ellis to Lyttleton, 7 March 1760, WHL, box 15 ("promises," "Lieutenant," "remonstrated"); *Penn Gazette,* 3 July 1760 ("Steps"); *SCG,* 29 March 1760 ("spear").

40. As Christina Snyder observes, in several Indigenous cultures, "a ceremonial

leader "maintained a bundle of sticks, breaking one each day ("the broken days") to count down the days to an important event." Also, see John Howard Payne to unknown, 1835, reprinted as "The Green-Corn Dance," *Continental Monthly*, January 1862, 17–29." Snyder, "Once and Future Moundbuilders," 97–98.

41. As one observer noted, the "broken days are those appointed for their meeting" in regard to peace or not and were represented by "a number of sticks, equal to the number of days are sent to each town, and every day one stick is broke and cast away." *New York Daily Advertiser, or The Daily Advertiser*, 27 October 1788.

42. Henry Ellis to William Henry Lyttleton, 7 March 1760, WHL, box 15 (broken days, "Breach"); *New York Daily Advertiser, or The Daily Advertiser*, 27 October 1788 ("hour"); South Carolina Council Minutes, 4 September 1749, CO 5/459, folders 130–37 ("please").

43. "A Map of the Southern Indian District in America," 1764, Plantations General ("Exploits," "Bloodshed"); *Penn Gazette*, 19 June 1760 ("Relations"); *SCG*, 22 March 1760 ("itched," "Mischief").

44. Such landed responsibilities of the Cherokee king were inherited by one of Escotchaby's successors, William McIntosh, in the 1820s and 1830s. However, McIntosh abused such territorial powers for "speculative designs." He deceived Cherokee leaders in his effort to "yield their land to the United States' Commissioners." McIntosh went so far as to suggest "the idea of the Cherokees, Creeks, Choctaws, and Chickasaws . . . to surrender up their country, and emigrate west of the Mississippi river, and there to settle themselves under one government." For this betrayal Cherokee leaders decreed that McIntosh "be discharged from ever having any voice in our Councils hereafter, as a chief connected with this nation," and he later paid for his betrayal with his life. Payne, vol. 6, book 2, 31–35.

45. At the initial peace, the Coweta king told the Cherokee king "to go westward to the Great Lick and there the Land Mark of the Cherokee run by there; and that the Creek man said to the Cherokee to go Eastward to the Savannah River, and there the Land Mark of the Creeks run by there." Charles Hicks to John Ross, 4 May 1826, Payne, vol. 7, folder 1.

46. Launey to Col. W. Lindsay, 18 June 1838, Payne, vol. 5, folder 19 ("intrusion"); Charles Hicks to John Ross, 4 May 1826, Payne, vol. 7, folder 1 ("high shoal"); *SCG*, 20 June 1768 ("mark out"); Taitt, "David Taitt's Journal of a Journey through the Creek Country," 29 April 1772, 548–49 ("Enquire").

47. *SCG*, 22 March 1760 (Cherokee king); Henry Ellis to William Henry Lyttleton, 11 February 1760, WHL, box 14 ("Head Warrior"); Edmond Atkin to Lyttleton, 13 February 1760, WHL, box 14 ("Head Warrior," "effectually"); *SCG*, 12–19 July 1760 ("war names"); Charles Hicks to John Ross, 4 May 1826, Payne, vol. 7, folder 1.

48. Edmond Atkin to Henry Ellis, 25 January 1760, Henry Ellis Papers.

Chapter Four

1. Provincial Congress with Head Men of Coweta and Cusseta, 10–11 October 1759, *EAID*, 11:300–308.

2. Council in Savannah with the Creek Indians and Head Men, 10 October 1759, *CRG*, 7:160–67 ("Uncle," "Man"); Board of Commissioners to King George II, 21 December 1756, Board of Trade and Secretaries of State: America and West Indies, Original Correspondence, Secretary of State: South Carolina, 1734–1776 ("Minor," "Head"); Provincial Congress with Head Men of Coweta and Cusseta ("Nakedness").

3. Provincial Congress with Head Men of Coweta and Cusseta.

4. Ibid.

5. Cherokee prisoners described the reason for going to war against the English as "the ill usage they had received" from British agents, specifically "Coytmore and Bell of Keowee Fort, who got Drunk, came into their Houses, and beat them, and otherwise evilly intreated them." They asserted that "most of the Traders had also used them very ill": in addition to the encroachments upon Cherokee lands, the Cherokees lost "twenty of their people, who were killed by the Virginians when they went to the assistance of their Brothers the English against the French" in 1758. South Carolina Council Minutes, 20 June 1760, CO 5/474, folder 74.

6. Henry Ellis to William Henry Lyttleton, 27 August 1759, WHL, box 11 ("set out"); Ellis to Lyttleton, 7 December 1759, WHL, box 13 ("warm," "prevail"); Edmond Atkins to Lyttleton, 4 November 1758, WHL, box 9 ("Mankiller").

7. Edmond Atkin to Henry Ellis, 25 January 1760, Henry Ellis Papers.

8. White Outerbridge to William Henry Lyttleton, 3 September 1759, WHL, box 12 (Sempoyaffee as "guardian"); Juan Josef Eligio de la Puente, 26 December 1777, General de Indias_(Escotchaby as guardian, "governed"); Corkran, *Creek Frontier*, 172–73 (three uncles/guardians); Henry Ellis and Georgia Council with Upper and Lower Creeks, 30 June 1760, *CRG*, 7:325 (Old Stumpe); Outerbridge to Lyttleton, 2 July 1759, WHL, box 11 ("Cherokees"); *SCG*, 21 July 1759 ("Lieutenant," "Headman"); *New-Hampshire Gazette*, 31 August 1759 ("Lieutenant," "Headman").

9. It seems the competition between Sempoyaffee, Escotchaby, and Togulki continued well after the war, when in 1768 the two brothers again publicly humiliated Togulki as one "who has forgot the advice of his father . . . [who] always considered the English as our fathers and with his last breath, he recommended to his people to hold the English fast." Instead Togulki was "a Snake in the Coil Spreading the Poison of his Breath all around him, it is he who makes the Young People mad." Proceedings of a Congress at Augusta, 12–14 November 1768, Gage, vol. 137.

10. Letter from William Bacon Stevens, 10 May 1760, William Bacon Stevens Papers (Fool Harry, "rebelled"); Provincial Congress with Head Men of Coweta and Cusseta, 10–11 October 1759, *EAID*, 11:300–308 ("deputed"); Board of Commissioners to King George II, 21 December 1756, CO 5/383–86 ("protection"); *SCG*, 8 September 1759 (Young-Twin's Conspiracy); Jean-Bernard Bossu to Marquis de l'Estrade 2 May 1759, in Bossu, *Travels in the Interior of North America*, 151–55 ("honor"); "Joseph Wright's Journal in the Lower Creeks," 20 July 1758, WHL, box 8 ("ill").

11. Hahn, *Invention of the Creek Nation*, 244 (neutrality/diplomacy); *SCG*, 24 May 1760 ("extend," "purpose"); James Glen to Edward Fenwicke, 1 June 1756, WHL, box 1 ("prices"); White Outerbridge to William Henry Lyttleton, 3 September 1759,

WHL, box 12 ("Spaniards"); Lyttleton to Lords Commissioners of the Board of Trade, 25 December 1756, CO 5/383–86 ("one hand"); Corkran, *Creek Frontier,* 176 (trade); Green, *Politics of Indian Removal,* 20–22 (political playoff system).

12. Headmen of the Lower Creeks to Governor John Reynolds, 17 September 1756, *EAID,* 11:244–45 ("spoils"); Georgia Council Talk with the Handsome Fellow of Okfuskee, 16 November 1756, *EAID,* 11:247–49; Board of Commissioners to George II, 21 December 1756, CO 5/383–86; "Journal of an Indian Trader," 22 April 1755, *DRIA I,* 63–68; Henry Ellis to the Board of Trade, 11 March 1757, *EAID,* 11:250–51 ("Cruel").

13. James Glen to Edward Fenwicke, 1 June 1756, WHL Box 1 ("principal"); Board of Commissioners to King George II, 21 February 1760, CO 5/383–86 (Sempoyaffee and Galphin); Edmond Atkin to William Henry Lyttleton, 7 March 1760, WHL, box 15 (Sempoyaffee and Galphin); Henry Ellis to Lyttleton, 31 October 1757, WHL, box 6 ("renew'd"); Provincial Congress with Upper and Lower Creeks, 3 November 1757, *EAID,* 265–69 (twenty-one *talwas*); George Galphin to Lyttleton, 5 April 1759, WHL, box 10 ("Interest").

14. Daniel Pepper to William Henry Lyttleton, 18 November 1756, *DRIA I,* 252–57 ("Disdain"); "Journal of an Indian Trader," February 1755, *DRIA I,* 57–58 ("peace"); Lyttleton to Captain Paul Demere, 20 March 1759, Letterbooks of William Henry Lyttleton (Mobile, "publick"); Edmond Atkin to Lyttleton, 17 June 1759, WHL, box 11 (Ufylegey); Atkin to Lyttleton, 13 February 1760, WHL, box 14 (Toulouse); Atkin to Lyttleton, 5 February 1760, WHL, box 14 ("Guns"); Atkin to Henry Ellis, 25 January 1760, Henry Ellis Papers (Second Man).

15. As James Hill demonstrates, "between the late 1760s and the early 1780s, hundreds of Creeks made the long journey to Havana," ferried by Spanish fisherman going to and from Cuba. However, it was Coweta who "initiated and dominated the Creek-Cuba connection." Hill, "'Bring Them What They Lack,'" 38–39, 46.

16. Juan Josef Eligio de la Puente, 26 December 1777, General de Indias; *SCG,* 23 October 1762.

17. At the town of Tellico, several traders "carrying the Flour to Fort Loudon" were killed. Meanwhile "a Party of Cherokee's . . . Return'd . . . with 22 Scalps of white Men, to the Town of Settico." South Carolina Council Minutes, 19 October 1759, CO 5/474, folder 20; *New York Mercury,* 2 July 1759.

18. Account of an Indian Woman Called the Buffalo Skin, 1 August 1759, Letterbooks of William Henry Lyttleton ("Wampum," "Loudoun"); South Carolina Council Minutes, 19 October 1759, CO 5/474, folder 20 (Cherokee attacks); *New York Mercury,* 2 July 1759 (Cherokee attacks); Raymond Demere to William Henry Lyttleton, 1 June 1759, Letterbooks of William Henry Lyttleton ("Mischief").

19. James Germany to John Rae and Isaac Barksdale, 10 June 1756, WHL, box 2 ("Hoop," "ruin," "usage"); *New York Gazette,* 21 April 1760 (Coweta king, "fellows," "plunder," "hatchet").

20. *Penn Gazette,* 22 March 1760 ("gangs," Fool Harry, "Young Lieutenant"); Conference at Mucolassah, 20 August 1759, WHL, box 13 ("Strap," "Nottoweagas"); Henry Ellis to William Henry Lyttleton, 7 December 1759, WHL, box 13 ("warm").

21. In the wake of Cherokee violence against the colonies in late 1759, the governor of South Carolina, William Henry Lyttleton, spearheaded an expedition into Cherokee Country that brought Cherokee leaders to the treaty table. However, the Cherokee ripped up the treaty in early 1760 when they failed "to give full satisfaction for some white people they had recently killed" and "broke out [in] War; murdered their Traders; and fell upon the back Settlers." As John Vann, one of the surviving traders among the Cherokee, observed after he was "attacked by a Party of Cherokees at his own House," he "apprehended it dangerous either to continue there, or retreat without Assistance." The Cherokee conflict culminated in Cherokee peoples besieging Fort Loudon and Fort Prince George, which was followed by the killing of Cherokee hostages at Prince George, the capitulation of the English garrison at Loudon, and the killing of the surrendering garrison for breaking the articles of capitulation. Henry Ellis to the Beloved Men and Head Warriors of the Upper and Lower Creeks, 9 February 1760, Telamon Cuyler Historical Manuscripts, box 38, folder Ellis 35 ("satisfaction"); *Penn Gazette,* 3 April 1760 (Vann, sieges); *New-London Summary, or, The Weekly Advertiser,* 3 October 1760 (surrender); *New York Mercury,* 19 May 1760 (killings). For a fuller discussion of the Cherokee War, see Tortora, *Carolina in Crisis.*

22. *SCG,* 8 March 1760 ("war-spear," "blood"), 24 March 1760 (Estatoe, goods, "deviate"), 24 May 1760 ("hatchet"), 7 March 1761 ("70").

23. Raymond Demere to William Henry Lyttleton, 9 July 1757, Letterbooks of William Henry Lyttleton (Old Hop); Alexander Cameron to John Stuart, 19 March 1771, Indian Affairs, CO 5/72, folder 219 (tobacco, "clear up"); White Outerbridge to Lyttleton, 12 February 1760, WHL, box 14 (Pidgeon, siege); *New York Gazette,* 21 April 1760 (Hoyahney, "bullets").

24. Scholars have examined the Mortar's role before, during, and after the Seven Years' War in trying to foment a pan-Indian resistance against the British Empire. None of this scholarship, however, has grappled with the fact that the Mortar occupied the office of a Cherokee king. For further information about the Mortar's intrigues, see Hatley, *Dividing Paths,* 126; Juricek, *Endgame for Empire,* 235, 267, Oliphant, *Peace and War on the Anglo-Cherokee Frontier,* 78; Corkran, *Creek Frontier,* 183–93.

25. For more particulars about Anglo-American fears of a Muscogee-Cherokee alliance and pan-Indian resistance more generally, see Dowd, *Groundless,* and Owens, *Red Dreams and White Nightmares.*

26. Creek Traders to William Henry Lyttleton, 31 July 1756, in McDowell, *Documents Relating to Indian Affairs, 1754–1765,* 152 ("Slaves," "Meetings"); Hahn, *Invention of the Creek Nation,* 252; Raymond Demere to Lyttleton, 26 March 1759, Letterbooks of William Henry Lyttleton (Tellico, "Suffer," "head," Coosawhatchie, "halfway"); Demere to Lyttleton, 12 May 1759, Letterbooks of William Henry Lyttleton (Moytoy, "Stay'd"); Account of an Indian Woman Called the Buffalo Skin, 1 August 1759, Letterbooks of William Henry Lyttleton (Ettuca, "halfway"); Tortora, *Carolina in Crisis,* 62–63 (Mortar's Cherokee-Creek settlements); South Carolina Council Minutes, 20 June 1760, CO 5/474, folder 74 ("stratagem").

27. English authorities mistakenly believed that Escotchaby, as a Cherokee king,

worked with the Mortar to turn Muscogee and Cherokee peoples against the colonies. As reported in the summer of 1760: "The Mortar and the Young Lieutenant of Coweta, who are the abettors and supporters of the Cherokee faction, seem to gain ground among the young people, who are fond of getting war names." *SCG*, 12–19 July 1760.

28. Daniel Pepper to William Henry Lyttleton, 28 June 1757, *DRIA 2*, 387–89 ("overrunning," "destroy"); Raymond Demere to Lyttleton, Letterbooks of William Henry Lyttleton (Chote); *SCG*, 24 May 1760 ("bloody"), 11 February 1761 ("good talk").

29. Escotchaby informed British authorities multiple times about Cherokee threats against Fort Loudon. For instance Governor Lyttleton remarked in early 1759 that "the Lieutenant of the Cowetas . . . with twelve more of the same Town are now at the Chickesaws Camp near Fort Moore . . . [and] informs me that . . . the French commandment [and Cherokees] there [were] very intent on planning an Expedition against Fort Loudoun." William Henry Lyttleton to Raymond Demere, 20 March 1759, Letterbooks of William Henry Lyttleton.

30. Mays, *Amherst Papers*, 111–12 (Atkin); *SCG*, 22 March 1760 ("Party," "Way"); Daniel Pepper to William Henry Lyttleton, 27 June 1757, Letterbooks of William Henry Lyttleton ("Garrison"); White Outerbridge to Lyttleton, 2 July 1759, WHL, box 11 ("disturb'd"); *SCG*, 24 March 1760 ("down upon us"); *Penn Gazette*, 3 April 1760, ("Discoveries"); Edmond Atkin to Lyttleton, 13 February 1760, WHL, box 14 (scout); 11 February 1760, WHL, box 14 ("Lives"); Cashin, *Lachlan McGillivray, Indian Trader*, 194–95 (Escotchaby's heroics); *Penn Gazette*, 23 April 1761; *New York Mercury*, 18 February 1760.

31. It should be noted that since Escotchaby served as Coweta's *tustenogy*, he may in fact have allowed the young men of his talwa to take part in certain, albeit restrained, actions against the Cherokee, rather than doing everything in his power to prevent them from doing so, as I suggest within the text. All of this is a testament to the fact that we just do not know, due to the fragmentary source base; one or the other could have been true, or even both.

32. Raymond Demere to William Henry Lyttleton, 10 April 1758, Letterbooks of William Henry Lyttleton (Settico); Edmond Atkins to Lyttleton, 4 November 1758, WHL, box 9 (Mankiller); Boulware, *Deconstructing the Cherokee Nation*, 104 (Little Estatoe killings); Provincial Council Talks with Lower Creek War Party, 14 April 1760, *EAID*, 11:313–16 ("fitted"); Henry Ellis & Georgia Council talk with Whehofee and Tupahatkee, 28 April 1760, *CRG*, 7:292–94 ("Skirmish").

33. John Stuart to the Lords Commissioners of Trade and Plantations, n.d., Plantations General, CO 323/17, folder 170 ("Eye"); 10 May 1760, William Bacon Stevens Papers ("people against"); *SCG*, 24 April 1761 ("protected"); *Boston News-Letter*, 5 March 1761 ("corn"); William Bull to Board of Trade, 29 January 1761, BD-SC, CO 5/377, folder 50 ("Provisions"); Edmond Atkin to William Henry Lyttleton, 7 March 1760, WHL, box 15 ("rewards," "endeavours"); *Penn Gazette*, 3 July 1760 ("Steps"); Henry Ellis to the Board of Trade, 15 May 1760, *CRG*, 16:250 (Estatoe, Keowee); Kelton, *Cherokee Medicine, Colonial Germs*, 123 (Estatoe, Keowee).

34. *SCG,* 14 October 1760 ("Channel"); *New York Mercury,* 16 February 1761; *London Chronicle: or, Universal Evening Post,* 17–19 November 1761.

35. *SCG,* 24 May 1760 ("preserve"); Raymond Coytmore to William Henry Lyttleton, 23 January 1760, Indian Affairs, CO 5/57, folder 313 (Okfuskee killings); South Carolina Council Minutes, 20 June 1760, CO 5/474, folder 74 (Okfuskee killings); Juricek, *Colonial Georgia and the Creeks,* 283–85 (Okfuskee killings); *New York Mercury,* 26 March 1760/1761 (Okfuskee killings); *SCG,* 14 March 1761 (Okfuskee killings); *Penn Gazette,* 3 July 1760 ("disaffected," "strongly," "Practices," "Affairs"); *SCG,* 5 July 1760 ("Fool Harry"), 12–19 July 1760 ("unanimously"), 14 March 1761 ("disposition").

36. August 1761, *CRG,* 7:553–57 ("News," "Concern"); *Penn Gazette,* 30 July 1761 ("Concern"); Reply to Cowetas and Cusseta, 4 August 1761, *CRG,* 7:553–57 ("Day"); *London Evening Post,* 6–8 August 1761; William Bull to the Board of Commissioners for Trade, 19 June 1761, Records in the British Public Records Office, vol. 29.

37. *SCG,* 6 March 1762 ("uneasiness," "credit"); Edmond Atkin to Henry Ellis, 25 January 1760, Henry Ellis Papers; *SCG,* 30 May 1761, 14 March 1761; Governor Thomas Boone to the Young Lieutenant of Coweta, 12 May 1762, *EAID,* 14:185–87 ("bad Talks," "throw").

38. The congress in November 1763 was one of the largest gatherings of Indigenous and European peoples in the history of the American South. John Juricek has provided the most thorough account of the Augusta proceedings. See Juricek, *Endgame for Empire.*

39. Hahn, *Invention of the Creek Nation,* 230 ("climate").

40. Hahn, *Invention of the Creek Nation,* 230 (independence); Journal of the Southern Congress at Augusta in Georgia, 19 ("few"), 20 ("intentions").

41. Tortora, *Carolina in Crisis,* 184 ("dominated"); Juricek, *Endgame for Empire,* 53–55.

42. This explains why Escotchaby and/or Sempoyaffee accompanied English surveyors in 1763, 1765, and 1768 when marking the new boundary lines. Lower Creek headmen to John Stuart, 1 October 1768, *EAID,* 12:63.

43. Juricek similarly adopts this interpretation, in which "no doubt Galphin and [Lachlan] McGillivray, along with their partner John Rae, were high on the list of suspect traders" who influenced the *micos* of the Lower *talwas* to cede lands during the Augusta congress. As Juricek concludes, *micos* only agreed to the "land-for-amnesty deal" at the "loaded suggestion from Wright, Galphin, and McGillivray [who] led them to see the matter in this light." While Edward Cashin gives the Lower *micos* a little more agency, arguing that the treaty cession was "worked out by the Indians and their trusted friends, specifically Lachlan McGillivray and George Galphin," he concedes that the Lower *talwas* acceded to imperial demands in the end. Juricek, *Endgame for Empire,* 56–57; Cashin, *Lachlan McGillivray, Indian Trader,* 213–14.

44. Tortora, *Carolina in Crisis,* 184; Juricek, *Endgame for Empire,* 53–55; John Stuart to James Grant, 15 March 1769, *FHO* ("Land Affairs"); Corkran, *Creek Frontier,* 238–39 ("drafted," "headmen," "cheerful," "offenses," "eliminate").

45. Journal of the Southern Congress at Augusta in Georgia, 8 ("affair"), 28 ("Spaniards"); John Stuart's Conference with Lower Creeks, 14 October 1768, Ballindalloch, reel 18 ("speakers"); Cashin, *Lachlan McGillivray, Indian Trader,* 213–14 (Galphin with Lower Creeks); John Stuart to the Southern Governors, 20 October 1763, *CRG,* vol. 39 ("tampered"); Congress at Augusta, 1763, *CRG,* vol. 39 (Galphin lands/boundary line, "disturbances," "forwarn"); Distribution of Presents to the Indians at the Augusta Congress, 19 November 1763, Indian Affairs, CO 5/-- ("Galphin's"); John Stuart to Jeffrey Amherst, 3 December 1763, Jeffrey Amherst Papers, vol. 7 (Silver Bluff as repository).

46. List of the Towns of the Lower Creek Nation, 1 December 1764, Plantations General, CO 323/20, document 82 ("Principal"); "A List of the Towns & Number of Gun Men in the Creek Nation," 8 July 1764, Gage, vol. 21 ("most influence"); List of the Lower Creeks, 1764, Ballindalloch, reel 18 ("govern").

47. Juan Josef Eligio de la Puente, 26 December 1777, General de Indias.

48. Hahn, *Invention of the Creek Nation,* 258 ("threat"), 267 ("beginning"); John Stuart to the Earl of Hillsborough, 27 January 1770, *EAID,* 12:482 ("displeased," "Encroachments").

Chapter Five

1. James Wright and John Stuart to the Upper Creeks, 27 December 1765, *EAID,* 12:17 (Payne-Hogg killings, "hunting," "Woods"); John Stuart to Togulki and Head Men of the Creeks, 2 February 1764, Gage, vol. 13 ("Contempt," "account"); *SCG,* 28 January 1764 (Limpike).

2. James Wright and John Stuart to the Upper Creeks, 27 December 1765 ("Son"); *Penn Gazette,* 3 May 1764 ("protected"); Stuart to James Grant, 2 July 1767, Ballindalloch, reel 13 ("ferment"); Journal of the Superintendent's Proceedings with the Indians and Traders at Augusta in Georgia about the Price of Goods, 30 April 1767, Gage, vol. 137 ("die").

3. John Stuart's Conference with Lower Creeks, 14 October 1768, Ballindalloch, reel 18.

4. Ibid. ("distress," "acquaint"); John Stuart to James Grant, 16 December 1768, Ballindalloch, reel 15 (Stuart to Grant, "Majesty," "Country men"); Grant to Stuart, 5 February 1769, Ballindalloch, reel 18 (pardon); Stuart to Grant, 15 March 1769, Ballindalloch, reel 18 (pardon, "Prevail").

5. A Talk from Escotchaby or Young Lieutenant of the Lower Creeks to John Stuart, 26 April 1770, *DAR,* 2:86–87.

6. Journal of the Superintendent's Congress held at Augusta, 12–14 November 1768, Gage, vol. 137.

7. Pierce Ginnott to Frederick Haldimand, 15 March 1768, Sir Frederick Haldimand Unpublished Papers, Add. MS 21728 (Bay of Tampa); John Stuart to James Grant, 16 December 1768, Ballindalloch, reel 15 ("correspondence"); Stuart to Grant, 6 December 1768, Indian Affairs, CO 5/75, Folder -- ("furnish"); Letter by Juan Josef Eligio de la Puente, 26 December 1777, General de Indias ("Youth"); Stuart to

the Earl of Dartmouth, 21 December 1773, *EAID*, 12:338–39 ("render"), Hill, "'Bring Them What they Lack,'" 36–37 (frequent Spanish fishermen).

8. This interpretation of Coweta's "peculiar dispersal" as a center of political authority among the Lower *talwas* is a hallmark of the existent scholarship, including Hahn, *Invention of the Creek Nation*, 225 ("dispersal"); Juricek, *Endgame for Empire*, 3–4; Braund, *Deerskins and Duffels*, 140; *EAID*, 12:2, 79.

9. Pierce Ginnott to Frederick Haldimand, 15 March 1768, Sir Frederick Haldimand Unpublished Papers, Add. MS 21728 ("richly," "congress"); Spanish agents in Cuba identified Escotchaby's "sons" several times, either traveling with Escotchaby to Havana or making the journey by themselves. Similar to the confounding relationship between Sempoyaffee and Limpike, Escotchaby's sons-by-blood should have had little to no affiliation with him and were instead part of their mother's clan and *huti*. This again suggests that we still know so little about the family and kinship dynamics of the Muscogee world. With that said, it is also plausible that the Spanish misidentified Escotchaby's "sons" who may instead have been his nephews, given that nephews within a matrilineal society like the Muscogee often learned from and shadowed their maternal uncles.

10. John Stuart to James Grant, 16 December 1768, Ballindalloch, reel 15 ("Point"); Stuart to Grant, 4 August 1769, Ballindalloch, reel 17 ("presents"); John Simpson to Grant, 2 February 1767, Ballindalloch, reel 12 (Thlawhulgu); Certificate of Rafael de la Luz, 24 January 1776, General de Indias ("horses," "Congress").

11. As Grant observed about Spanish reasons for reaching out to Muscogee peoples during the 1760s and 1770s: "I was well-informed that their sole motive for going to that expense was with a view to keep up a friendly correspondence with the savages: for by that means only their fishery can be carried on with safety, and that fishery is an object of consequence to Spain in point of subsistence to the inhabitants of Cuba, and of one species of provision for ships stationed at the Havanah and for such vessels as sail from thence to Europe." James Grant to Earl of Hillsborough, 12 December 1770, *DAR*, 2:294.

12. John Stuart's Conference with the Lower and Upper Creeks, 14 October 1768, Ballindalloch, reel 18 ("Sea Coast," "Friends," "concerning"); Taitt, "David Taitt's Journal of a Journey through the Creek Country," 28 April 1772, 548–49 (Havana); John Stuart to James Grant, 4 August 1769, Ballindalloch, reel 17 (Pumpkin King); John Simpson to Grant, 3 February 1767, Ballindalloch, reel 12; Talk from the Pumpkin King to Stuart, 3 May 1769, in Boehm, *Records of the British Public Records Office*, reel 5, vol. 70, 373–74 ("Liberty").

13. Treaty at Savannah, 20 October 1774, Gage, vol. 137 ("Lieutenant's Settlement"); Juricek, *Endgame for Empire*, 123 (intercepting hunters), 187 (Standing Peach Tree, "Lieutenant's Settlement"); Braund, *Deerskins and Duffels*, 136 (Galphin and White Boy); Return of the Lower Creeks, December 1764, Plantations General, CO 323/20, document 82 (Little Coweta, Bigskin Creek, Chouaglas); Taitt, "David Taitt's Journal of a Journey through the Creek Country," 28 April 1772, 548–49 (Clay-Catskee); 11 June 1772 and 23 June 1772, Silver Bluff Trading Post Account Book (White Boy accounts); Corkran, *Creek Frontier*, 266 (Edmund Barnard); John Stuart

to Thomas Gage, 2 July 1768, Gage, vol. 78 ("Buzzard's Roost"); Taitt, "David Taitt's Journal of a Journey through the Creek Country," 14 February 1774, 502–3 ("advantageous").

14. Taitt, "David Taitt's Journal of a Journey through the Creek Country," 28 April 1772, 548–49 ("houses"); Charles Stuart to John Stuart, 17 June 1770, *DAR*, 108–10; George Galphin to John Stuart, 2 June 1768, Gage, vol. 78 ("Things," "Powder," "Name").

15. James Grant to John Stuart, 1 February 1769, *FHO* ("utility"); Grant to Thomas Gage, 25 August 1768, Sir Frederick Haldimand Unpublished Papers, Add. MS 21728 (Gordon, St. Marks); Grant to Haldimand, 3 October 1768, Sir Frederick Haldimand Unpublished Papers, Add. MS 21728 ("credible"); Grant to John Stuart, 4 September 1769, Ballindalloch, reel 18 (McMurphy); Grant to John Gordon, 18 September 1769, Ballindalloch, reel 18 (Picolata); George Galphin to Grant, 26 March 1770, Ballindalloch, reel 19 (St. John's); Wright, *Creeks and Seminoles*, 48–49 (Florida trade); Hill, "'Bring Them What They Lack,'" 50 (St. Marks).

16. English officials observed that the Lower *talwas* claimed the territories of East Florida, particularly around St. Marks and the Appalachee River area, "upon the right of Conquest." During the late seventeenth and early eighteenth centuries, Muscogee peoples "conquered and extirpated the Apalache Indians; and demolished the Spanish Forts and Settlements in that Country." Stuart, "Map of the Southern Indian District in America," 1764, Plantations General, CO 323/17, folder 240.

17. For a definitive biography of Tunape, see Hill, "'Bring Them What They Lack."

18. Daniel McMurphy to James Grant, 14 December 1769, Ballindalloch, reel 17; Grant to John Gordon, 6 December 1769, Ballindalloch, reel 18; Daniel McMurphy to Grant, 14 December 1769, Ballindalloch, reel 17; Stuart, "Map of the Southern Indian District in America" ("settlement"); John Stuart to Grant, 16 December 1768, Ballindalloch, reel 15 ("Neighbourhood"); Hill, "'Bring Them What They Lack,'" 36–37 (Tunape), 47 (relationship with Coweta), 48 (St. Marks settlement); Wright, *Creeks and Seminoles*, 111 (Tunape, St. Marks settlement, Escotchaby).

19. 1 September 1767, *CRG*, 10:302–3 ("Convince"); Talk from the Lower Creeks to John Stuart, 19 September 1767, Gage, vol. 72 (Galphin); Cashin, *Lachlan McGillivray, Indian Trader*, 238 (Savery, incident); Cashin, *William Bartram and the American Revolution*, 60 ("trigger," "hot heads").

20. For further information about John Stuart's failed Plan of 1764, see Stuart, "Map of the Southern Indian District in America"; Alden, *John Stuart and the Southern Colonial Frontier;* and Snapp, *John Stuart and the Struggle for Empire.*

21. John Stuart and Peter Chester, governor of West Florida, were less tactful in their correspondence with imperial authorities, writing to Sir Frederick Haldimand and others that "the Traders in the Creek Nation are at the highest pitch of Licentiousness and disorder" and demanding "a British Act of Parliament . . . to pass taking the management of the whole trade out of the hands of these wretches." The Earl of Hillsborough even represented the issue in London for the need "of a proper regulation for the Indian Commerce [that] has long been the subject of very just Complaints and the source of disorders that cannot fail to have the most

fatal consequences," ultimately to little effect. Stuart to Haldimand, 21 June 1772, Sir Frederick Haldimand Unpublished Papers, Add. MS 21672; Governor Peter Chester to the Earl of Dartmouth, 4 June 1774, *DAR*, 8:126–28; Earl of Hillsborough to John Stuart, 3 July 1771, *EAID*, 14:316–17.

22. Paulett, *Empire of Small Places*, 159 (failed reforms); Piker, *Okfuskee*, 149–50 (failed reforms); Braund, *Deerskins and Duffels*, 110–12 (failed reforms); Juricek, *Endgame for Empire*, 80, 125 (failed reforms); Stuart, "Map of the Southern Indian District in America" ("redress"); Post-talk Conference with Upper Creeks, *CRG*, 254–61 ("Numbers," "Evils").

23. Memorial of the Traders to the Creek and Cherokee Nations to Governor James Wright, June 1771, *DAR*, 3:125–27; John Stuart to William Bull, 2 December 1769, *EAID*, 12:92 ("Frauds"); Governor James Wright to Escotchaby, Young Lieutenant of the Cowetas, n.d., CO 5/661, folder 192 ("scarcer"); Charles Stuart to John Stuart, 26 December 1770, *DAR*, 2:303–6 ("confine"); Braund, *Deerskins and Duffels*, 106, 136 (out-settlements); Piker, *Okfuskee*, 152 (out-settlements); John Stuart to James Grant, 1 December 1769, Ballindalloch, reel 17 ("Detriment"); David Taitt, 22 January 1774, Sir Frederick Haldimand Unpublished Papers, Add. MS 21672 ("fitting out"); Wright to Emistisiguo, 5 September 1768, *CRG*, 11:571–82 ("accordingly"); Wright, *Creeks and Seminoles*, 56–57, 63 (debts, scarcity).

24. One trader went so far as to generalize the influx of unlicensed traders as "the great number of worthless traders . . . [who] contributed to hurt the Trade. Towns that used formerly to kill 1800 hides, have not this year killed 500, yet they expected the same quantity of goods as usual, without any probability of ever being able to pay for them: The general cry then was, that the trade would be ruined unless proper regulations were enforced, and an effectual check given to the admission of people of the worst characters, from all quarters, into the nation as traders." *South Carolina & American General Gazette*, 22 May 1767.

25. Charles Stuart to John Stuart, 17 June 1770, *DAR*, 2:108–10 (debts); Braund, *Deerskins and Duffels*, 105–6 (debts); Journal of the Superintendent's Proceedings with the Indians and Traders at Augusta, 28 May 1767, Gage, vol. 137 (violence); Taitt, "David Taitt's Journal of a Journey through the Creek Country," 28 March 1772, 532–34 (Tallassiehatchie); Memorial of the Traders to the Creek and Cherokee Nations to James Wright, June 1771, *DAR*, 3:125–27 ("ruin," "intolerable"); Corkran, *Creek Frontier*, 281 (debts).

26. Philemon Kemp to Governor James Wright, 9 June 1771, *DAR*, 3:118–21 ("mountain"); Two Talks from the Mortar and Handsome Fellow for the Upper and Lower Creeks, 14 July 1763, *CRG*, 9:70–77 ("numerous," "Buffalo," "betwixt").

27. Galphin to the Georgia Governor, Council, and Assembly, January 1764, *CRG*, 9:114–116 (Long Cane); Green, *Politics of Indian Removal*, 4 (*talofas*); James Grant to Thomas Gage, 27 August 1767, Gage, vol. 69 ("plundered"); Howmatcha to Escotchaby, 27 August 1767, Gage, vol. 69 ("Disturbance," "fellows"); John Stuart to Gage, 26 September 1767, Gage, vol. 70 (reimbursement); Stuart to Gage, 27 November 1767, Gage, vol. 7 (prosecutions).

28. James Wright to the Earl of Hillsborough, 8 December 1770, *DAR*, 1:225

("Delinquents," "high time"); *South Carolina & American General Gazette,* 7 August 1767 ("value," "dreadful"); James Habersham to the Head Men and Warriors of the Creek Nation, with accompanying Affidavits, 29 October 1771, *CRG,* 12:70–77 (Oconee, "tyed"); James Habersham to Hillsborough, 21 April 1772, Habersham Family Papers (Carey); John Stuart to Governor Peter Chester, 30 August 1771, *DAR,* 3:174–175 ("cause").

29. Talk from Escotchaby to John Stuart, 26 April 1770, *DAR,* 2:86–87; Stuart to Thomas Gage, 24 May 1770, Gage, vol. 92.

30. It should be noted that Muscogee peoples, including Sempoyaffee and Escotchaby, went to war against the Choctaw in 1765, partly at the instigation of British agents who hoped to distract the *talwas* from taking out their frustrations upon the colonies. This conflict started as primarily a war between the Upper *talwas* and Choctaw, after the killing of the vaunted Choctaw leader Red Captain. At several points during the Muscogee-Choctaw War, one side or the other tried to broker peace, but factions within the *talwas,* as well as Governor James Wright, encouraged the violence to continue. As Wright confided to his superiors in 1774: "I must hope this war will continue between them for these wretches cannot rest without some bloody amusement; and if they were at peace with the Choctaws I should be very apprehensive they would look for amusement in the province of Georgia." This was despite the efforts of many *micos* to restore peace, as Sempoyaffee and Escotchaby tried to do in May 1766 when opposing Emistisiguo's "going to War" against the Choctaw and desiring the *micos* of the Upper *talwas* "to make it up" but to no avail. Governor Johnstone and Provincial Council, 24 April 1765, *EAID,* 12:289; Juricek, ed., *EAID,* 12:327; Governor James Wright to the Earl of Hillsborough, 8 December 1770, *DAR 1,* 225; Wright to the Earl of Dartmouth, 17 June 1773, *DAR,* 6:156–58; Stephen Forrester to Governor Johnstone, 25 May 1766, *EAID,* 12:297.

31. Braund, *Deerskins and Duffels,* 131 (balance, "volatile"); Piker, *Okfuskee,* 176–77, 185–86 (generation tension); George Galphin to James Grant, 26 March 1770, Ballindalloch, reel 19 ("mad," "white people"); Talk from the Lower Creeks to John Stuart, 19 September 1767, Gage, vol. 72 ("power"); John Stuart to Grant, 1 December 1769, Ballindalloch, reel 17 ("Frontiers"); Philemon Kemp to Georgia Governor with Talks from Emistisiguo and the Gun Merchant, 9 June 1771, *DAR,* 3:118–21.

32. Braund, "Guardians of Tradition and Handmaidens to Change," 245 (masculinity crisis); John Stuart to the Lords Commissioners of Trade and Plantations, n.d., Plantations General, CO 323/17, folder 170 ("manhood"); Stuart to Upper Creek Headmen, 20 January 1772, *EAID,* 12:423 ("practice"); Edward Barnard, James Jackson, P. Welsh, and J. Waters to Stuart, 20 July 1767, Gage, vol. 69 ("Steal").

33. Governor Peter Chester to the Earl of Hillsborough, 9 March 1771, *DAR,* 3:65–66 ("surrounded"); Philemon Kemp to Governor James Wright, 9 June 1771, *DAR,* 3:118–21 ("rights"); *South Carolina & American General Gazette,* 30 October 1767 ("Virginia"), 23 May 1770 (Wrightsborough); 9 December 1771, *CRG,* 12:148–54 ("Whipped"); George Galphin to John Stuart, 2 June 1768, Gage, vol. 78 ("War").

34. George Galphin to James Grant, 26 March 1770, Ballindalloch, reel 19 ("pease"); John Stuart's Conference with the Lower and Upper Creeks, 14 October

1768, Ballindalloch, reel 18 ("power"); Stephen Forrester to Grant, Spring 1768, Ballindalloch, reel 4 ("taken," "Warr"); James Wright to the Young Lieutenant of Coweta, 2 October 1770, *DAR,* 1:225; Talk from Escotchaby or the Young Lieutenant of the Lower Creeks to John Stuart, 26 April 1770, *DAR,* 2:86–87 ("colour").

35. Thomas Gage to the Earl of Hillsborough, 7 October 1772, in Carter, *Correspondence of General Thomas Gage,* 1:335 ("exterminated"); Headmen of the Lower Creeks to John Stuart, 19 September 1767, Indian Affairs, 73–75 ("disturbance"); Stuart to James Grant, 22 July 1765, Ballindalloch, reel 18 ("Hint"); George Roupell to Stuart, 10 December 1767, Gage, vol. 73 ("private"); Talk from James Wright to Emistisiguo, 5 September 1768, *CRG,* 10:571–82 (St. Mary's boundary line).

36. John Stuart to Thomas Gage, 21 January 1766, Gage, vol. 47 ("Bounds"); Talk from James Wright to Emistisiguo, 5 September 1768, *CRG,* 10:571–82; Talk of the Headmen of the Cowetas to Wright, 8 June 1766, *CRG,* 28:159–61; Journal of the Superintendent's Proceedings of Congress held at Augusta, 12–14 November 1768, Gage, vol. 137 (Quakers, "Number"); Wright to James Grant, 20 October 1768, Ballindalloch, reel 18 ("disposed," "Body," "prevail").

37. Talk from James Wright to Emistisiguo, 5 September 1768, *CRG,* 11:571–82 ("Countrey"); Taitt, "David Taitt's Journal of a Journey through the Creek Country," 30 April 1772, 550 (cattle); Taitt, "David Taitt's Journal of a Journey through the Creek Country," 521 ("Hireling"); Taitt, "David Taitt's Journal of a Journey through the Creek Country," 2 March 1772, 514 ("River"); Post-talk Conference with the Upper Creeks, n.d., *CRG,* vol. 28, pt. 2, 254–61; James Wright to James Grant, 20 October 1768, Ballindalloch, reel 18 ("Mr. Galphin's"); "Creek Complaints to David Taitt over Nonperformance of Terms of 1773 Treaty," 3 January 1774, *EAID,* 12:134 ("Baggs," "Congress").

38. For more specifics, see Rindfleisch, *George Galphin's Intimate Empire.*

39. Braund, *Deerskins and Duffels,* 151 (debtors); James Habersham, 2 May 1775, *Letters of Hon. James Habersham,* 21 (ten thousand pounds); Claim of George Galphin for Self and Other Indian Traders—Certificate of the Secretary of the Georgia Governor and Council, 6 June 1775, Le Conte Genealogical Collection (ten thousand pounds); "Creek Complaints to David Taitt over Nonperformance of Terms of 1773 Treaty," 3 January 1774, *EAID,* 12:134 (Sempoyaffee).

40. Petition of Lachlan McGillivray, John Rae, and George Galphin, 1 January 1765, *CRG,* 9:269–70 (fifty thousand acres, Ogeechee); 19 February 1768, *CRG,* 17:269–70 ("Protestant"); 9 December 1771, *CRG,* 12:148–54 (Carey, *mico* deaths); James Habersham to James Wright, 12 March 1772, *Letters of Hon. James Habersham,* 169–70 ("kill"); 6 February 1770, *CRG,* 109–10 ("uneasiness").

41. Taitt, "David Taitt's Journal of a Journey through the Creek Country," 30 April 1772, 550 (Galphin land grant, "granted"); 29 September 1783, in Dumont, *Colonial Georgia Genealogical Data,* 40 (eighty-eight thousand); Talk of the Second Man of the Cussetaws to Governor John Houston and Georgia Executive Council, 14 April 1784, CIT, 145–47 ("23 miles"); "Kings, Headmen, and Warriors of the Creek Nation to Our Sister Mataway," 27 August 1772, in Dumont, *Colonial Georgia Genealogical Data,* 40 (land cession, signatories); Memorandum, 25 February 1773, book BBB, Georgia Colonial Conveyance Books ("attorney").

42. "At a Convention of the Over Hills Cherokee Chiefs and Beloved Men at Toogalie," 7 March 1771, CO 5/661, folders 194–96 ("Debts," "settled"); John Stuart to the Earl of Hillsborough, 12 June 1772, *DAR*, 5:114–17 ("conquest," "property"); "At a Meeting of the Cherokee Indians at Fort Charlot," 8 June 1771, CO 5/661, folders 211–12 ("well"); Taitt, "David Taitt's Journal of a Journey through the Creek Country," 29 April 1772, 548–49 ("two young men"); Stuart to Frederick Haldimand, 13 September 1772, Sir Frederick Haldimand Unpublished Papers, Add. MS 21672 (Creek-Cherokee tensions); Augusta Traders to President James Habersham, 16 April 1772, *DAR*, 5:72–73 ("affair").

43. Proclamation of Governor James Wright, 24 October 1774, in Force, *American Archives*, 1:889–91 ("Province"); James Wright to the Earl of Dartmouth, 10 August 1773, *DAR*, 6:202; James Habersham to the Earl of Hillsborough, 21 April 1772, Habersham Family Papers ("Colony"); David Taitt to John Stuart, 17 March 1772, in Taitt, "David Taitt's Journal of a Journey through the Creek Country," 521; Memorial of the Traders to the Creek and Cherokee Nations to Governor James Wright, June 1771, *DAR*, 3:125–27 ("ruin").

44. Memorial of the Traders to the Creek and Cherokee Nations to Governor James Wright; David Taitt to John Stuart, 16 March 1772, in Taitt, "David Taitt's Journal of a Journey through the Creek Country," 521 ("Consent," "Debts," "Goods").

45. Braund, *Deerskins and Duffels,* 151 ("jurisdiction"); James Habersham to George Galphin, 12 August 1772, *Letters of Hon. James Habersham,* 199–200 ("Trouble"); "At a Meeting of the Cherokee Indians near Fort Charlot," 8 June 1771, Board of Trade and Secretaries of State: America and West Indies, Original Correspondence, Board of Trade: Georgia, 1734–1784, Colonial Office Records, CO 5/651, folder 146 ("Lands").

46. Juricek, *Endgame for Empire,* 177–78; Lower Creek Chiefs to John Stuart, 19 September 1772, *EAID,* 12:113–14 (Escotchaby's address).

47. The natural scientist William Bartram provided one of the few testimonials to the proceedings of the 1773 congress. As he remarked at the conclusion of the treaty: "The preparatory business of the surveyors being now accomplished . . . [and] anxious for travelling . . . joined with me the caravan, consisting of surveyors, astronomers, artisans, chain-carriers, markers, guides, and hunters, besides a very respectable number of gentlemen, who joined us, in order to *speculate* in the lands." Slaughter, *William Bartram,* 54.

48. John Stuart to Thomas Gage, 24 November 1772, *EAID,* 12:116 ("tired"); James Wright to the Earl of Dartmouth, 10 August 1773, *DAR,* 6:202 ("beloved"); James Habersham to George Galphin, 1 October 1772, Habersham Family Papers, folder 4 (Cherokee secret); Slaughter, *William Bartram,* 388 (Tugaloo, "dissolve"); Lower Creek Chiefs to Stuart, 19 September 1772, *EAID,* 12:113–14 (gifts "Steelyard," "desires"); Slaughter, *William Bartram,* 57 ("point," "course," "err," "liar"), 439–40 ("Parties"); Wright to Dartmouth, 17 June 1773, *DAR,* 4:156–58; Haynes, *Patrolling the Border,* 40–41 (steelyard trade).

49. Slaughter, *William Bartram,* 52–53 ("demand," "force," "amicable"); Juricek, *Endgame for Empire,* 182 ("divide"); David Taitt to John Stuart, 9 September 1773, Sir

Frederick Haldimand Unpublished Papers, Add. MS 21672 ("ill," "Account"); Taitt to Stuart, 20 September 1775, Indian Affairs, CO 5/74, document 119–20 ("leaving off," "rash").

50. In addition to Howmatcha, we know the identities of three other young men "named Silloya and Nottawega . . . and Sousea." *South Carolina Gazette; and Country Journal*, 11 October 1774.

51. Petitions for Settling the Ceded Lands from Georgia, South Carolina, North Carolina, and Pennsylvania, 15 July 1773, *CRG*, 12:371–76 (flood of settlers); David Taitt to Frederick Haldimand, 22 January 1774, Sir Frederick Haldimand Unpublished Papers, Add. MS 21672.

52. It should be noted that historian Joshua Haynes understands these attacks to be the beginning of, or an early part of, Muscogee "border patrols" that policed their territories to try and stop English encroachments. In fact Haynes argues that the violence of the early to mid-1770s, led by "Coweta and a few other towns," is what precipitated the "rise of Creek border patrols." Haynes, *Patrolling the Border*, 22, 45–46, 60.

53. John Stuart to the Earl of Dartmouth, 13 February 1774, *DAR*, 8:48–49 (violence); *GGZ*, 2 February 1774 ("stockade," "mangled"); Stuart to Thomas Gage, 12 May 1774, *EAID*, 12:143–45 ("disavowed"); *GGZ*, 25 May 1774 ("physic").

54. *Virginia Gazette*, 24 March 1774 ("Terrour"); Speech of William Bull, *South Carolina Gazette; and Country Journal*, 8 March 1774 ("general War"); James Wright to the Earl of Dartmouth, 12 March 1774, *CRG*, 28:186–90 ("Furious"); *Belfast News Letter*, 15–19 April 1774 ("hatchet"); Peace Talk from the Creek Indians, 27 June 1774, in Force, *American Archives*, 1:451.

55. Several historians, such as Kevin Kokomoor and John Juricek, call this conflict the "Ceded Lands crisis." Kokomoor, *Of One Mind and of One Government*, 16; Juricek, *Endgame for Empire*, 187-201.

56. *South Carolina Gazette; and Country Journal*, 15 March 1774, ("grieved," "twice"); David Taitt to Frederick Haldimand, 22 January 1774, Sir Frederick Haldimand Unpublished Papers, Add. MS 21672 ("War"); Governor James Wright to the Earl of Dartmouth, 13 January 1774, *DAR*, 13:30–32 ("stop"); Wright to Dartmouth, 4 May 1774, *DAR*, 7:101 ("twice").

57. Samuel Thomas to David Taitt, 10 December 1774, Gage, vol. 122 ("hunt"); Juan Josef Eligio de la Puente to the Marquis de la Torre, 6 March 1773, General de Indias ("Arms," "San Marcos," "crude," "Venom"); Account of Rafael de la Luz, 16 March 1775, General de Indias (Escotchaby and family); Report of Don Rafael de la Luz, 2 May 1775, General de Indias ("22 English," "obedience"); Alexander Cameron to John Stuart, 2 August 1774, Indian Affairs, CO 5/75, folder 174 ("promised"); Report of Don Rafael de la Luz, 2 August 1775, General de Indias (Tampa Bay); Wright, *Creeks and Seminoles*, 106 (Coweta-Spanish negotiations).

58. Peace Talk from the Creek Indians, 27 June 1774, in Force, *American Archives*, 1:451 (embargo); Alexander Cameron to John Stuart, 3 June 1774, *EAID*, 14:356–58 ("Power," "Influence"); Conference between Governor James Wright and the Upper Creek Indians, 14 April 1774, *DAR*, 8:90–95 ("shut up," "stand," "stop"); Emistisiguo

to Stuart, 4 February 1774, Indian Affairs, CO 5/75, folders 133–34 ("Part," "paths").

59. Talk from the Lower and Middle Cherokees and Their Beloved Women to the Creeks of Coweta, 21 February 1774, *EAID*, 14:348–49.

60. *GGZ*, 2 March 1774; Haynes, *Patrolling the Border*, 54.

61. Fee was "apprehended by John Anderson . . . and one Williams," who was "wounded with an axe." *South Carolina Gazette; and Country Journal*, 17 May 1774.

62. *SCG*, 4 April 1774 ("Fee," "Errand"); *South Carolina Gazette; and Country Journal*, 17 May 1774 ("men"); *GGZ*, 13 April 1774 ("iron"); Conference between Governor James Wright and the Upper Creek Indians (the Elk); *South Carolina Gazette; and Country Journal*, 29 March 1774 (Buck); Piecuch, *Three Peoples, One King*, 33 (the Elk, Thomas Fee).

63. One of the three Cowetas who were executed was Oktulgi, who was "shot by the Cusseta people, and lived four Days after he received the Wound." But even on his deathbed, Oktulgi still "desired his Relations to revenge his Death on the Virginians, and not give out until every one of his Relations should fall." David Taitt to John Stuart, 7 July 1774, Indian Affairs, CO 5/75.

64. George Galphin to Escotchaby, 23 March 1774, *EAID*, 12:137–38 ("Friend," "Power," "poor"); *GGZ*, 25 May 1774; *SCG*, 27 June 1774 (satisfaction," "Murderers").

65. Governor James Wright and John Stuart to the Earl of Dartmouth, 21 October 1774, *DAR*, 7:193 ("Treaty," Le Cuffee); Treaty with the Upper and Lower Creeks at Savannah, 20 October 1774, *EAID*, 12:153–55 ("Hut"); Peace Talk from the Creek Indians, 27 June 1774, in Force, *American Archives*, 1:45.

Chapter Six

1. Address by Henry Hamilton to the Creek Nation, 13 November 1775, in *Colonial and State Records of North Carolina*, 10:329–30 (Galphin's office/commission); David Holmes to John Stuart, 26 September 1776, Indian Affairs, CO 5/75 (letters); Thomas Brown to Stuart, 29 September 1776, Indian Affairs, CO 5/75 ("Virginians," "apprehended").

2. Certificate of Rafael de la Luz, 24 January 1776, General de Indias; George Galphin to Council of Safety, 26 May 1776, South Carolina Department of Archives and History, Record #56: Series S213089, Box 0003, Folder 00010, Item 000.

3. Haynes, *Patrolling the Border*, 71.

4. John Stuart to Lower and Upper Creek Chiefs, 15 August 1775, *EAID*, 12:169–70 ("Dispute," "Disposition"); George Galphin to Willie Jones, 26 October 1776, in Force, *American Archives*, 3:648–50 ("persuade"); Address by the Commissioners of Indian Affairs for the United States to the Creek Nation, 13 November 1775, in *Colonial and State Records of North Carolina*, 10:330–31 ("ammunition").

5. Lower Creek Reply to John Stuart, 29 September 1775, *EAID*, 12:177–78.

6. Galphin to Jones, 26 October 1776; Patrick Carr, "A Journal of My Proceedings from Ogeechee to the Creek Nation and Back Again," 23 September 1775, Henry Laurens Papers ("come out," "starve"); John Stuart to the Lower and Upper Creek

Chiefs, 15 August 1775, *EAID,* 12:169–70 ("white"); Talk from the Patucy Mico to George Galphin, 4 November 1778, GGL 1779 ("white path"); Talk from Ostenalley Mico of Okfuskee to Galphin, n.d., Benjamin Franklin Papers; Henry Laurens to the Georgetown Committee, 15 March 1776, in *HL,* 11:165 (Stukychee); Haynes, *Patrolling the Border,* 64 (neutrality, trade).

7. Thomas Brown to John Stuart, 29 September 1776, Indian Affairs, CO 5/75 ("Virginians"); Galphin to Jones, 26 October 1776 ("meet them," "Doctor"); Piecuch, *Three Peoples, One King,* 114 (Georgia Assembly); George Galphin to Henry Laurens, 26 October 1778, in *HL,* 14:452–54; Galphin to Laurens, 13 October 1777, in *HL,* 11:552–53 ("Indian Line"); Petition of the Inhabitants of the Parish of St. George and St. Paul, including the Ceded Lands, to General Charles Lee, 31 July 1776, in Force, *American Archives,* 1:685 ("exterminate"); John Wells Jr. to Laurens, 28 August 1778, in *HL,* 14:242–43 ("Fire").

8. Snyder, "Conquered Enemies, Adopted Kin, and Owned People," 261 (Broad); Piecuch, *Three Peoples, One King,* 76 (fall 1776 attacks); David Taitt to John Stuart, 7 July 1776, *DAR,* 12:159–61 ("revenge"); Journal of a Conference between the American Commissioners and the Creeks at Augusta, 16–19 May 1776, *EAID,* 12:183–90 (nephew, "minds"); Talk of the Lower Town Chiefs, 8 November 1775, Indian Affairs, CO 5/75 ("path"); A Talk from Opoitley Mico of the Tallassees, the Tallassee King's Son, and Ematla or Fools Factor, 22 February 1778, GGL 1779 ("black beads," "Blood").

9. William McIntosh to Patrick Tonyn, 29 May 1777, EFL, CO 5/540, 607–9 ("thirty," Tiger clan); David Taitt to John Stuart, 5 June 1777, Indian Affairs, CO 5/78, folder 157 ("Chiefs," Mad Dog); Taitt to Tonyn, 15 August 1777, EFL, CO 5/540, 695–96 ("irritated"); Stuart to Lord George Germain, 22 August 1777, *DAR,* 14:168–69 ("number," "harass," "rebel"); Stuart to William Howe, 23 August 1777, Carleton Papers, vol. 6, 649 (famine); George Galphin to Henry Laurens, 19 October 1777, GGL 1779 ("steady"); Taitt to Stuart, 12 July 1777, Indian Affairs, CO 5/75, 682–83 ("single"); Ingram, *Indians and British Outposts in Eighteenth-Century America.*

10. For more particulars of the violence between 1776 and 1778, see Searcy, *Georgia-Florida Contest in the American Revolution.*

11. John Stuart to Lord George Germain, 6 October 1777, *DAR,* 14:192–95 ("armed," "injury"); David Taitt to Stuart, 23 May 1777, *DAR,* 14:93–95 ("220," "going to see," "fort"); Taitt to Stuart, 12 July 1777, Indian Affairs, CO 5/75, 682–83 (Coosa boats); Talk from the Cussitah King, Dog Lieutenant, Tallassee King, Escotcabie, and Sempoyaffee, 6 February 1777, *DAR,* 13:52 ("Attack").

12. David Taitt to John Stuart, 23 May 1777, *DAR,* 14:93–95 ("Choctaws"); William McIntosh to Patrick Tonyn, 29 May 1777, EFL, CO 5/540, 607–9 ("war hoop"); Taitt to unknown, 5 June 1777, Indian Affairs, CO 5/78, folder 157 (McGillivray, "message"); Taitt to Stuart, 7 July 1776, *DAR,* 12:159–61 (Emistisiguo); Talk from the Cussitah Town in the Creek Nation to John Stuart, 10 March 1777, Indian Affairs, CO 5/78, folder 111 (Cusseta, Tallassee).

13. John Rutledge to Henry Laurens, 8 August 1777, *HL,* 11:434–35 (Handsome Fellow, "Goods," eagle tail, "threw"); John Lewis Gervais to Laurens, 16 August

1777, in *HL*, 11:461 ("prisoners," "War"); Rutledge to unknown, 30 August 1777, John Rutledge Papers ("Emissaries," "vengeance"); Piecuch, *Three Peoples, One King,* 113 (killing of Dooley's brother); Haynes, *Patrolling the Border,* 73 (Handsome Fellow imprisonment).

    14. George Galphin to Henry Laurens, 22 December 1777, in *HL*, 12:175–77 ("Drove"); Galphin to Laurens, 13 October 1777, in *HL*, 11:552–53 (goods, "Drove"); William McIntosh to Alexander Cameron, 6 July 1777, in Boehm, *Records of the British Public Records Office,* reel 7, vol. 78 ("Long Crop"); Talk from the Head Men Nea Mico and Nea Clucko to Galphin, 13 October 1777, GGL 1779 ("Women").

    15. The Cowetas wisely advised McIntosh, who "wanted to have returned" immediately to Cusseta, to instead wait, and "would not consent to it until the Cussitahs are brought to there senses." John Stuart to Lord George Germain, 6 October 1777, *DAR*, 14:192–95.

    16. Ibid. (Coweta, "guarded"); John Stuart to William Howe, 4 February 1778, Henry Clinton Papers (Coweta); David Taitt to Patrick Tonyn, 15 August 1777, EFL, CO 5/540, 695–96 ("behavior," "irritated," "Scouting"); George Galphin to Henry Laurens, 13 October 1777, in *HL*, 11:552–53 ("Deliver," "Peaceable"); Stuart to Lord George Germain, 22 August 1777, *DAR*, 14:168–69 ("number"); Tonyn to Germain, 26 December 1777, *DAR*, 14:276 ("property"); Stuart to William Knox, 26 August 1777, Indian Affairs, CO 5/78, folder 220 ("spoilt").

    17. David Taitt to John Stuart, 5 June 1777, Indian Affairs, CO 5/78, folder 157 (nephew); Blackmon, *Dark and Bloody Ground,* 121–22 (nephew); Corkran, *Creek Frontier,* 303–4 (nephew); Stuart to Lord George Germain, 5 March 1778, *DAR*, 15:54–55 ("rangers"); John Lewis Gervais to Henry Laurens, 21 September 1778, John Lewis Gervais Papers ("killed"); John Houston to Laurens, 1 October 1778, in *HL*, 14:375–76 ("Part," "broke"); Alexander McGillivray to Stuart, 9 March 1778, Carleton Papers, 9:998 (Chehaw, "point"); Stuart to William Knox, 9 October 1778, *DAR*, 13:360 ("terror"); Minutes of the Executive Council, 26 August 1778, in Candler, *Revolutionary Records of the State of Georgia,* 2:90 ("appearances"); Piecuch, *Three Peoples, One King,* 114–17 (other *talwas* join the war in 1778); Haynes, *Patrolling the Border,* 63–64.

    18. Timothy Barnard to John Stuart, 9 November 1778, Indian Affairs, CO 5/75, 161–66 ("intends"); Stuart to Lord George Germain, 19 May 1778, *DAR*, 15:121–22 (St. Augustine); Alexander Cameron to Germain, 18 December 1779, Indian Affairs, CO 5/75, 329 (staging base); Piecuch, *Three Peoples, One King,* 151–54 (Southern Strategy); Talk from Will's Friend and the Half-Breed to George Galphin, 9 June 1778, GGL 1779 ("Virginia People").

    19. In the aftermath of the battle at Fincastle in summer 1776, newspapers reports, eyewitness accounts, and rumors from western Georgia all differed in describing whether it was the "Cherokee [or] Creek Indians" who "fought . . . a party of the Fincastle militia." *Pennsylvania Evening Post,* 13 August 1776; *Pennsylvania Ledger; or the Virginia, Maryland, Pennsylvania, & New-Jersey Weekly Advertiser,* 17 August 1776, 31 August 1776.

    20. As Henry Laurens remarked in the wake of the expeditions against the Cherokee, "Colonel Williamson & his parties have driven back . . . the lower Towns [and]

killed as many as could be come at in fight & taken some Prisoners. . . . They have also destroyed Sennecca, Keowee, Warrachy, Estatoe, Toxaway, & Sugar Town together with the Crops of Corn & other grain found in fields & Barns." Account of a Battle between the Militia of Fincastle County, Virginia, and the Cherokee and Creek Indians, 2 August 1776, in Force, *American Archives,* 1:464 ("blood"); Henry Laurens to John Laurens, 14 August 1776, in *HL,* 11:228–31 ("Williamson," "Keowee").

21. John Stuart to General Thomas Gage, 15 November 1775, in Force, *American Archives,* 3:714–15 ("ancient"); Galphin to Jones, 26 October 1776 ("broke out," "horse-loads," "sent off"); Account of a Battle between the Militia of Fincastle County, Virginia, and the Cherokee and Creek Indians ("blood"); Henry Laurens to John Laurens, 14 August 1776 (Keowee).

22. John Stuart to Lord George Germain, 14 June 1777, *DAR,* 14:114–15 ("distressed," "eyes," "great many"); Stuart to William Howe, 11 July 1777, Carleton Papers, 6:602 ("Corn"); Boulware, *Deconstructing the Cherokee Nation,* 160 (refugees, "accounts"); Stuart to Germain, 23 January 1778, Indian Affairs, CO 5/79, folder 64 ("assisted"); Alexander Cameron to Germain, 18 December 1778, Indian Affairs, CO 5/75, 329 ("Expedition"); Haynes, *Patrolling the Border,* 72 (Cherokee refugees).

23. As James Hill observes, "Havana hosted three different groups of Creeks per year, which cost the Spanish treasury over 1,700 pesos annually between 1774 and 1778. Most of the visitors were Lower Creeks of various backgrounds," but none more esteemed than "Coweta leader Escochabe." Hill, "'Bring Them What They Lack,'" 59–60.

24. Escotchaby's negotiations with the Spanish were nearly sabotaged in October 1776 when a Spanish fisherman and his crew murdered a Muscogee man. As the Spanish governor de la Torre reported to his superiors in Madrid, a "Captain of the Spanish Boat" killed the man because of a "jealousy over a female Indian who was aboard during one of his trips." After the killing hostility "spread through the Towns of Cabeta. It has caused such anger amongst those inhabitants against our Nation, as has been learned by some (of our) Fisherman, that it would be very risky to have our Boats arrive on the Coast until the passage of time has cooled their desire for vengeance." De la Torre then actively searched for the fisherman, that "one man" who nearly pushed Coweta to "have declared Bloody War against the Spaniards." De la Torre to Jose de Galvez, 9 October 1776, General de Indias; Patrick Tonyn to Lord George Germain, 10 June 1776, EFL, CO 5/556.

25. South Carolina Council of Safety to Georgia Council of Safety, 24 July 1775, in *HL,* 10:243–44 ("Dozen"); Saunt, *West of the Revolution,* 188, 204–5 (Escotchaby's 1775 visit to Havana, "needs"); Certificate of Rafael de la Luz, 24 January 1776, General de Indias ("horses," "Boats"); de Torre to Jose de Galvez, 11 April 1776, General de Indias ("Boats"); Juan Josef Eligio de la Puente, 28 December 1777, General de Indias; John Stuart to William Howe, 17 July 1777, Carleton Papers, 6:602 (Tibulayche); Richard Henderson to George Galphin, 12 June 1778, GGL 1779; *Virginia Gazette,* 25 December 1779 ("Apalachee," "tobacco"); Hill, "'Bring Them What They Lack,'" 66 (Spanish serious).

26. David Holmes and Thomas Scott to John Stuart, 19 October 1777, Carleton

Papers, 7:706 ("Old," "Censure"); Declarations of the Boat Captain Jose Mermudez and the Cacique Tunape, 22 December 1777, General de Indias ("Priest"); Talk from Ostenalley Mico of Okfuskee to George Galphin, n.d., Benjamin Franklin Papers ("Jeagay"); Galphin to Henry Laurens, 8 March 1778, *HL*, 525–26 (Fine Bones); Talk by an Oakfusky Fellow a Friend of the White Lieutenant to George Galphin, 19 July 1778, GGL 1779 (talk); Piecuch, *Three Peoples, One King*, 113 (Havana visits); Hill, "'Bring Them What They Lack,'" 36–37 (Havana visits).

27. Don Francisco Ruiz del Canto, 26 September 1779, General de Indias.

28. Ibid.; Instruction of Don Juan Francisco Ruiz del Canto, 16 December 1779, General de Indias.

29. We have no idea how or why Escotchaby died, for he seemed in good health a few months earlier. But with all his travels between Coweta and East Florida in December 1779 to confront Estimape, he may have contracted an illness, or he may have succumbed to old age. Don Francisco Ruiz del Canto, 16 December 1779, General de Indias.

30. While we have the fragments of Escotchaby's death, there is no evidence for what happened to Sempoyaffee. Again, in the absence of documentation, all we can do is speculate as to his fate. It may be plausible that his omission from the Portado del Archivo General de Indias—which details the confrontations between Escotchaby and Estimape in 1779—suggests that he died sometime before then. While Sempoyaffee remained active in the fighting during the war, if he had been killed in battle, Muscogee *micos* or British authorities would have mentioned as much, like they did when Emistisiguo was killed near Savannah in summer 1781. In effect the silence surrounding Sempoyaffee's death may lead us to conclude he died a normal death of old age or illness. Thomas Brown to the Earl of Shelburne, 25 September 1781, *DAR*, 21:122.

31. It should be noted, though, that in the wake of Sempoyaffee's disappearance and Escotchaby's death, a faction of the Cowetas—likely those who supported Sempoyaffee and Escotchaby—resumed their defiant stance against the Americans. Several of Coweta's young men also joined in the defense of the British garrison at Pensacola in 1781, collaborated with Emistisiguo and some of the Upper *talwas* to attack Georgia in 1781 and 1782, and entertained talks with the Cherokee and "Northern Indians" to unite against the revolutionaries. And when Coweta received news that the British were agreeing to peace with the Americans, Fine Bones of Coweta stated, "We cannot take a Virginian . . . by the hand we cannot look them in the face," and he "desired that the Governor . . . and the Superintendent would inform the Great King that if he meant to throw away the Land—to send Vessels to take them off as they were determined to follow their friends." Piecuch, *Three Peoples, One King*, 255, 304–5; Green, "Creek Confederacy in the American Revolution," 54; Thomas Brown to unknown, 1 June 1783, Indian Affairs, CO 5/82; Brown to Lord George Germain, 6 April 1782, Indian Affairs, CO 5/75, 674–77; William McIntosh to Brown, April 1783, Indian Affairs, CO 5/82; Patrick Tonyn, Brigadier General McArthur, and Thomas Brown Talk to the Creek Indians, 15 May 1783, Indian Affairs, CO 5/75, 679–81.

32. Instruction of Don Juan Francisco Ruiz del Canto, 16 December 1779,

General de Indias ("Died"); Treaty of Augusta with the Creeks, 1 November 1783, *EAID*, 18:372–73 ("forgotten").

Conclusion

1. DuVal, *Independence Lost,* 351; Report from Henry Knox, Secretary of War, to the President of the United States, George Washington, 6 July 1789, in US Congress, *American State Papers,* 1:15–16 ("war," "inroads," "interference"); Alexander McGillivray to Thomas Pinckney, 26 February 1789, in US Congress, *American State Papers,* 1:20 ("spirits").

2. Thomas Brown to Sir Frederick North, 24 October 1783, Indian Affairs, CO 5/82, folder 403 ("elected"); DuVal, *Independence Lost,* 341 (Tallassee King); Haynes, *Patrolling the Border,* 115 (Nea Mico).

3. *Daily Advertiser, or New York Advertiser,* 27 October 1788 ("defence"); John Galphin to General Jared Irwin, 21 August 1793, in US Congress, *American State Papers,* 1:371 ("limits," "free"); DuVal, *Independence Lost,* 254 ("independent"); Haynes, *Patrolling the Border,* 83–84, 89 ("resistance"), 201 ("autonomy," "coalescence"); *Federal Gazette, and Philadelphia Evening Post,* 22 June 1789 ("dispute"); *Pennsylvania Packet, and Daily Advertiser,* 20 June 1788 ("Congress," "unhappy"), 7 July 1790; George Galphin to Andrew Pickens and Henry Osborn, 27 May 1789, in US Congress, *American State Papers,* 1:35–36 ("lands"); "A Treaty of Peace and Friendship between the United States of America and the Creek Nation of Indians," *Pennsylvania Packet, and Daily Advertiser,* 13 August 1790 ("Treaty"); Wright, *Creeks and Seminoles,* 115–17 (McGillivray and nationalization); Kokomoor, *Of One Mind and of One Government,* 15–17.

4. Carter, "Observations of John Stuart and Governor James Grant of East," 829–30.

BIBLIOGRAPHY

Unpublished Primary Sources

Andrew Pickens Papers, 1782–1804. Microform 51–121. South Carolina Historical Society, Charleston.

Belfast News Letter, 1738–1865. PRONI MIC/19. Public Records Office of Northern Ireland, Belfast.

Belfast (Ireland) Newspaper Collection, 29 July 1729–27 December 1776. MS B: Belfast Newspapers. South Caroliniana Library. University of South Carolina, Columbia.

Benjamin Franklin Papers, Part XIII: Miscellaneous Franklin Materials, 1640–1791, Mss B.F85inventory13. American Philosophical Society. Philadelphia.

Board of Trade and Secretaries of State: America and West Indies, Original Correspondence, Board of Trade: East Florida, 1763–1777. Colonial Office Records, EFL, CO 5/540–58. British National Archives, Kew: Great Britain.

Board of Trade and Secretaries of State: America and West Indies, Original Correspondence, Board of Trade: Georgia, 1734–1784. Colonial Office Records, CO 5/636–52. British National Archives, Kew: Great Britain.

Board of Trade and Secretaries of State: America and West Indies, Original Correspondence, Board of Trade: South Carolina, 1733–1775. Colonial Office Records, CO 5/363–80. British National Archives, Kew: Great Britain.

Board of Trade and Secretaries of State: America and West Indies, Original Correspondence, North Carolina: Sessional Papers—Assembly, 1771–1774. Colonial Office Records, CO 5/357. British National Archives, Kew: Great Britain.

Board of Trade and Secretaries of State: America and West Indies, Original Correspondence, Proprieties: Board of Trade Correspondence, Q Nos. 50–208. Colonial Office Records, CO 5/1265. British National Archives, Kew: Great Britain.

Board of Trade and Secretaries of State: America and West Indies, Original Correspondence, Secretary of State: East Florida, 1768–1783. Colonial Office Records, CO 5/566. British National Archives, Kew: Great Britain.

Board of Trade and Secretaries of State: America and West Indies, Original Correspondence, Secretary of State: Georgia, 1735–1784. Colonial Office Records, CO 5/654–65. British National Archives, Kew: Great Britain.

Board of Trade and Secretaries of State: America and West Indies, Original Correspondence, Secretary of State: Indian Affairs, 1763–1784. Colonial Office Records, CO 5/65–82. British National Archives, Kew: Great Britain.

Board of Trade and Secretaries of State: America and West Indies, Original Correspondence, Secretary of State: Military and Naval Dispatches. Colonial Office Records, CO 5/61. British National Archives, Kew: Great Britain.

Board of Trade and Secretaries of State: America and West Indies, Original Correspondence, Secretary of State: South Carolina, 1734–1776. Colonial Office Records, CO 5/383–87. British National Archives, Kew: Great Britain.

Board of Trade and Secretaries of State: America and West Indies, Original Correspondence, Secretary of State: South Carolina, 1730–1784. Colonial Office Records, CO 5/388–97. British National Archives, Kew: Great Britain.

Board of Trade and Secretaries of State: America and West Indies, Original Correspondence, Shipping Returns: East Florida, 1765–1769. Colonial Office Records, CO 5/573. British National Archives, Kew: Great Britain.

Board of Trade and Secretaries of State: America and West Indies, Original Correspondence, Shipping Returns: South Carolina, 1736–1775. Colonial Office Records, CO 5/510–11. British National Archives, London Kew.

Board of Trade and Secretaries of State: America and West Indies, Original Correspondence, South Carolina: Sessional Papers—Council, 1749–1755. CO 5/471. British National Archives, Kew: Great Britain.

Board of Trade and Secretaries of State: America and West Indies, Original Correspondence, South Carolina: Sessional Papers—Council in Assembly, 1757–1760. Colonial Office Records, CO 5/474. British National Archives, Kew: Great Britain.

Boehm, Randolph, ed. *Records of the British Public Records Office, Colonial Office, Series 5 Part I: Westward Expansion, 1700–1783*, vols. 1–8 [microfilm]. Frederick, MD: University Publications of America, 1983.

Bonar, William. A Draught of the Creek Nation. Records of the Colonial Office, Maps and Plans: Series I—North American Colonies, North and South Carolina. CO 700/Carolina21. British National Archives, Kew: Great Britain.

British Headquarters Papers of the British Army in America (Carleton Papers), 1747–1783 [microfilm]. Washington, DC: Recordak Corporation Microfilming Service, 1957.

British Public Records Office, Records of the Colonial Office, America and West Indies: Indian Affairs, Series 1, vols. 65–82, 225 [microfilm]. University of Oklahoma, Norman.

Candler, Allen D., ed. *The Colonial Records of the State of Georgia*, vols. 33–39 [microfilm]. Georgia Department of Archives and History, Atlanta.

Charles Cornwallis Papers: American Militia Campaigns, 1780–1781. Domestic Records of the Public Record Office, PRO 30/11/2. British National Archives. Kew: Great Britain.

Chekilli Speech, 11 June 1735, MS #143, Georgia Historical Society, Savannah.

Cherokee Vertical Files—Fragment of a Daily Journal Kept by an Unidentified Officer Relating to the Cherokee Expedition of 1776. South Carolina Historical Society, Charleston.

Cobham Lyttleton Family Papers, 1607–1949. Roll PR0099. South Carolina Department of Archives and History, Columbia.

Creek Indian Letters, Talks and Treaties, 1705–1837. WPA Georgia Writers' Project, MS #1500. Hargrett Rare Book and Manuscript Library, University of Georgia. Athens.

Dalhousie Muniments Papers, 1746–1759. MS mfm R. 1085a–b. South Caroliniana Library, University of South Carolina, Columbia.

George Galphin Letters, 1777–1779, in Henry Laurens Papers. Roll 17: Papers Concerning Indian Affairs. South Carolina Historical Society, Charleston.

George Galphin Letters, 1778–1780. Edward E. Ayer Manuscript Collection, Vault Box Ayer MS 313. Newberry Library, Chicago.

Georgia Colonial Conveyance Books. Georgia Historical Society, Savannah.

Georgia Gazette, 1763–76 [microfilm]. University of North Texas, Denton.

Georgia and Indian Land Cessions, ca. 1770. Southern States Manuscript Maps. Maps 6-E-11. William L. Clements Library, University of Michigan, Ann Arbor.

Habersham Family Papers, 1712–1842. MS #1787, Georgia Historical Society, Savannah.

Henry Clinton Papers, 1736–1850. William L. Clements Library, University of Michigan, Ann Arbor.

Henry Ellis Papers, 1757–60. MS #942. Georgia Historical Society, Savannah.

Henry Laurens Papers, Kendall Collection, in William Gilmore Simms Papers. MS P. South Caroliniana Library, University of South Carolina, Columbia.

James Glen Papers, 1738–77. MS Plb. South Caroliniana Library, University of South Carolina, Columbia.

James Grant of Ballindalloch Papers, 1740–1819. Microfilm 687. David Library of the American Revolution. Washington Crossing, PA.

James Edward Oglethorpe Papers, 1730–85. MS 0595. Georgia Historical Society, Savannah.

Jeffrey Amherst Papers, 1758–64. William L. Clements Library, University of Michigan, Ann Arbor.

John Gerard William DeBrahm. "A Map of South Carolina and a Part of Georgia." HMap1780d4. Hargrett Rare Book and Manuscript Library, University of Georgia, Athens.

John Howard Payne Papers, 1794–1842. Edward E. Ayer Manuscript Collection. Vault Ayer MS 689. Newberry Library, Chicago.

John Lewis Gervais Papers, 1772–1801. In Henry Laurens Papers, 1742–1792. Roll 19. South Carolina Historical Society, Charleston.

John Rutledge Papers, 1739–1800. Manuscript mfm R. 281. South Caroliniana Library, University of South Carolina, Columbia.

Journal of an Expedition in 1776 against the Cherokee, under the command of Captain Peter Clinton, South Carolina Historical Society Pamphlet, 973.3 1850 Fairies. South Carolina Historical Society, Charleston.

Journal of the Southern Congress at Augusta in Georgia, 1763. Charleston: Peter Timothy, 1763. British National Archives, Kew: Great Britain.

Keith M. Read Collection, 1732–1905. MS #921. Hargrett Rare Book and Manuscript Library, University of Georgia, Athens.

Last Will and Testament of George Galphin. 6 April 1776, 000051.L 51008. South Carolina Department of Archives and History, Columbia.

Le Conte Genealogical Collection, 1900–1943. MS #71. Hargrett Rare Book and Manuscript Library, University of Georgia, Athens.

The Letter Books of the Society for the Propagation of the Gospel in Foreign Parts, 1702–1786, MS microfilm 45–296. South Carolina Historical Society, Charleston.

The Letterbooks of William Henry Lyttleton, 1756–1759. South Carolina Department of Archives and History, Columbia.

London Chronicle or Universal Evening Post. 17th and 18th Century Burney Collection Database. British Library, London.

London Gazette. 17th and 18th Century Burney Collection Database. British Library, London.

London Evening Post. 17th and 18th Century Burney Collection Database. British Library, London.

A Map of the Indian Nations in the Southern Department, 1766. HMap1766d4. Hargrett Rare Book and Manuscript Library, University of Georgia, Athens.

Mouzon, Henry. An Accurate Map of North and South Carolina with Their Indian Frontiers. HMap1775s6. Hargrett Rare Book and Manuscript Library, University of Georgia, Athens.

New York Mercury [microfilm]. MS film 245. David Library of the American Revolution, Washington Crossing, PA.

Pennsylvania Gazette, 1728–1800. South Caroliniana Library. University of South Carolina, Columbia.

Records in the British Public Record Office Relating to South Carolina, 1663–1782 [micro-film]. British National Archives, Kew: Great Britain.

Records of the Colonial Office, Maps and Plans, Series I—North American Colonies. CO 700. British National Archives, Kew: Great Britain.

Records of the Colonial Office: Original Correspondence, Plantations General, 1689–1952. British Public Records Office, CO 323. British National Archives, Kew: Great Britain.

Report of Colonels Christian and Lewis, Expedition against the Overhill Cherokees, Bullitt Family Papers—Oxmoor Collection, 1683–2003. MSS A B937c, Folder 410, Filson Historical Society. Louisville, KY.

Savery, Samuel. Sketch of the Boundary Line between Georgia and the Creek Indian Nation. MPG 1/337. British National Archives. Kew: Great Britain.

Silver Bluff Trading Post Account Book, 1767–1772. MS #269. Georgia Historical Society, Savannah.

Sir Frederick Haldimand Unpublished Papers, 1758–1784. Add. MS 21661–21892. British Library, London.

South Carolina & American General Gazette, 1765–1781. MS C. South Caroliniana Library, University of South Carolina, Columbia.

South Carolina Gazette, 1732–1775. MS CscG. South Caroliniana Library, University of South Carolina, Columbia.

South Carolina Gazette; and Country Journal, 1765–1775. MS CscG. South Caroliniana Library, University of South Carolina, Columbia.

South Carolina Journals of His Majesty's Council, 1721–1774. ST0704-ST0712. South Carolina Department of Archives and History, Columbia.

Stephens, William. *A State of the Province of Georgia, 10 November 1740*. London: W. Meadows, 1742. Eighteenth-Century Collections Online

Telamon Cuyler Historical Manuscripts, 1754–1905. MS #1170, Series 1. Hargrett Rare Book and Manuscript Library, University of Georgia, Athens.

Thomas Gage Papers, 1754–1807, American Series. William L. Clements Library, University of Michigan, Ann Arbor.

Transcriptions of Records from Portada del Archivo General de Indias, Texas Tech University Center in Seville, Spain. Edward E. Ayer Manuscript Collection. MS #1236, Newberry Library, Chicago.

Virginia Gazette, 1732–1780. MS 900200.P900049. South Carolina Department of Archives and History, Columbia.

William Bacon Stevens Papers, 1736–1849. MS #759. Georgia Historical Society, Savannah.

William Henry Lyttleton Papers, 1756–1760. William L. Clements Library, University of Michigan, Ann Arbor.

Published Primary Sources

Adair, James, and Kathryn E. Holland Braund, eds. *The History of the American Indians*. Tuscaloosa: University of Alabama Press, 2005.

Bossu, Jean-Bernard. *Travels in the Interior of North America, 1751–1762*. Translated and edited by Seymour Feiler. Norman: University of Oklahoma Press, 1962.

Boston News-Letter. America's Historical Newspapers, New York Public Library.

Britt, Albert Sidney, Jr., and Anthony Roane Dees, eds. *Selected Eighteenth-Century Manuscripts*, vol. 20 of *Collections of the Georgia Historical Society*. Savannah: Georgia Historical Society, 1980.

Candler, Allen D., ed. *The Colonial Records of the State of Georgia*, vols.1–32. Atlanta: Franklin-Turner, 1904–.

———, ed. *The Revolutionary Records of the State of Georgia*, vols. 1–3. Atlanta: Franklin-Turner, 1908.

Carter, Clarence Edwin, ed. *The Correspondence of General Thomas Gage, 1763–1775, Volume I–II*. New Haven: Yale University Press, 1931.

———, ed. "Observations of John Stuart and Governor James Grant of East Florida on the Proposed Plan of 1764 for the Future Management of Indian Affairs." *American Historical Review* 20, no. 4 (1915): 815–31.

Chicken, George. "Journal of Colonel George Chicken." In *Travels in the American Colonies*, edited by Newton Dennison Mereness, 75–194. New York: Macmillan, 1916.

Colonial and State Records of North Carolina. 26 vols. Documenting the American South. Chapel Hill: University of North Carolina, 1886–1907.

Coulter, E. Merton, ed. *The Journal of William Stephens 1741–1745, Vol. I–II*. Athens: University of Georgia Press, 1958–59.

Davies, K. G., ed. *Documents of the American Revolution, 1770–1783, Volumes I–XXI*. Shannon, Ireland: Irish University Press, 1972–1979.

Dumont, William H., ed. *Colonial Georgia Genealogical Data, 1748–1783*. Washington, DC: National Genealogical Society, 1971.

Easterby, James Harold, ed. *The Journal of the South Carolina Commons House of Assembly, 1736–1757.* 14 vols. Columbia: South Carolina Department of Archives and History, 1951–1983.

The Federal Gazette, and Philadelphia Evening Post. America's Historical Newspapers, New York Public Library.

Fitch, Tobias. "Journal of Captain Tobias Fitch, 1725." In *Travels in the American Colonies,* edited by Newton Dennison Mereness, 175–214. New York: Macmillan, 1916.

Force, Peter, ed. *American Archives: Documents of the American Revolution 1774–1776,* Series 5, vols. 1–3. Washington, DC: Government Printing Office, 1837.

Foster, Thomas, ed. *The Collected Works of Benjamin Hawkins, 1790–1810.* Tuscaloosa: University of Alabama Press, 2003.

Gatschet, Albert S. *A Migration Legend of the Creek Indians.* Philadelphia: Brinton, 1884.

Habersham, James. *The Letters of Hon. James Habersham, 1756–1775.* Collections of the Georgia Historical Society, vol. 6. Savannah: Savannah Morning News Print, 1904.

Hamer, Philip M., and David R. Chesnutt, ed. *The Papers of Henry Laurens.* 16 vols. Columbia: University of South Carolina Press, 1968–2003.

Hill, James, ed. *The Indian Frontier in British East Florida: Letters to Governor James Grant from Soldiers and Indian Traders at Fort St. Marks of Apalache, 1763–1784.* Florida History Online, University of North Florida. http://www.unf.edu/floridahistory online/Projects/Grant/index.html.

———, ed. *The Indian Frontier in British East Florida: Spanish Correspondence Concerning the Uchiz Indians, 1771–1783.* Florida History Online, University of North Florida. www.unf.edu/floridahistoryonline/Projects/uchize/index.html.

Jacobs, Wilbur R., ed. *The Appalachian Indian Frontier: The Edmond Atkin Reports and Plan of 1755.* Columbia: University of South Carolina Press, 1954.

———, ed. *Indians of the Southern Colonial Frontier: The Edmund Atkin Report and Plan of 1755.* Columbia: University of South Carolina Press, 1954.

"John Bartram: A Diary of a Journey through the Carolinas, Georgia, and Florida from July 1, 1765 to April 10, 1766." *Transactions of the American Philosophical Society* 33, no. 1 (1942): iv–120.

King, Duane H., ed. *The Memoirs of Lt. Henry Timberlake: The Story of a Soldier, Adventurer, and Emissary to the Cherokees, 1756–1765.* Chapel Hill: University of North Carolina Press, 2007.

Letters of Benjamin Hawkins, 1796–1806, Collections of the Georgia Historical Society, vol. 9. Savannah: Morning News Press, 1916.

McDowell, William L. Jr., ed. *Documents Relating to Indian Affairs, May 21, 1750–August 7, 1754.* Colonial Records of South Carolina, Series 2. Columbia: South Carolina Department of Archives and History, 1958.

———, ed. *Documents Relating to Indian Affairs, 1754–1765.* Colonial Records of South Carolina, Series 2. Columbia: South Carolina Department of Archives and History, 1970.

Mays, Edith, ed. *Amherst Papers, 1756–1763, The Southern Sector.* Bowie, MD: Heritage Books, 1999.

Milfort, Louis Leclerc. *Memoirs; or, a Quick Glance at My Various Travels and My Sojourn in the Creek Nation.* Translated by Ben C. McCary. Savannah: Beehive, 1959.

Nairne, Thomas. *Nairne's Muskhogean Journals: The 1708 Expedition to the Mississippi River*. Edited by Alexander Moore. Jackson: University Press of Mississippi, 1988.

New-Hampshire Gazette. Early Eighteenth-Century Collections Online, Gale-Cengage. Farmington Hills, MI.

The New-London Summary, or, The Weekly Advertiser. America's Historical Newspapers, New York Public Library.

New York Daily Advertiser, or The Daily Advertiser. America's Historical Newspapers, New York Public Library.

Pennsylvania Evening Post. America's Historical Newspapers, New York Public Library.

The Pennsylvania Ledger; or the Virginia, Maryland, Pennsylvania, & New-Jersey Weekly Advertiser. America's Historical Newspapers, New York Public Library.

The Pennsylvania Packet, and Daily Advertiser. America's Historical Newspapers. New York Public Library.

Pope, John. *A Tour through the Southern and Western Territories of the United States of North America; the Spanish Dominions on the River Mississippi, and the Floridas; the Countries of the Creek Nations; and many Uninhabited Parts*. Richmond: Dixon, 1792.

Reese, Trevor R., ed. *Our First Visit in America: Early Reports from the Colony of Georgia, 1732–1740*. Savannah: Beehive, 1974.

Rowland, Dunbar, and Albert Godfrey Sanders, eds. and trans. *Mississippi Provincial Archives, English, French, and Spanish Dominion, 1757–1820*. 4, vols. Jackson: University of Mississippi Press, 1911–1927.

Salley, A. S., ed. *The Journal of the Commons House of Assembly: Nov. 14, 1751–Oct. 7, 1752*, edited by A.S. Salley. Columbia: Historical Commission of South Carolina, 1951.

Saye, A. B., E. Merton, et al., eds. *A List of the Early Settlers of Georgia*, 2nd ed. Athens: University of Georgia Press, 1967.

Slaughter, Thomas P., ed. *William Bartram: Travels and Other Writings*. New York: Library of America, 1996.

Southeastern Native American Documents, 1730–1842. Digital Library of Georgia. University of Georgia, Athens.

Taitt, David. "David Taitt's Journal of a Journey through the Creek Country, 1772." In *Travels in the American Colonies*, edited by Newton Dennison Mereness, 493–568. New York: Macmillan, 1916.

The Treaty of Paris, 30 September 1783. The Avalon Project: Documents in Law, History and Diplomacy, Yale Law School. https://avalon.law.yale.edu/18th_century/paris.asp.

United States Congress. *American State Papers: Indian Affairs, Series 2*, vols. 1–2. Buffalo, NY: Hein, 1998.

Urlsperger, Samuel. *Detailed Reports on the Salzburger Emigrants who Settled in America*. 17 vols. Translated and edited by George Fenwicke Jones and Renate Wilson. Athens: University of Georgia Press, 1968–83.

Vaughan, Alden T., ed. *Early American Indian Documents*. 27 vols. Washington, DC: University Publications of America, 1979–2004.

Vorsey, Louis de, Jr., ed. *DeBrahm's Report of the General Survey in the Southern District of North America*. Columbia: University of South Carolina Press, 1987.

Williams, Samuel Cole, ed. *Adair's History of the American Indians*. Nashville: Promontory, 1973.

Woodward, Thomas S. *Woodward's Reminiscences of the Creek, or Muscogee Indians.* Edited by Peter Brannon. Tuscaloosa: Weatherford, 1939.

Published Secondary Sources

JOURNAL ARTICLES

Bell, Amelia Rector. "Separate People: Speaking of Creek Men and Women." *American Anthropologist* 92, no. 2 (1990): 332–45.

Berkhofer, Robert F., Jr. "The Political Context of a New Indian History." *Pacific Historical Review* 40, no. 3 (1971): 357–82.

Bohaker, Heidi. "'Nindoodemag': The Significance of Algonquian Kinship Networks in the Eastern Great Lakes Region, 1600–1701." *William and Mary Quarterly,* 3rd ser., 61, no. 1 (2006): 23–52.

Braund, Kathryn E. Holland. "Guardians of Tradition and Handmaidens to Change: Women's Roles in Creek Economic and Social Life during the Eighteenth Century." *American Indian Quarterly* 14, no. 3 (1990): 239–58.

Force, Pierre. "The House on Bayou Road: Atlantic Creole Networks in the Eighteenth and Nineteenth Centuries." *Journal of American History* 100, no. 1 (2013): 21–45.

Galloway, Patricia. "Four Ages of Alibamon Mico, fl. 1700–1760." *Journal of Mississippi History* 65 (2003): 321–42.

Hardwick, Julie, Sarah M. S. Pearsall, and Karin Wulf. "Introduction: Centering Families in Atlantic Histories." *William and Mary Quarterly,* 3rd ser., 70, no. 2 (2013): 205–24.

Hatfield, April Lee. "Colonial Southeastern Indian History." *Journal of Southern History* 73, no. 3 (2007): 567–78.

Hill, James L. "'Bring Them What They Lack': Spanish-Creek Exchange and Alliance-Making in a Maritime Borderland, 1763–1784." *Early American Studies* 12, no. 1 (2014): 36–67.

Kidwell, Clara Sue. "Indian Women as Cultural Mediators." *Ethnohistory* 39, no. 2 (1992): 97–107.

Lankford, George E. "Red and White: Some Reflections on Southeastern Symbolism." *Southern Folklore* 50, no. 1 (1993): 53–80.

Mt. Pleasant, Alyssa, Caroline Wigginton, and Kelly Wisecup. "Materials and Methods in Native American and Indigenous Studies: Completing the Turn." *William and Mary Quarterly,* 3rd ser., 75, no. 2 (2018): 207–36.

Moore, W. O., Jr. "The Largest Exporters of Deerskins from Charles Town, 1735–1775." *South Carolina Historical Magazine* 74, no. 3 (1973): 144–50.

Pearsall, Sarah M. S., Julie Hardwick, Karin Wulf, and James H. Sweet, eds. "Centering Families in Atlantic History." Special issue, *William and Mary Quarterly* 3rd ser., 70, no. 2 (2013).

Piker, Joshua. "Colonists and Creeks: Rethinking the Pre-Revolutionary Southern Backcountry." *Journal of Southern History* 70, no. 3 (2004): 503–40.

———. "'White & Clean' & Contested: Creek Towns and Trading Paths in the Aftermath of the Seven Years' War." *Ethnohistory* 50, no. 2 (2003): 315–33.

Salley, A. S. "The Creek Indian Tribes in 1725." *South Carolina Historical Magazine* 32, no. 3 (1931): 241–42.

Saunt, Claudio. "The Native South: An Account of Recent Historiography." *Native South* 1, no. 1 (2008): 52–54.

Snyder, Christina. "Conquered Enemies, Adopted Kin, and Owned People: The Creek Indians and Their Captives." *Journal of Southern History* 73, no. 2 (2007): 255–88.

———. "The Once and Future Moundbuilders." *Southern Cultures* 26, no. 2 (2020): 97–114.

Speck, Frank G. "The Creek Indians of Taskigi Town." In *Memoirs of the American Anthropological Association Vol. 2, Part II*, 99–164. Lancaster, PA: New Era, 1907.

Stoler, Ann Laura, Ramon A. Gutierrez, Lori D. Ginzberg, Dirk Hoerder, Mary A. Renda, and Robert J. McMahon. "Empires and Intimacies: Lessons from (Post) Colonial Studies." *Journal of American History* 88, no. 3 (2001): 829–96.

Swanton, John R., "The Green Corn Dance." *Chronicles of Oklahoma* 10, no. 2 (1932): 170–95.

ARTICLES—CHAPTERS IN A LARGER WORK

Brown, Kathleen. "The Anglo-Indian Gender Frontier." In *Negotiators of Change: Historical Perspectives on Native American Women*, edited by Nancy Shoemaker, 26-48. New York: Routledge, 1995.

Cashin, Edward J. "'But Brothers, It Is Our Land We Are Talking About': Winners and Losers in the Georgia Backcountry." In *An Uncivil War: The Southern Backcountry during the American Revolution*, edited by Ronald Hoffman, Thad W. Tate, and Peter J. Albert, 240–75. Charlottesville: University of Virginia Press, 1985.

Green, Michael D. "The Creek Confederacy in the American Revolution: Cautious Participants." In *Anglo-Spanish Confrontations on the Gulf Coast during the American Revolution*, edited by William S. Coker and Robert R. Rea, 54–66. Pensacola, FL: Gulf Coast History and Humanities Conference, 1982.

Hahn, Steven C. "The Cussita Migration Legend: History, Ideology, and the Politics of Mythmaking." In *Light on the Path: The Anthropology and History of the Southeastern Indians*, edited by Thomas J. Pluckhahn and Robbie Ethridge, 57–93. Tuscaloosa: University of Alabama Press, 2006.

Hewitt, J. N. B., and John R. Swanton. "Notes on the Creek Indians." In *Smithsonian Institution Bureau of American Ethnology Bulletin 123: Anthropological Papers, No. 10*, 119–59. Washington, DC: Government Printing Office, 1939.

McLoughlin, William G. "Cherokee Anomie, 1794–1810: New Roles for Red Men, Red Women, and Black Slaves." In *American Encounters: Natives and Newcomers from European Contact to Indian Removal, 1500–1850*, 1st ed., edited by James H. Merrell and Peter C. Mancall, 452–76. New York: Routledge, 2007.

Myer, William E. "Indian Trails of the Southeast." In *42nd Annual Report of the Bureau of American Ethnology to the Secretary of the Smithsonian Institution*, 727–857. Washington, DC: Government Printing Office, 1928.

Sheidley, Nathaniel. "Hunting and the Politics of Masculinity in Cherokee Treaty-Making, 1763–75." In *Empire and Others: British Encounters with Indigenous Peoples*,

1600–1850, edited by Martin Daunton and Rick Halpern, 167–85. Philadelphia: University of Pennsylvania Press, 1999.

Stoler, Ann Laura. "Tense and Tender Ties: The Politics of Comparison in North American History & (Post) Colonial Studies." In *Haunted by Empire: Geographies of Intimacy in North American History,* edited by Ann Laura Stoler, 23–70. Durham, NC: Duke University Press, 2006.

MONOGRAPHS AND BOOK-LENGTH STUDIES

Adams, Mikaela. *Who Belongs? Race, Resources, and Tribal Citizenship in the Native South.* Oxford: Oxford University Press, 2016.

Alden, John R. *John Stuart and the Southern Colonial Frontier: A Study of Indian Relations, War, Trade, and Land Problems in the Southern Wilderness, 1754–1775.* Ann Arbor: University of Michigan Press, 1944.

Anderson, Emma. *The Betrayal of Faith: The Tragic Journey of a Colonial Native Convert.* Cambridge, MA: Harvard University Press, 2007.

Beiler, Rosalind. *Immigrant and Entrepreneur: The Atlantic World of Caspar Wistar, 1650–1750.* University Park: Pennsylvania State University Press, 2008.

Blackhawk, Ned. *Violence over the Land: Indians and Empire in the Early American West.* Cambridge, MA: Harvard University Press, 2008.

Blackmon, Richard D. *Dark and Bloody Ground: The American Revolution along the Southern Frontier.* Yardley, PA: Westholme, 2012.

Boulware, Tyler. *Deconstructing the Cherokee Nation: Town, Region, and Nation among Eighteenth-Century Cherokees.* Gainesville: University Press of Florida, 2011.

Braund, Kathryn. *Deerskins and Duffels: The Creek Indian Trade with Anglo-America, 1685–1815.* 2nd ed. Lincoln: University of Nebraska Press, 2008.

Brooks, Lisa. *Our Beloved Kin: A New History of King Philip's War.* New Haven: Yale University Press, 2018.

Brown, Jennifer S. H. *Strangers in Blood: Fur Trade Company Families in Indian Country.* Vancouver: University of British Columbia Press, 1980.

Carson, James Taylor. *Making an Atlantic World: Circles, Paths, and Stories from the Colonial South.* Knoxville: University of Tennessee Press, 2007.

Cashin, Edward. *Lachlan McGillivray, Indian Trader: The Shaping of the Southern Colonial Frontier.* Athens: University of Georgia Press, 1992.

———. *William Bartram and the American Revolution on the Southern Frontier.* Columbia: University of South Carolina Press, 2000.

Catton, Theodore. *Rainy Lake House: Twilight of Empire on the Northern Frontier.* Baltimore: Johns Hopkins University Press, 2017.

Child, Brenda J. *Boarding School Seasons: American Indian Families, 1900–1940.* Lincoln: University of Nebraska Press, 1998.

Cleves, Rachel Hope. *Charity and Sylvia: A Same-Sex Marriage in Early America.* New York: Oxford University Press, 2014.

Corkran, David H. *The Creek Frontier, 1540–1783.* Norman: University of Oklahoma Press, 1967.

Crane, Elaine Foreman. *Killed Strangely: The Death of Rebecca Cornell.* Ithaca: Cornell University Press, 2009.

Denial, Catherine. *Making Marriage: Husbands, Wives, and the American State in Dakota and Ojibwe Country.* St. Paul: Minnesota Historical Society, 2013.

Demos, John. *The Unredeemed Captive: A Family Story from Early America.* New York: Vintage, 1995.

Doerfler, Jill. *Those Who Belong: Identity, Family, Blood, and Citizenship among the White Earth Anishinaabeg.* East Lansing: Michigan State University Press, 2015.

Dowd, Gregory Evans. *Groundless: Rumors, Legends, and Hoaxes on the Early American Frontier.* Baltimore: Johns Hopkins University Press, 2015.

Dubcovsky, Alejandra. *Informed Power: Communication in the Early American South.* Cambridge, MA: Harvard University Press, 2016.

Dunbar, Erica Armstrong. *Never Caught: The Washingtons' Relentless Pursuit of Their Runaway Slave, Ona Judge.* New York: Atria, 2017.

DuVal, Kathleen. *Independence Lost: Lives on the Edge of the American Revolution.* New York: Random House, 2016.

Ethridge, Robbie. *Creek Country: The Creek Indians and Their World.* Chapel Hill: University of North Carolina Press, 2003.

————, ed. *Mapping the Mississippian Shatter Zone: The Colonial Indian Slave Trade and Regional Instability in the American South.* Lincoln: University of Nebraska Press, 2009.

Farge, Arlette. *The Allure of the Archives.* New Haven: Yale University Press, 2013.

Foster, H. Thomas, II. *Archaeology of the Lower Muscogee Creek Indians, 1715–1836.* Tuscaloosa: University of Alabama Press, 2009.

Frank, Andrew. *Creeks and Southerners: Biculturalism on the Early American Frontier.* Lincoln: University of Nebraska Press, 2005.

Fuentes, Marisa J. *Dispossessed Lives: Enslaved Women, Violence, and the Archive.* Philadelphia: University of Pennsylvania Press, 2016.

Fullagar, Kate. *The Warrior, the Voyager, and the Artist: Three Lives in an Age of Empire.* New Haven: Yale University Press, 2020.

Gallay, Alan. *The Indian Slave Trade: The Rise of the English Empire in the American South, 1670–1717.* New Haven: Yale University Press, 2003.

Ghosh, Durba. *Sex and the Family in Colonial India: The Making of Empire.* New York: Cambridge University Press, 2006.

Gordon-Reed, Annette. *The Hemingses of Monticello: An American Family.* New York: Norton, 2009.

Grantham, Bill. *Creation Myths and Legends of the Creek Indians.* Gainesville: University Press of Florida, 2002.

Graybill, Andrew. *The Red and the White: A Family Saga of the American West.* New York: Liveright, 2014.

Green, Michael D. *The Politics of Indian Removal: Creek Government and Society in Crisis.* Lincoln: University of Nebraska Press, 1985.

Griffith, Benjamin W., Jr. *McIntosh and Weatherford: Creek Indian Leaders.* Tuscaloosa: University of Alabama Press, 1998.

Hahn, Steven C. *The Invention of the Creek Nation, 1670–1763.* Lincoln: University of Nebraska Press, 2004.

————. *The Life and Times of Mary Musgrove.* Gainesville: University of Florida Press, 2012.

Hall, Joseph M., Jr. *Zamumo's Gifts: Indian-European Exchange in the Colonial Southeast.* Philadelphia: University of Pennsylvania Press, 2009.

Hancock, David. *Citizens of the World: London Merchants and the Integration of the British Atlantic Community, 1735–1785.* Cambridge: Cambridge University Press, 1997.

Hartman, Saidiya. *Lose Your Mother: A Journey Along the Atlantic Slave Route.* New York: Farrar, Straus & Giroux, 2007.

Hatley, Tom. *The Dividing Paths: Cherokees and South Carolinians through the Revolutionary Era.* Oxford: Oxford University Press, 1995.

Haynes, Joshua S. *Patrolling the Border: Theft and Violence on the Creek-Georgia Frontier, 1770–1796.* Athens: University of Georgia Press, 2018.

Hudson, Angela Pulley. *Creek Paths and Federal Roads: Indians, Settlers, and Slaves and the Making of the American South.* Chapel Hill: University of North Carolina Press, 2010.

———. *Real Native Genius: How an Ex-Slave and a White Mormon Became Famous Indians.* Chapel Hill: University of North Carolina Press, 2015.

Hudson, Charles. *The Southeastern Indians.* Knoxville: University of Tennessee Press, 1976.

Hurtado, Albert L. *Intimate Frontiers: Sex, Gender, and Culture in Old California.* Albuquerque: University of New Mexico Press, 1999.

Hyde, Anne F. *Empires, Nations, and Families: A History of the North American West, 1800-1860.* Lincoln: University of Nebraska Press, 2011.

Ingram, Daniel. *Indians and British Outposts in Eighteenth-Century America.* Gainesville: University Press of Florida, 2012.

Inman, Natalie. *Brothers and Friends: Kinship in Early America.* Athens: University of Georgia Press, 2017.

Isaac, Rhys. *Landon Carter's Uneasy Kingdom: Revolution and Rebellion on a Virginia Plantation.* New York: Oxford University Press, 2005.

Juricek, John T. *Colonial Georgia and the Creeks: Anglo-Indian Diplomacy on the Southern Frontier, 1733–1763.* Gainesville: University of Florida Press, 2010.

———. *Endgame for Empire: British-Creek Relations in Georgia and Vicinity, 1763–1776.* Gainesville: University Press of Florida, 2015.

Kelton, Paul. *Cherokee Medicine, Colonial Germs: An Indigenous Nation's Fight against Smallpox, 1518–1824.* Norman: University of Oklahoma Press, 2015.

Kimmerer, Robin Wall. *Braiding Sweetgrass: Indigenous Wisdom, Scientific Knowledge, and the Teaching of Plants.* Minneapolis: Milkweed, 2013.

Kokomoor, Kevin. *Of One Mind and of One Government: The Rise and Fall of the Creek Nation in the Early Republic.* Lincoln: University of Nebraska Press, 2019.

LeMaster, Michelle. *Brothers Born of One Mother: British-Native American Relations in the Colonial Southeast.* Charlottesville: University of Virginia Press, 2012.

Lewis, Jan. *The Pursuit of Happiness: Family and Values in Jefferson's America.* Cambridge: Cambridge University Press, 1985.

Little, Ann M. *The Many Captivities of Esther Wheelwright.* New Haven: Yale University Press, 2016.

Matson, Cathy. *Merchants and Empire: Trading in Colonial New York.* Baltimore: Johns Hopkins University Press, 1998.

McDonnell, Michael. *Masters of Empire: Great Lakes Indians and the Making of America.* New York: Hill & Wang, 2015.

Mihesuah, Devon A. *Natives and Academics: Researching and Writing about American Indians.* Lincoln: University of Nebraska Press, 1998.

———. *So You Want to Write About American Indians? A Guide for Writers, Students, and Scholars.* Lincoln: University of Nebraska Press, 2005.

Morgan, Jennifer L. *Laboring Women: Reproduction and Gender in New World Slavery.* Philadelphia: University of Pennsylvania Press, 2004.

Oatis, Steven J. *A Colonial Complex: South Carolina's Frontiers in the Era of the Yamasee War, 1680–1730.* Lincoln: University of Nebraska Press, 2008.

Oberg, Michael Leroy. *Professional Indian: The American Odyssey of Eleazer Williams.* Philadelphia: University of Pennsylvania Press, 2015.

———. *Uncas: First of the Mohegans.* Ithaca: Cornell University Press, 2003.

Oliphant, John. *Peace and War on the Anglo-Cherokee Frontier, 1756–63.* Baton Rouge: Louisiana State University Press, 2001.

O'Neill, Lindsay. *The Opened Letter: Networking in the Early Modern British World.* Philadelphia: University of Pennsylvania Press, 2015.

Owens, Robert M. *Red Dreams and White Nightmares: Pan-Indian Alliances in the Anglo-American Mind, 1763–1815.* Norman: University of Oklahoma Press, 2015.

Palmer, Jennifer L. *Intimate Bonds: Family and Slavery in the French Atlantic.* Philadelphia: University of Pennsylvania Press, 2016.

Paulett, Robert. *An Empire of Small Places: Mapping the Southeastern Anglo-Indian Trade, 1732–1795.* Athens: University of Georgia Press, 2012.

Pearsall, Sarah M. S. *Atlantic Families: Lives and Letters in the Later Eighteenth Century.* Oxford: Oxford University Press, 2008.

Perdue, Theda. *Cherokee Women: Gender and Culture Change, 1700–1835.* Lincoln: University of Nebraska Press, 1998.

Perry, Adele. *Colonial Relations: The Douglas-Connolly Family and the Nineteenth-Century Imperial World.* Cambridge: Cambridge University Press, 2015.

Peterson, Dawn. *Indians in the Family: Adoption and the Politics of Antebellum Expansion.* Cambridge, MA: Harvard University Press, 2017.

Piecuch, Jim. *Three Peoples, One King: Loyalists, Indians, and Slaves in the Revolutionary South, 1775–1782.* Columbia: University of South Carolina Press, 2008.

Piker, Joshua. *The Four Deaths of Acorn Whistler: Telling Stories in Colonial America.* Cambridge, MA: Harvard University Press, 2013.

———. *Okfuskee: A Creek Town in Colonial America.* Cambridge, MA: Harvard University Press, 2004.

Plane, Ann Marie. *Colonial Intimacies: Indian Marriage in Early New England.* Ithaca: Cornell University Press, 2000.

Pulsipher, Jenny Hale. *Swindler Sachem: The American Indian Who Sold His Birthright, Dropped out of Harvard, and Conned the King of England.* New Haven: Yale University Press, 2018.

Ramsey, William L. *The Yamasee War: A Study of Culture, Economy, and Conflict in the Colonial South.* Lincoln: University of Nebraska Press, 2008.

Rindfleisch, Bryan C. *George Galphin's Intimate Empire: The Creek Indians, Family, and Colonialism in Early America.* Tuscaloosa: University of Alabama Press, 2019.

Romney, Susanah Shaw. *New Netherland Connections: Intimate Networks and Atlantic Ties in Seventeenth-Century America.* Chapel Hill: University of North Carolina Press, 2014.

Rothman, Joshua D. *Notorious in the Neighborhood: Sex and Families across the Color Line in Virginia, 1787–1861.* Chapel Hill: University of North Carolina Press, 2003.

Rothschild, Emma. *The Inner Life of Empires: An Eighteenth-Century History.* Princeton: Princeton University Press, 2011.

Rountree, Helen C. *Pocahontas, Powhatan, and Opechancanough: Three Indian Lives Changed by Jamestown.* Charlottesville: University of Virginia Press, 2006.

Saunt, Claudio. *Black, White, and Indian: Race and the Unmaking of an American Family.* Oxford: Oxford University Press, 2006.

———. *A New Order of Things: Property, Power, and the Transformation of the Creek Indians, 1733–1816.* Cambridge: Cambridge University Press, 1999.

———. *West of the Revolution: An Uncommon History of 1776.* New York: Norton, 2015.

Scott, Rebecca J., and Jean M. Hebrard. *Freedom Papers: An Atlantic Odyssey in the Age of Emancipation.* Cambridge, MA: Harvard University Press, 2012.

Searcy, Martha Condray. *The Georgia-Florida Contest in the American Revolution, 1776–1778.* Tuscaloosa: University of Alabama Press, 2003.

Shannon, Timothy J. *Indian Captive, Indian King: Peter Williamson in America and Britain.* Cambridge, MA: Harvard University Press, 2018.

Shefveland, Kristalyn Marie. *Anglo-Native Virginia: Trade, Conversion, and Indian Slavery in the Old Dominion, 1646–1722.* Athens: University of Georgia Press, 2016.

Sleeper-Smith, Susan. *Indian Women and French Men: Rethinking Cultural Encounter in the Western Great Lakes.* Amherst: University of Massachusetts Press, 2001.

Smith, Marvin T. *Coosa: The Rise and Fall of a Southeastern Mississippian Chiefdom.* Gainesville: University Press of Florida, 2000.

Smithers, Gregory D. *Native Southerners: Indigenous History from Origins to Removal.* Norman: University of Oklahoma Press, 2019.

Snapp, Russell J. *John Stuart and the Struggle for Empire on the Southern Frontier.* Baton Rouge: Louisiana State University Press, 1996.

Stern, Jessica Yirush. *The Lives in Objects: Native Americans, British Colonists, and Cultures of Labor and Exchange in the Southeast.* Chapel Hill: University of North Carolina Press, 2017.

Stoler, Ann Laura. *Along the Archival Grain: Epistemic Anxieties and Colonial Common Sense.* Princeton: Princeton University Press, 2009.

———. *Carnal Knowledge and Imperial Power: Race and the Intimate in Colonial Rule.* Berkeley: University of California Press, 2002.

Stoler, Ann Laura, and Frederick Cooper, eds. *Tensions of Empire: Colonial Cultures in a Bourgeois World.* Berkeley: University of California Press, 1997.

Stremlau, Rose. *Sustaining the Cherokee Family: Kinship and the Allotment of an Indigenous Nation.* Chapel Hill: University of North Carolina Press, 2011.

Swanton, John R. *Creek Religion and Medicine*. Bison Books. Lincoln: University of Nebraska Press, 2000.

———. *Early History of the Creek Indians and Their Neighbors*. Washington, DC: Government Printing Office, 1922.

Sweet, Julie Ann. *Negotiating for Georgia: British-Creek Relations in the Trustee Era, 1733–1752*. Athens: University of Georgia Press, 2005.

Thomas, Daniel H. *Fort Toulouse: The French Outpost at the Alabamas on the Coosa*. Tuscaloosa: University of Alabama Press, 1989.

Tortora, Daniel J. *Carolina in Crisis: Cherokees, Colonists, and Slaves in the American Southeast, 1756–1763*. Chapel Hill: University of North Carolina Press, 2015.

Trivellato, Francesca. *The Familiarity of Strangers: The Sephardic Diaspora, Livorno, and Cross-Cultural Trade in the Early Modern Period*. New Haven: Yale University Press, 2009.

Trouillot, Michel-Rolph. *Silencing the Past: Power and the Production of History*. Boston: Beacon, 1995.

Van Kirk, Sylvia. *Many Tender Ties: Women and Fur Trade Society, 1670–1870*. Winnipeg: Watson & Dwyer, 1980.

Wright, J. Leitch, Jr. *Creeks and Seminoles: The Destruction and Regeneration of the Muscogulge People*. Lincoln: University of Nebraska Press, 1990.

INDEX